FRIEDRICH HÖL

SELECTED POEMS AND

JOHANN CHRISTIAN FRIEDRICH HÖLDERLIN was born in 1770 in Lauffen, south-west Germany. He was educated first at boarding school, and then at Tübingen seminary, where he met and became friends with G. W. F. Hegel and F. W. J. Schelling. Despite deciding not to enter the Church, he completed his studies and on graduation in 1793 found employment as a private tutor to the son of Charlotte von Kalb, friend of the poet Friedrich Schiller. It was in his second tutorial post, in the house of a Frankfurt banker named Gontard, that he became romantically involved with his employer's wife, Susette. He became passionately attached to the young woman, who returned his affection, praising her as 'Diotima'. Hölderlin began writing poetry at school, and not long after graduating from the seminary he began his only novel, *Hyperion*. It has been suggested that he explored the profound trauma of his parting with Susette Gontard in 1798 through the latter part of this work, and the pain of this event seems to have contributed to the onset of mental illness. In 1802, he returned home from a tutorial post in Bordeaux in a very disturbed state of mind, and, though he recovered for a short while, this condition soon returned. After a brief period of institutionalization, he was taken into the care of a carpenter named Zimmer, with whose family Hölderlin lived in Tübingen until his death in 1843.

Hölderlin's abiding passion was for the ideal of classical Greece. He felt he had a mission to try to regenerate Germany by using his writing to instil in the country some of the Hellenic greatness he admired, and it was a source of considerable sadness to him that he was unable to fulfil this dream. While his talent was not widely recognized during his lifetime he has come to be regarded as one of the finest writers in the German language, producing a body of lyric poetry (primarily in classical forms, though later unpublished work was of a freer nature) and the epistolary novel *Hyperion oder der Eremit in Griechenland* (1797–9), which was set against the backdrop of the unsuccessful Greek revolt against the Turks in 1770.

MICHAEL HAMBURGER has written, translated and edited across the fields of German, French, Italian and Romanian literature. Educated at Westminster and Christ Church, Oxford, he lectured at University College,

London, and the University of Reading, and has held visiting posts at universities and colleges in America and Great Britain. He has received many awards and honours, including two honorary doctorates, several prizes for his translations and, in 1992, an OBE. He has produced poetry throughout his writing life, his *Collected Poems 1941–1994* being published in 1995 and his critical work on the subject, *The Truth of Poetry*, in 1970, by Penguin. He has also written his memoirs, *String of Beginnings* (1991), and published many critical works and translations.

JEREMY ADLER is Professor of German at King's College London. He studied German at Queen Mary College (University of London) and was a Lecturer in German at Westfield College before being awarded a Personal Chair. He is a sometime fellow of the Institute of Advanced Study, Berlin, and a sometime scholar of the Herzog August Bibliothek, Wolfenbüttel. He has written books on Goethe's novel *The Elective Affinities* (1987), produced (with Ulrich Ernst) a catalogue of visual poetry, *Text als Figur* (third edition, 1990), and edited the collected works of August Stramm (1990). With Richard Fardon he edited Franz Baermann Steiner's *Selected Writings* (1999) and recently edited Steiner's collected poems (2000). His *Franz Kafka*, in the Penguin Illustrated Lives series, was published in 2002. He has published several volumes of poetry, including *The Wedding and Other Marriages* (1980), *At the Edge of the World* (1995) and *The Electric Alphabet* (third edition, 2001). Jeremy Adler is married and lives in London.

FRIEDRICH HÖLDERLIN

SELECTED POEMS AND FRAGMENTS

Translated by MICHAEL HAMBURGER
Edited by JEREMY ADLER
With a new preface and an introduction by MICHAEL HAMBURGER

PENGUIN BOOKS

PENGUIN BOOKS

Published by the Penguin Group
Penguin Books Ltd, 80 Strand, London WC2R ORL, England
Penguin Group (USA) Inc., 375 Hudson Street, New York, New York 10014, USA
Penguin Group (Canada), 90 Eglinton Avenue East, Suite 700, Toronto, Ontario, Canada M4P 2Y3
(a division of Pearson Penguin Canada Inc.)
Penguin Ireland, 25 St Stephen's Green, Dublin 2, Ireland (a division of Penguin Books Ltd)
Penguin Group (Australia), 250 Camberwell Road, Camberwell,
Victoria 3124, Australia (a division of Pearson Australia Group Pty Ltd)
Penguin Books India Pvt Ltd, 11 Community Centre,
Panchsheel Park, New Delhi – 110 017, India
Penguin Group (NZ), 67 Apollo Drive, Mairangi Bay, Auckland 1310, New Zealand
(a division of Pearson New Zealand Ltd)
Penguin Books (South Africa) (Pty) Ltd, 24 Sturdee Avenue, Rosebank, Johannesburg 2196, South Africa

Penguin Books Ltd, Registered Offices: 80 Strand, London WC2R ORL, England

www.penguin.com

This edition first published by Anvil Press Poetry 1994
Published in Penguin Classics with a new preface and introduction 1998

040

Translation copyright © Michael Hamburger, 1966, 1980, 1994
Preface copyright © Michael Hamburger, 1998
This selection copyright © Jeremy Adler, 1994
Foreword copyright © Jeremy Adler, 1998
All rights reserved

The moral right of the editor and translator has been asserted

Set in 9.25/11.25 pt Monotype Ehrhardt
Typeset by Rowland Phototypesetting Ltd, Bury St Edmunds, Suffolk
Printed and bound in Great Britain by Clays Ltd, Elcograf S.p.A.

www.greenpenguin.co.uk

CONTENTS

Foreword ix
Preface xi
Introduction xvii
Bibliographical note xliv

ODES AND EPIGRAMS (1797–1799) 1
EPIGRAMS (1797)
  Good Advice 3
  Descriptive Poetry 3
To Diotima 3
Diotima ('Bliss of the heavenly Muse . . .') 3
Bonaparte 5
Empedocles 5
To the Fates 7
Diotima ('You suffer and keep silent and, strange to
    them . . .') 7
To Her Genius 9
Plea for Forgiveness 9
Then and Now 9
The Course of Life ('High my spirit aspired . . .') 11
Brevity 11
Human Applause 11
Home ('Content the boatman turns . . .') 13
Good Faith 13
Her Recovery ('Nature, she who's your friend . . .') 13
The Unpardonable 15
To the Young Poets 15
To the Germans ('Do not laugh . . .') 15
The Sanctimonious Poets 17
Sunset 17
To Our Great Poets 17

Socrates and Alcibiades 19
EPIGRAMS (1799)
  Sophocles 19
  The Angry Poet 19
  The Root of All Evil 19

THE LATER ODES (1798–1803) 21
Man 23
Hyperion's Song of Fate 25
In my boyhood days . . . 27
The Spirit of the Age 29
Evening Fantasy 31
In the Morning 33
The River Main 35
My Possessions 37
To Princess Augusta of Homburg 41
Go down, then, lovely sun . . . 43
To the Germans ('Never laugh at . . .') 45
Rousseau 49
Heidelberg (Alcaic version) 51
The Neckar 53
Home ('Content the boatman turns . . .') 55
Love 57
The Course of Life ('More you also desired . . .') 59
Her Recovery ('Nature, look, your most loved . . .') 61
The Farewell (second version) 63
Diotima ('You suffer and keep silent, unknown . . .') 65
Return to the Homeland 67
The Ancestral Portrait 69
The Departed 71
Exhortation (second version) 73
Nature and Art or Saturn and Jupiter 75
Sung beneath the Alps 77
The Poet's Vocation 79
Voice of the People (second version) 83
The Blind Singer 87
Chiron 91
Tears 95
To Hope 97

Vulcan 97
The Poet's Courage (first version) 99
Timidness 101
The Fettered River 103
Ganymede 105

HEXAMETERS AND ELEGIES (1800–1801) 109
The Archipelago 111
Menon's Lament for Diotima 127
The Traveller 137
Stuttgart 143
Bread and Wine 151
Homecoming 159

THE HYMNS (1799–1803) 169
The Ages of Life 171
Half of Life 171
The Nook at Hardt 173
As on a holiday . . . 175
At the Source of the Danube 177
The Journey 183
Germania 189
The Rhine 197
Celebration of Peace 209
The Only One (first version) 219
The Only One (second version) 225
Patmos 231
Patmos (fragments of the later version) 243
Remembrance 251
The Ister 253
Mnemosyne (third version) 259

FRAGMENTS OF OTHER HYMNS (1800–1805) 263
German Song 265
Home ('And no one knows . . .') 267
For when the grape-vine's sap . . . 269
On fallow foliage . . . 269
What is the life of men . . . 271
What is God? . . . 271
To the Virgin Mary 273

The Titans 283
At one time I questioned the Muse . . . 287
But when the heavenly . . . 289
The Eagle 295
You firmly built alps . . . 299
Whatever is Nearest (third version) 301
Colombo 305
When there's a flaming . . . 313
For from the abyss . . . 313
Narcissi . . . 315
In Socrates' Time 317
Greece (third version) 317

LAST POEMS (1807–1843) 323
If from the distance . . . 325
On the Birth of a Child 327
The world's agreeable things . . . 329
To Zimmer ('The lines of life . . .') 329
Conviction 329
The Merry Life 329
The Walk 333
Spring ('New day descends . . .') 333
Summer ('When then the blooms . . .') 335
Summer ('Still you can see . . .') 335
Autumn ('Nature's bright gleam . . .') 337
Winter ('When past, unseen . . .') 337
Spring ('When springtime from the depth . . .') 339

Index of German first lines 341
Index of English first lines 345
Index of German titles 349
Index of English titles 351

FOREWORD

Michael Hamburger's Hölderlin translations have established themselves
as a classic. No German poet has been better, more devotedly served by
an English poet and translator. Hölderlin's metres and free rhythms,
achieved through an intense dialogue with classical verse, find a true voice
in these versions. Without exactly following Hölderlin's own translation
theory, Michael Hamburger's verse limpidly enables an 'alien' style to
'go native'. He thereby makes what is strange even in the German tongue
amazingly accessible. In three successive editions, published in 1966,
1980 and 1994, he repeatedly enlarged the number of poems available in
English, until, discounting the early rhymes and blank verse, he had
translated practically the whole mature output. Having thus expanded
his work, it proved impossible for him to shorten it for a Penguin Classic,
and so, at his suggestion, and the publisher's invitation, I took on the
job. We have worked as follows. Responding to my initial draft selection
from the Anvil Press edition of 1994, which kept to the projected word
limit, Michael Hamburger named all those excluded poems that he
considered essential, as well as several others, where he left me a free
hand. This formed the basis for my final choice, achieved by further
cutting and adding. Thanks to the understanding of Paul Keegan at
Penguin, this has led to a book much more substantial than was originally
planned. The selection has been guided by a few simple principles: to
include everything in the original bilingual Penguin Hölderlin, which
has long been out of print; to represent all the great poems which any
reader has the right to expect in an edition such as this; and to convey
the range of the whole corpus as fully as possible. That has meant printing
a substantial number of the odes; all the hexameters and elegies; practically
all the hymns; and a major body of fragments and late poems. The
emphasis on late work, on the fragmentary strange beauty of Hölderlin's
later years, reflects the changed image of Hölderlin that has developed
since Michael Hamburger first began translating him. The end-notes of
the Anvil edition are omitted, replaced by a few explanatory footnotes.
The most painful cuts are Hölderlin's play, *The Death of Empedocles*, and
the nine 'Pindar Fragments and Commentary'. The former deserves

separate publication. The latter are due to appear in a companion volume
of Hölderlin's essays and letters.

Jeremy Adler

PREFACE

This selection from my Hölderlin versions replaces the 1966 Hölderlin in the Penguin Poets series, for which literal prose translations were required. In fact I had already done verse translations of all but one of the poems included in that book, and sensitive readers will have heard the rhythms of the originals in most of my would-be prose. My very first book of Hölderlin versions, published in 1943, was the only one for which I made no attempt to render the metres of Hölderlin's odes, elegies and hexameters.

These classical metres and strophes have always remained more or less exotic in English, not only because in Greek and Latin they were based on a measurement of quantity believed to be lost and irrecoverable since. In German there was a well-established tradition of such imitation or adaptation well before Hölderlin's time; and in English, too, there have been sporadic attempts to revive these forms, from the Countess of Pembroke's Sapphics in her version of the Psalms to the odd experiments by eighteenth- and nineteenth-century poets including Cowper, Coleridge, Tennyson, Clough and Swinburne, and the twentieth-century poets Vernon Watkins and W. H. Auden, both of whom knew Hölderlin's poems. As for Hölderlin's resort to these forms, after earlier, mainly rhymed and iambic verse not represented in any of my selections, it remains inseparable from his strenuous grappling with Greek antiquity, therefore from his poetic vision and his most urgent concerns. It was in the short Alcaic or Asclepiadean odes of 1797 that he found his distinct voice as a poet; and it was by way of Pindar that he evolved the 'free verse' of his most daringly innovative poems.

The verse renderings in the present book are taken from the third edition – enlarged once more – of *Hölderlin: Poems and Fragments*, published by Anvil Press, London, in 1994. After almost half a century of intermittent work on my Hölderlin translations and successive editions to which I had added new versions, as well as correcting or trying to improve earlier ones, I could not bring myself to reverse that process by reducing the contents of this last edition to about half of its 719 pages of texts. I am most grateful to Professor Jeremy Adler for not only taking on this operation, but doing so in consultation with me; and to Paul Keegan of Penguin Books for responding to our plea for more space than had originally been allowed for the selection, so that the excisions most painful to me could be avoided.

My Introduction to the larger Anvil edition is reprinted here virtually unchanged, in the hope that references to works that could not be included in the selection, such as the fragments of the verse tragedy *The Death of Empedocles*, will be more helpful than irritating to readers of this book.

In an earlier Preface – to the first edition of *Poems and Fragments* (1967) – I felt it necessary to write at some length about my practice as a translator, at a time when poet–translators were expected to favour a freedom to re-interpret, recast and even omit that has never been my way. I had probably been needled by Robert Lowell's description of my kind of translator as 'taxidermists'. Here it is enough to reaffirm that there will always be radically different approaches to the translation of poetic texts, roughly corresponding to Dryden's 'metaphrase', 'paraphrase' and 'imitation'; and that each of these serves a distinct purpose, with gains and losses that will continue to be weighed up and debated. About my practice I will say only that it aims at the greatest possible closeness not only to the semantic gist of the originals but their movement, their dynamic and way of breathing. If I have not been quite consistent in this, neither was Hölderlin, whose 'modulation of tones' extended from the sublime and heroic to the utmost plainness and 'naivety', from intense enthusiasm to 'stillness of beauty'.

Hölderlin's own spelling has been retained in the German texts. Although Hölderlin was never a dialect poet, his diction and spelling show traces of his regional, Swabian, vernacular. 'Th' for modern 't' in certain words and 'ey' for modern 'ei' were general usage in his time. Single or double 'k' for modern 'ck' and 'e' for modern 'ä' may point to Hölderlin's pronunciation of the words in question. A single 'l' for modern double 'll' will also be encountered, and so on.

Despite his Hellenism and the almost global range of allusion in his later visionary poems, Hölderlin's regional allegiances linked his earliest poems to the very last, written when his visionary explorations had brought him back home, to the second childhood of his so-called madness. At the age of 18 or 19 he wrote the one ode included in the earlier Penguin volume which I was unable to translate metrically, a poem in praise of the Swabian astronomer Johannes Keppler or Kepler (1571–1630), in a metre not taken over from any Greek poet but from Hölderlin's earliest German master and predecessor, Klopstock:

Kepler

Unter den Sternen ergehet sich
   Mein Geist, die Gefilde des Uranus
      Überhin schwebt er und sinnt; einsam ist
         Und gewagt, ehernen Tritt heischet die Bahn.

Wandle mit Kraft, wie der Held, einher!
   Erhebe die Miene! doch nicht zu stolz,
      Denn es naht, siehe es naht, hoch herab
         Vom Gefild, wo der Triumph jubelt, der Mann,

Welcher den Denker in Albion,
   Den Späher des Himmels um Mitternacht
      Ins Gefild tiefern Beschauns leitete,
         Und voran leuchtend sich wagt' ins Labyrinth,

Daß der erhabenen Themse Stolz
   Im Geiste sich beugend vor seinem Grab,
      Ins Gefild würdigern Lohns nach ihm rief:
         'Du begannst, Suevias Sohn! wo es dem Blik

Aller Jahrtausende schwindelte;
   Und ha! ich vollende, was du begannst,
      Denn voran leuchtestest du, Herrlicher!
         Im Labyrinth, Stralen beschwurst du in die Nacht.

Möge verzehren des Lebens Mark
   Die Flamm' in der Brust – ich ereile dich,
      Ich vollends! denn sie ist groß, ernst und groß,
         Deine Bahn, höhnet des Golds, lohnet sich selbst.'

Wonne Walhallas! und ihn gebar
   Mein Vaterland? ihn, den die Themse pries?
      Der zuerst ins Labyrinth Stralen schuf,
         Und den Pfad, hin an dem Pol, wies dem Gestirn.

Heklas Gedonner vergäß ich so,
  Und, gieng ich auf Ottern, ich bebte nicht
    In dem Stolz, daß er aus dir, Suevia!
      Sich erhub, unser der Dank Albions ist.

Mutter der Redlichen! Suevia!
  Du stille! dir jauchzen Aeonen zu,
    Du erzogst Männer des Lichts ohne Zal,
      Des Geschlechts Mund, das da kommt, huldiget dir.

In starry regions my mind perambulates, hovers over Uranian fields, and ponders, solitary and daring is my course, demanding a brazen stride.

Mightily, like the hero, wander about! Lift up your face! But not too proudly, for there approaches, look, there approaches down from the field high up, where triumph exults, that man

Who led the thinker in Albion, the spy of the midnight heavens, into the field of deeper contemplation, and who, lighting the way, ventured into the labyrinth,

So that the pride of exalted Thames, bowing in spirit before his grave, called after him into the field of more worthy reward: 'You began, Swabia's son, where the gaze

Of all the millennia grew dizzy; and hah! I complete what you began; for it was you, glorious one, that lighted the way in the labyrinth, conjuring beams into the night.

Though the flame in my breast devour the marrow of my life, I shall catch you up, I shall complete it! For it is great, solemn and great, your course, scorning gold, rewarding itself.'

Bliss of Walhalla! And did my homeland give birth to him? Him, whom the Thames praised? Who was the first to cast beams into the labyrinth and traced the path of the stars to the Pole.

Thus should I forget the thundering of Hekla and, if I walked on adders, I should not quake in the pride that from you, Swabia, he arose, and the thanks of Albion are ours.

Mother of the truthful, Swabia! You, the quiet! The aeons cry out to you in joy; you reared numberless men of light; the mouth of the generation to come does homage to you.

The exclamatory rhetoric of this juvenile poem, not yet purged by the example of classical poets, made it ineligible for anything but pedestrian metaphrase on the one hand, the freest of imitations on the other. Yet neither Kepler nor Isaac Newton would ever have been celebrated in

Hölderlin's early pantheon if Kepler had not been a fellow Swabian. (The Nordic Walhalla of one line, quite uncharacteristic of Hölderlin, is another borrowing from Klopstock and other immediate precursors.) Hölderlin's self-identification with his hero goes so far that the ode opens as a *persona* poem, rather than with the address or invocation obligatory in an ode.

Gaps in Hölderlin's fragmentary later poems have not been filled with taxidermic stuffing. The Introduction should explain how and why so many of Hölderlin's texts failed to become complete or definitive. The anomaly has to do both with his extraordinarily hectic development, which demanded constant revision and rejection of earlier achievements, and with the fact that he was never able to place and authorize a book of his poems. The first book collection of poems by him was made by others in 1826, when the poet had ceased to be Hölderlin and become 'Scardanelli, or something of the sort', as he put it, refusing to have any part in the selecting or editing and disowning the publication. That is why the editing of his later work has continued up to the present time, and the volume of the current 'Frankfurt' edition that will contain the most fragmentary of his texts did not appear in time for my last revision of the texts and translations.

M.H.
Suffolk, 1996

INTRODUCTION

Johann Friedrich Hölderlin was born in the small Swabian town Lauffen on the Neckar on 20 March 1770. His father, the manager of estates belonging to the Lutheran Church, died soon after, in 1772. After his mother's remarriage in 1774, the family moved to Nürtingen, where her second husband was burgomaster. Hölderlin attended the local grammar school until 1784. His stepfather, too, had died in 1779, leaving Hölderlin uncommonly dependent on his mother.* He remained deeply, if ambivalently, attached to her; but also to his grandmother, his younger sister and his half-brother, Karl Gock. In 1784 Hölderlin became a boarder at the Lower Monastery School at Denkendorf, two years later at the Upper Monastery School at Maulbronn. (Despite the name, both were Protestant institutions.)

From 1788 to 1793 he studied for his ordination at the Theological Seminary at Tübingen, the 'Stift'. There he founded a Poetry Club together with his friends Neuffer and Magenau, who shared his enthusiasm for the French Revolution, and formed friendships with two other fellow students who were to become eminent philosophers, Hegel and Schelling. As early as 1787 he became engaged to Luise Nast, the cousin of a school friend, but broke off the engagement in 1790. At Tübingen he fell in love with Elise Lebret, but by this time he knew that he would not take up the career planned for him by his mother and might never be in a position to support a family. In the autumn of 1789 he had gone so far as to ask his mother's permission to leave the university, but was persuaded to stay on, wrote theses on the History of the Fine Arts in Greece and on Parallels between the Proverbs of Solomon and Hesiod's *Works and Days*, as well as a great deal of poetry, obtained his degree of 'Magister' and passed his final examinations in theology.

Though Hölderlin was never to become a Lutheran minister, the kind of education he received has an immediate bearing on his poetry. The

*Several biographers and psychologists have made much of that dependence, even tracing his later 'schizophrenia' to the emotional tensions of his childhood and adolescence. One Freudian study of that kind is Dr Jean Laplanche's *Hölderlin et la Question du Père* (Paris, 1961).

would-be harmonious blending of theological and classical studies that characterized the Denkendorf, Maulbronn and Tübingen institutions had a formative effect on his conception of poetry and of the poet's function, though it was not their blending but their incompatibility that was to preoccupy him. There may even be a vital connection between the peculiarities of Swabian religious traditions, such as the millenarian and mystical doctrines of Bengel and Oetinger, and some of Hölderlin's chiliastic visions. The French scholar Robert Minder wrote an ingenious summary of theological traditions which he traced not only to Hölderlin but also to Hegel and Karl Marx.*

Another critic, L. S. Salzberger, argued that Hölderlin's was 'the typical Renaissance view of the *poeta theologus* or *sacer vates*' relating it to that of poets from Tasso, Ronsard and Sir Philip Sidney to Milton and Klopstock. The inner gate of the Tübingen Stift bore the inscription *Aedes Deo et Musis Sacrae*, and it was Hölderlin's privilege and burden to dedicate himself to the same dual service at a time when this Renaissance tradition was virtually extinct, religious allegiances harder and harder to reconcile with humanistic and aesthetic ones. The subject of the comparative study that Hölderlin wrote at Tübingen is also significant. Because of his essential syncretism, it could be said of Hölderlin, as Hazlitt said of Milton, that 'he had his thoughts constantly fixed on the contemplation of Hebrew theocracy, and of a perfect commonwealth', even though it was the theocracy of an idealized ancient Greece that Hölderlin much more often invoked until his 'return to the source' in middle life; and also that 'his religious zeal infused its character into his imagination, so that he devoted himself with the same sense of duty to the cultivation of his genius, as he did to the exercise of virtue, or the good of his country'. Although there is no documentary evidence that Hölderlin ever read Milton, I have pointed to some striking concordances in the work of the two poets, especially Milton's *Samson Agonistes* and Hölderlin's *Empedocles* fragments.† To Hazlitt's description of the *sacer vates* – with complications, in Hölderlin's case, due to his fervent pantheism, at one stage, and his need in early years to come to terms with the latest developments in German philosophy – we must add a radicalism and intransigence that prevented both Milton and Hölderlin from making a trade of their religious vocations. Both were deterred by 'a conscience that would retch', as Milton put it, though their reasons for preferring a

---

*'*Herrlichkeit*' chez Hegel, ou le Monde des Pères Souabes. In *Etudes Germaniques*, July–Dec. 1951, pages 225–90.
†*The Sublime Art. Notes on Milton and Hölderlin*. In *Reason and Energy*. London. 1070.

'blameless silence' may have been as different as the characters of the two men in other regards, their beliefs and their aspirations. The differences between Milton's England and Hölderlin's Württemberg in an era of post-Enlightenment, post-classicism, repressed revolutionary ferment and the Napoleonic wars, are so glaring that they need no comment here.

Even in his childhood Hölderlin had been moody, hyper-sensitive and subject to waves of extreme depression or elation. He was devoted not only to his friends but to a cult of friendship widespread in late eighteenth-century Germany and so effusive that twentieth-century biographers and critics, such as Pierre Berteaux, could mistake it for homosexuality; but he found it hard to be sociable in a more general way. His ode 'Mein Vorsaz' ('My Resolution'), written when he was seventeen, shows how acutely aware he was at this early time that his vocation and ambition set him apart even from his closest friends:

> O friends, my friends, who love me so loyally,
>> What can so dim, so trouble my lonely gaze?
>> What makes my wretched heart seek refuge
>>> Here in this gloomy and deathly stillness?
>
> I flee the tender clasp of your hands, avoid
>> The soulful, happy touch of a brother's lips.
>> Oh, don't be angry, friends, forgive me! –
>>> Look at my innermost self, then judge me! –
>
> Is it hot thirst for manly perfection, then?
>> A craving, hushed, for fame and a hecatomb?
>> A feeble urge to Pindar's flight? Or
>>> Strenuous striving for Klopstock's greatness?
>
> Ah, friends, where can I hide, to what corner of
>> This earth escape, and wrapped in perpetual night,
>> Weep there? For never shall I know the
>>> Flight of those men round the world, in no time.
>
> And yet I will, I'll climb the most glorious path!
>> Climb on, climb on in ardent and reckless dreams
>> Of joining them; I will, though, dying,
>>> Faintly I mutter, forget me, children!

Klopstock – acclaimed in his lifetime as 'the German Milton' – was Hölderlin's earliest model. Klopstock not only wrote his Christian epic *Der Messias* in classical hexameters, but imitated or adapted Greek and Latin ode forms, one of which, the Alcaic, Hölderlin chose for this early poem and returned to for his more mature work, after discarding the rhymed stanzas taken over from his second master, Schiller. As for Pindar, he outlasted both of Hölderlin's German masters, leading him to his most daring departures from all the conventions of German verse – structural, metric and even syntactic. The Pindar translations I felt it necessary to re-translate from Hölderlin's German were the last piece of work completed by Hölderlin before the collapse of his poetic ambition.

His early ambition, a Hellenism more fervent and radical than any built into the educational system, and a political radicalism even less compatible with it, turned Hölderlin away from the career for which he had been trained since childhood, with subsidies from both Church and State. His alternative was the humble drudgery, but relative independence, of a private tutor. Despite pressure from his mother, who took care to keep him dependent on her financially throughout the crises that followed inevitably, Hölderlin refused again and again to take up the ministry for which he was qualified. With the help of friends and of Schiller, who became his hero and patron for a number of years, he obtained the position of private tutor to the son of Charlotte von Kalb, whose literary interests and connections made her a congenial employer. At her home in Waltershausen, where he lived from the winter of 1793 to the following summer, Hölderlin worked on a first version of his novel *Hyperion*. In the autumn he took his pupil to Jena, attended Fichte's philosophical lectures, saw a good deal of Schiller and met several other prominent German writers, including Goethe. An early fragment of the novel was published by Schiller in his periodical *Thalia*.

Meanwhile Hölderlin's pupil proved intractable. Charlotte von Kalb sent them both to Weimar, then made provision for Hölderlin to live independently in Jena and Nürtingen until the summer of 1795. He continued his work on *Hyperion*, on the philosophical and idealistic 'hymns' he was writing in those years – rhymed poems very close to Schiller's in manner and dedicated to 'the ideals of humanity' – and on a translation from Ovid.

In December 1795 he was appointed tutor to the children of J. F. Gontard, a wealthy banker in Frankfurt, whose wife Susette became the 'Diotima' of Hölderlin's poems. If, as research has suggested, at Waltershausen Hölderlin had entered into an affair with Wilhelmine

Marianne Kirms, a young widow who acted as a companion to Charlotte von Kalb, and fathered her daughter born in July 1795 – to die of smallpox in the following year – nothing of this transpired in Hölderlin's extant letters of any period. Though Susette's social and marital status called for even greater discretion, no such reticence inhibited him from celebrating his love for Susette in letters, poems and the final version of *Hyperion*. Susette was more to him than a lover or mistress. She was the Platonic Diotima who transfigured Hölderlin's life and poetry. That is how he understood, explained and proclaimed the change; and his work bears it out. After the wordiness and stock metaphors of the rhymed 'hymns' propelled by enthusiasm without experience, in Frankfurt he found his true voice as a poet, the poise of the brief epigrams and almost epigrammatic odes with which my selection begins. The diffuse rhetoric of generalized enthusiasm had begun to crystallize.

In 1796 Susette, her four children, her mother-in-law and Hölderlin were forced to leave Frankfurt for Westphalia to escape the invading French army, while Gontard stayed behind to attend to his business. In Kassel they were joined by Wilhelm Heinse, the author of *Ardinghello*, a novel that influenced Hölderlin's view of ancient Greece by its penetration into what Nietzsche was to call the 'Dionysian' layers of the culture, as distinct from the Apollonian balance, symmetry and 'noble simplicity' which Winckelmann had emphasized. It was to Heinse that Hölderlin later addressed and dedicated his most explicitly Dionysian poem, the elegy 'Bread and Wine'. The relationship with Susette, who reciprocated Hölderlin's love, must have been easier during that emergency, in Gontard's absence.

After their return to Frankfurt in the following year, Hegel also became a tutor there. Hölderlin met Goethe once more, at Schiller's recommendation, but the rather formal interview was not to Hölderlin's advantage, and Goethe remained unaware or unappreciative of Hölderlin's best work. The first volume of *Hyperion* was published in 1797.

Hölderlin's novel has many of the peculiarities of his poems, especially the tendency towards a cyclic or spiralling progression that has been compared both to Hegel's dialectic in philosophy and to the sonata form in music. (Hölderlin was to make a structural principle of what he called 'the modulation of tones' in poetry.) This tendency may have something to do not only with aesthetics and philosophy – though at this period Hölderlin did keep up with the latest philosophical developments, also writing essays whose terminology is close to that of Fichte, Hegel and Schelling – but with Hölderlin's extreme vacillations of mood, which he summed up in his complaint, 'if only one were not so periodical!' In his tragic odes, as in his novel, Hölderlin's pantheism, his desire to be at one with the cosmos, continually comes up against his awareness not only of the differences between human and non-human nature, but of the isolation into which human beings are precipitated by their consciousness. This awareness, exacerbated by the philosophical preoccupations of Hölderlin's contemporaries and obsessions with the dichotomy of 'Nature' and 'Art', or nature and civilization, that had become acute in the writings of Rousseau, accounts for those moments in *Hyperion* which shock the reader by their bitterness, their sharp dualism and almost nihilistic despair.

'Man is a god when he dreams, a beggar when he reflects', Hyperion writes in the novel. Dreaming here is the state of mind that permits pantheistic communion; reflection, the self-consciousness that cuts off the individual from the rest of creation. It is the alternation of these states of mind, with characteristic modulations and variations more or less related to the hero's political and amorous experiences, and a gradual progression towards synthesis or reconciliation, that gives *Hyperion* a structure unlike that of any comparable novel. (Hölderlin also resorted to an astronomical term, the 'eccentric orbit', to describe his characteristic mode of progression.) Hyperion's dualism is elaborated in another passage.

There is an oblivion of all existence, a silencing of all individual being, in which it seems that we have found all things.

There is an oblivion of all existence, in which it seems that we have lost all things, a night of the soul in which not the faintest gleam of a star, not even the phosphorescence of rotten wood, can reach us.

When Hyperion is plunged into this negative state of mind – and all his experiences as a fighter for the liberation of Greece from the Turks, as of a lover and friend, are conducive to it – what had been 'all' before suddenly turns into 'nothing'. He becomes like one of those persons whom he pities for being 'in the grip of that Nothing which rules over us, who are thoroughly aware that we are born for Nothing, believe in a Nothing, work ourselves to the bone for a Nothing, until we gradually dissolve into Nothing . . .'.

Hölderlin's love for Susette, like his Hyperion's for the Diotima of the novel, was religious because it was a unifying principle and power, a binding together with Platonic extensions well beyond the personal sphere. As such it is celebrated not only in the poems to and about Diotima and in *Hyperion* but in poems with no personal context at all. Hölderlin's departure from the Gontard household in the autumn of 1798, after an unpleasant confrontation with his employer, plunged Hölderlin back into the dichotomy, to the point of undermining his already precarious idealism. Both his idealism and his humanism rested on the One and All of antiquity, rather than on the rationalism of modern progressive creeds. Even before the enforced separation from Susette, Hölderlin's reflection told him that the relationship was socially impossible, if only because he was little more than a beggar in the husband's eyes. (Private tutors were only in the process of becoming more than servants.) Hölderlin was to apologize to Susette for letting the Diotima of the novel die – one instance of his extraordinary prescience in everything to do with his own deepest concerns. Premonitions of his own tragic 'course of life' never left him for long, even before the rupture. Now his work was to enter a distinctly tragic phase.

Very significantly, his own definition of tragedy hinged on the same antithesis of union and separation. 'A lyrical poem', he wrote, 'is the continuous metaphor of a feeling.' A tragic poem, on the other hand, 'is the metaphor of an intellectual point of view'; and this intellectual point of view 'can be no other than the awareness of being at one with all that lives'. The hero of Hölderlin's own unfinished tragedy, Empedocles, resembles Hölderlin in being a pantheist with a mission to inspire and unite a whole people; but in *The Death of Empedocles* the stress had to fall on the hero's total separation from all that he loves, not only from the Agrigentines and his favourite disciple but even from Nature and the gods, from the very cosmos with which he had felt at one. After his vain attempts to finish that play, in successive versions that could not keep pace with his precipitous development as a poet or his intense thinking about the grounds and requirements of tragedy, his pantheism itself became modified by a sense of *hubris*, as though the downfall of his hero had taught him that cosmic mysteries must remain unspoken, unrevealed. Here it is relevant to quote his later, profound and cryptic, definition of the tragic (from his commentary on his translation of the *Oedipus Rex* of Sophocles): 'The representation of the tragic is mainly based on this, that what is monstrous and terrible in the coupling of god and man, in the total fusion of the power of Nature with the innermost depth of man, so that they are one at the moment of wrath, shall be made intelligible by showing how this total fusion into one is purged by their total separation.'

It was in 1797 that Hölderlin began work on his tragedy. An earlier dramatic project, *The Death of Socrates*, is mentioned in his letters, and several of his friends and contemporaries believed that he wrote a tragedy called *Agis*. Not a line remains of either work. The first version of *The*

Death of Empedocles, mainly written in 1798, consists of an almost complete first act and the greater part of a second, though there are gaps and passages never finalized even in this largest of the fragments. (All three versions were conceived as a five-act tragedy.) The second version, mainly of 1799, differs both in plot and execution from the first. Unlike the earlier and later versions, it is written not in blank-verse pentameters but in a shortened, predominantly iambic line that allows considerable rhythmic and metric variation, so much so that it has been described as free verse. Friedrich Beißner, editor of the *Große Stuttgarte Ausgabe* text, believed that Hölderlin may have completed more of the second version than the extant fragments.

Hölderlin did not publish so much as an extract from any of the three versions. Between the second and the third versions he wrote his reflections on this dramatic project and on tragedy in general, *Grund zum Empedokles*. The essay shows why the basic conception of the third version had to be totally different from that of the first and second. The planned introduction of a Chorus is only one feature of a much closer approximation in the last version to Hölderlin's Greek models, a shift that had begun in the second version, with its much greater stress on Empedocles' sin of *hubris*. As the essay confirms, in the process of writing the three versions Hölderlin grew more and more aware of the dramatist's need to remain partly detached from his hero – to be 'objective', as he called it, and able to place himself at one remove from that 'deepest inwardness' which the dramatic poem must convey even more dialectically than the tragic ode, Hölderlin's principle medium up to that time (apart from the novel, written in letter form, so as to permit the highest degree of subjectivity!).

Yet the main reason why Hölderlin finished no version of the play must be that he remained too closely identified with Empedocles, at the very period in his life when his own view of the poet as philosopher, prophet and priest – and as tragic hero – was subject to perpetual crisis and re-examination. The special significance for Hölderlin of Empedocles' mode of death – a physical fusion with the primal elements and return to the very womb of Earth – had already been intimated in his short ode 'Empedocles'; but the growing emphasis on his hero's guilt in the successive versions also has its parallels in later poems – most starkly and poignantly in the prose draft that breaks off his only strictly Pindaric hymn 'As on a holiday . . .', a poem written in the same year as the last version of the play, with many textual similarities. In the prose draft Hölderlin accuses himself of a *hubris* very much like that of which Manes accuses Empedocles:

when of
(a self-inflicted wound my heart is bleeding, and deeply lost
is peace of mind, and freely modest contentment,
And when unrest and deprivation drive me to
the superabundance of the banqueting table of gods,
when round about me . . .)

More remarkably still, Manes' characterization of the true saviour –
as opposed to the hubristic, over-reaching pantheist, Empedocles – seems
to point to that image of Christ which Hölderlin was to invoke in his
elegies and hymns (or cantos) of the next years. Another way of putting
it is that the play had to keep up with Hölderlin's own prodigious
development in the years between 1797 and 1800 and that each version,
therefore, ceased to be valid for him before it could be completed. It may
even be that, just as Empedocles had displaced Socrates in his sympathy
and imagination, another hero had displaced Empedocles by the time he
had clarified his ideas about the nature and needs of tragedy; but here it
is best to take up the biography again.

After his decision to leave the Gontard household in September 1798,
Hölderlin settled nearby, at Homburg. He kept up a correspondence with
Susette, mainly by hand delivery at secret meetings they were able to
arrange until May 1800. At Homburg Hölderlin resumed relations with
Isaak von Sinclair, whom he had first met in 1793, when Sinclair was a
law student and ardent republican. Sinclair was to prove a most loyal
and helpful friend to Hölderlin in the next few years. It was he who
introduced Hölderlin to the Landgrave of Homburg, whose daughter
Princess Auguste became an admirer of Hölderlin's works, to the point
of being in love with their author, within the limits set by her piety and
her rank. Apart from the ode addressed to her, she received the dedication
of Hölderlin's last book publication, his translations of Sophocles' *Oedipus
Rex* and *Antigone*. It was to the Landgrave, Friedrich V, that Hölderlin
was to dedicate his poem 'Patmos'. Its companion piece, 'The Rhine',
was dedicated to Sinclair. The Princess of Dessau to whom he addressed
another ode was Princess Auguste's married sister.

In November Sinclair invited Hölderlin to Rastatt, where Sinclair was
the Landgrave's representative at the Congress that was to have settled
questions of sovereignty arising from the shifting alliances and military
occupations of the Napoleonic wars. Hölderlin's revolutionary hopes and
his early admiration for Napoleon had already been shaken by Napoleon's
imperial ambitions – very much like those of Hölderlin's coeval Beethoven.

Sinclair's Republicanism or reformism was to precipitate another crisis for Hölderlin when his friend and patron was accused of a revolutionary conspiracy against the Prince Elector of Württemberg and tried for high treason in 1805. Although he was acquitted, Sinclair lost his function as a Minister to the Landgrave when the principality of Hessen–Homburg became part of the Grand Duchy of Hessen–Darmstadt in 1806.

1799 was a productive but critical year. For the first and last time Hölderlin tried desperately to establish himself as a self-supporting writer and find the place which he thought was due to him in the intellectual and cultural life of Germany. He planned a 'humanistic magazine', *Iduna*, to be devoted to the 'unification and reconciliation of the sciences with life, of art and good taste with genius, of the heart with the head, of the real with the ideal' – the very ends, in fact, that were his own most constant concern, basic to his view of the poet's religious and social function. His choice of contraries in the programme related his personal conflicts to a dichotomy widespread after the impact of Rousseau's thought, the cult of primitive genius in Herder and the literature of the *Sturm und Drang*, and the general tendency to posit an irreconcilable conflict between Nature and Art (or civilization). Schiller, too, was obsessed with it, as were the foremost German philosophers of Hölderlin's time. Goethe alone could claim to have overcome it, though, in its own way, Hölderlin's poetry achieved a fine balance of head and heart, of the real and the ideal, of 'Reason and Energy', as William Blake called two of his antinomies. The failure of Hölderlin's project – because of inadequate response from potential contributors, including Goethe – followed by that of his appeal to Schiller to find him an academic appointment, amounted to nothing less than his rejection by society. From now on Hölderlin felt himself to be a lonely outcast, like the Empedocles of his play or the Rousseau of his ode, and as a prophet without honour in his country. His poems of the next few years record the alienation, as do his letters of those years.

The second volume of *Hyperion* was published in 1799, and small batches of Hölderlin's poems continued to appear in yearbooks and miscellanies; but Hölderlin felt more and more isolated, more and more remote from the literature and culture of his time, which, in a letter, he was to describe as 'childlike'. Because of a growing impersonality and detachment in his work, there was a gradual transition from a predominantly tragic phase to a prophetic one, culminating in the visionary free-verse poems and fragments on which he worked even after his breakdown of 1802. The transition can be followed in his later odes, such as 'Exhortation' or 'Nature and Art'; and even the last version of *The Death of Empedocles* almost transcends tragedy, since the hero seems to have undergone a profound catharsis before the opening scene. It was as though in the years of extreme loneliness, frustration and self-questioning that followed his departure from Frankfurt – and there was also the humiliation inflicted on Hölderlin as a lover powerless to assert any claim or right, but knowing that Susette could well be even less able to recover from their separation than he was – Hölderlin could preserve his faith only by renouncing all his ambitions and attachments, virtually giving up his own self and becoming a disembodied voice crying out to 'future ages'. In 1801 he wrote to his half-brother:

I have struggled to the point of exhaustion to fix my faith and my vision upon that which is supreme in life; indeed, I had struggled amid sufferings which – to judge by all the evidence I know – were more overwhelming than any thing that men are capable of enduring, though they exert their utmost strength . . . At last, when my heart was already rent on more than one side, and yet held fast, I must also be led to embroil my thoughts in those evil doubts, that question so easily answered if only one's eyes are clear, namely what is more important, the eternal fountainhead of life or the temporal . . . But I continued to struggle till I found out the truth . . . There is only one quarrel in the world: which is more important, the whole or the individual part. And that quarrel, in every instance and application, is proved void in action, because the man who truly acts out of a sense of the whole is the more dedicated to peace for that very reason, more disposed to respect every individual person and thing, because his sense of humanity, the very quality that distinguishes him, will sooner permit him to fall into egoism – or whatever you choose to call it – than into pure generality.

A Deo principium. Whoever understands this, and lives up to it . . . that person is free and strong and full of joy.

This renewed faith sustained Hölderlin's prophetic, and increasingly impersonal, poetry, but it could not alleviate his deepening solitude. Thanking his sister in 1800 for writing to remind him of their family bonds, he told her that 'this sustains my heart, which in the end too often loses its own voice in a solitude all too complete, and withdraws from one's very self'. The voice of the heart – words that also occur in one of Hölderlin's odes – was more than a sentimental trope in a poet who believed that the capacity to feel is a prerequisite even for religious dedication. It was the loss of that capacity – after the loss of the one woman he had loved religiously – that marks the poems written not by

Hölderlin but by the person he became when his sufferings had broken him. Whether or not we call that condition 'catatonic stupor' – or 'schizophrenia', to use the later term – has little bearing on his poetry.

As far as his poetry is concerned, that quarrel between the whole and the part was truly resolved. If he had once been in acute danger of falling into 'pure generality' in his poems – the early poems not included here – because his youthful enthusiasm had shied away from particulars, the poetry of his prophetic phase became more and more physical, more and more sensuous, more and more concrete. Already in the successive drafts of his ode 'Des Morgens' (1799) we see how 'the leaves of the tree' becomes 'the poplar bends', then 'the birch tree bends', finally 'the beech tree bends'; but it is in the visionary landscapes of the free-verse hymns and fragments – whether drawn from memory or from imagination and literary sources, as for the Greek landscapes he never saw – that he succeeded best in 'respecting every individual person and thing', just because each is imbued with a 'sense of the whole'. His turning away from an idealized ancient Greece to local, regional or national concerns and the interpretation of modern history was part of the same process.

At Homburg he took up his Greek studies in a more critical and methodical manner than before, and began to formulate his insights into the differences between ancient and modern cultures, as well as into the laws governing epic, dramatic and lyric poetry. In the spring of 1800 he went home to Nürtingen, as he had done repeatedly between attempts to make an independent life for himself, then stayed at Stuttgart as the guest of his friend Christian Landauer, to whom he dedicated an elegy I have not translated, 'Der Gang aufs Land'. The poems written there include the ode 'Das Ahnenbild', a longer poem, 'An eine Verlobte' and the tiny elegy 'Die Entschlafenen'. I had omitted all these poems from earlier selections because they struck me as untypical, if not freakish. One of them is included now.* All these Stuttgart poems differ from others written by Hölderlin at this period in being neither tragic nor prophetic. They are celebrations of those human affections and continuities denied to Hölderlin by his circumstances and vocation. They were also occasional poems, written in response to the friendship and hospitality offered to a homeless guest. The 'ancestral portrait' of the ode is one of Christian Landauer's father, who had died in August of that year, while Hölderlin was staying in the house. The boy of the poem was his friend's only son, four years old at the time. What Hölderlin's relative realism in

*Another. 'Die Entschlafenen'. is in the Anvil edition. 1004.

this poem could not accommodate was that his friend's prosperity rested on a textile business founded by the same father, not on the agricultural and horticultural pursuits which the ode celebrates. Christian Landauer, though, would not have been Hölderlin's friend if he had not combined worldly astuteness with concerns more congenial to Hölderlin. If the ode stands out as the nearest thing to the domestic poetry, or the bucolics and idylls, otherwise beyond Hölderlin's range – 'Domestic Life' was a rejected title for the ode – his religious preoccupations were by no means in abeyance there. The dead father becomes a spirit – akin to the *lares* and *penates* of antiquity – in the penultimate strophe, by a construction so puzzling syntactically that I had to bridge it with guesswork; and a piety at once natural and spiritual informs the whole poem. The two strands intertwine in the child's drinking of his grandfather's wine – an image at once naively representational and fraught with religious symbolism. These attempts of Hölderlin's to merge his own preoccupations in those of 'ordinary' people are a prefiguration of his last, unrecognizable, phase and person. After the change he was to write two poems on the birth of a child.

From Stuttgart Hölderlin went to Nürtingen for Christmas, then set out for Hauptwyl in Switzerland to take up another engagement as a private tutor. As usual, Hölderlin travelled on foot most of the way, though it was January and he had to cross the Alps. He passed through Stuttgart again on the way, and his friends escorted him as far as Tübingen. By April his employer in Switzerland, Gonzenbach, whose two daughters were Hölderlin's pupils, terminated the engagement 'for family reasons'. Again, Hölderlin set out on one of his long walks, also rowing across Lake Constance, seeing the Danube, and revisiting his birthplace. His one Sapphic ode, 'Sung beneath the Alps', and the elegy 'Homecoming' celebrate the landscapes through which he had passed and his return to his family in April. Many impressions of the journeys also entered into his hymns and fragments. For the rest of the year he remained at Nürtingen, with visits to Stuttgart.

In January 1802 he set out for his last appointment as a tutor, in Bordeaux. There, too, he spent only a few months, returning home – on foot once more – in a state of acute disturbance and distress. On his outward journey, which took more than a month, he is known to have stopped in Strasbourg and Lyon, where he had to report as an alien. The long itinerary of his return, including a visit to Paris, has been the subject of endless speculation and debate. Pierre Berteaux, who questioned the madness imputed to Hölderlin after his return, argued that Hölderlin could have passed through Frankfurt and learned of Susette's illness, possibly even have seen her, before arriving in Stuttgart in mid-June; but Susette died on 22 June, by which time Hölderlin must have been back with his family. Berteaux also suggests that Hölderlin's mother found Susette's love letters to Hölderlin in the trunk he had sent home from Bordeaux, and that altercations about that precipitated Hölderlin's alleged rages. What is certain is that as soon as Hölderlin left his mother's house again for Stuttgart, after brief convalescence at home, he recovered sufficiently to work again. An estrangement from his whole family undoubtedly occurred at this time – and no wonder, in the light of what is now known of their behaviour towards him in later years, their petty squabbles about money up to and after his death, even over the monument to be placed on his grave.

After receiving the letter from Sinclair, written at the end of June, informing him of Susette's death, he took refuge again briefly at his mother's. Though Susette died of German measles caught from her children, her health had been in decline ever since her last meeting with Hölderlin in 1800.

There is a letter written by Hölderlin after his return from Bordeaux that tells us more about his state of mind at this time than all the biographical reconstructions or extant reports by acquaintances of his haggard appearance, his silences, unintelligible utterances and outbreaks of rage. The physical hardships of his travels, too, must have had something to do with the changes in his appearance. The letter, or draft of a letter, was to Casimir Ulrich Böhlendorff, written in November 1802:

Dear friend,

I have not written to you for a long time, and meanwhile have been in France and have seen the sad, lonely earth; the shepherds and shepherdesses of southern France and individual beauties, men and women, who grew up in the fear of political uncertainty and of hunger.

The mighty element, the fire of heaven and the silence of the people, their life in nature, their confinedness and their contentment, moved me continually, and as one says of heroes, I can well say of myself that Apollo has struck me.

In the regions bordering on the Vendée I was interested in a quality fiercely warlike, and purely masculine, to which the light of life becomes spontaneous, immediate in eye and limb, which experiences the sensation of death like a kind of virtuosity and satisfies its thirst for knowledge.

The athletic character of the southern peoples, in the ruins of the ancient spirit, made me more familiar with the true character of the Greeks: I came to understand their nature and their wisdom, their bodies, how they grew in their climate and the rule they used to preserve their exuberant genius from the violence of the element.

This determined their peculiarity as a people, their way of adopting foreign natures and of communicating with them, and it is from this that they derived their distinct individuality which seems alive, in so far as supreme understanding, to the Greeks, was the power to respond to reality; and this becomes comprehensible to us when we comprehend the heroic bodies of the Greeks; it is tenderness, like our own peculiarity as a people.

The contemplation of ancient statuary made an impression on me that brought me closer to an understanding not only of the Greeks, but of what is greatest in all art, which, even where movement is most intense, the conception most phenomenalized and the intention most serious, still preserves every detail intact and true to itself, so that assuredness, in this sense, is the supreme kind of representation.

After many shocks and disturbances of my mind it was necessary for me to settle down for a while, and for the time being I am staying in my home town.

Nature in these parts moves more powerfully, the more I study it. The thunder-storm, not only in its extreme manifestation, but precisely as a power and shape, among the other forms of the sky, light in its workings, nationally and as a principle that fashions a mode of fate, so that something is holy to us, its urgency in coming and going, what is characteristic in forests and the convergence in one region of different kinds of nature, so that all the holy places of the earth come together around one place, and the philosophic light around my window – these are now my joy; and may I bear in mind how I came here, as far as this place!

Dear friend, I think that we shall not gloss the poets up to our time, but that song altogether will assume a different character, and that we cannot make ourselves heard because we, after the Greeks, are beginning once more to sing nationally and naturally, that is, in a truly original way.

Please write to me soon. I need pure tones. Psyche among friends, the generation of thought in conversation and letters is necessary for artists ... Otherwise we have no thought for ourselves; but it belongs to the holy image which we are shaping. A sincere farewell.

Yours,
Hölderlin

That autumn Hölderlin received medical treatment at Stuttgart, but was reported to have grown composed whenever the doctor's son read out passages from Homer to him. At the end of September Hölderlin travelled to Regensburg, where the Landgrave and his Minister, Sinclair, were trying to negotiate an enlargement of the Landgrave's territory. Soon after, Hölderlin submitted an early version of his Sophocles translations to a publisher and worked on his poem 'Patmos', sent to Sinclair in January 1803. In June of that year he set out on another walk, to Murhardt in Württemberg, where he called on his old friend Schelling. That year his Sophocles translations were accepted for book publication – his first since the two volumes of *Hyperion*, and the only other he was to see into print.

Hölderlin's 'return to the source', his symbolic homecoming, is intimated in his dedication to Princess Auguste of his Sophocles book: 'Apart from these, if time permits, I will sing the forefathers of our princes, their seats, and the angels of our holy country.' It was in these years that he worked on his most ambitious project, a series of hymns or cantos that were to range over the cosmology, myths and history of ancient and modern times, from the revolt of the Titans to the discovery of America and Hölderlin's own era. The Virgin Mary and Columbus were the subject of extant drafts and fragments. Luther and Shakespeare were among the titles jotted down for poems never written or lost. Yet until the collapse of this endeavour he could not wholly renounce the Greek gods, and his last intense exertions were directed towards a visionary reconciliation of his Greek and Christian allegiances, even though this demanded an almost hopeless attempt to syncretize a pantheistic and polytheistic system with a higher monotheism.

In 1803, at Nürtingen, Hölderlin also prepared for publication the group of late short poems which appeared in a miscellany as 'Nachtgesänge' ('Canticles of Night') in 1804. They included the odes 'Chiron', 'Tears', 'To Hope', 'Vulcan', 'Timidness' and 'Ganymede', but also free-verse poems that had originated as parts of his longer hymns, 'The Ages of Life', 'Half of Life' and 'The Nook at Hardt'. By recognizing that such fragments could be published as separate poems, Hölderlin won a last victory over the taste and conventions of his own time. Nearly a century had to pass before such poems came into their own, as anticipations of Symbolist, Imagist and even Surrealist practices. Yet these very fragments are closely akin to those that Hölderlin extracted from Pindar, with his comments, as late as 1805. By 'originality' Hölderlin meant something quite different from 'modernity' or personal idiosyncracy; it had to do with 'going to the source'. If both his own poems and his Pindar versions strike us as 'modern', it is because they rely not on argument but on particulars charged with the most concentrated significance, on the mere naming of a person or thing or their invocation by signs, where less daring poets of Hölderlin's time or any other would have presented a sequence of arguments and metaphors. In the later versions of the hymns, too, there are instances not only of inverted or deliberately ambiguous syntax – justified by Hölderlin's insights into Greek poetry, especially Pindar's – but of a-syntactic sentences that serve as a poetic shorthand. The most astonishing contraction of all occurs in the later version of 'Patmos'. The later poems proceed by flashes of perception or allusion, true to the laws not of discourse or argument but of pre-articulate feeling and thought, a poetic 'architecture' which Hölderlin distinguished from the logical structure of expository prose.

In many cases it may well be that Hölderlin never got beyond drafts or sketches that would have been filled out at a later stage; and it is some of these that prefigure the work of twentieth-century poets like Ezra Pound, whose ambition and range in his *Cantos* are comparable to Hölderlin's in drafts like this one:

> So Mahomed*, Rinaldo,
> Barbarossa as a liberal spirit,
> The Emperor Heinrich.
> But we are mixing up
> the periods
>   Demetrius Poliorcetes
> Peter the Great
>   Heinrich's
> crossing of the Alps, and that
> with his own hand he gave the people food
> and drink and his son Conrad died of poison
> Example of one who changes an age
> reformer
> Conradin etc.
> all as representative
> of conditions
> * hear the horn of the watchman by night
> After midnight it is, at the fifth hour

Fortuitous as the resemblance may be, because Hölderlin's lines are only the nucleus of an unwritten poem, there is something about the quality of his historical imagination here that makes one think of Pound's *Cantos*; but also of Hölderlin's words in the letter to Böhlendorff about 'all the holy places of the earth coming together around one place', and the endeavour of a single mind, a single imagination, to embrace them all. Hölderlin put it more trenchantly still in the draft of one of his unfinished poems:

> And there I am
> All things at once

Another fragment of Hölderlin's contains hints of what he was trying to do before giving up his poetic ambition – perhaps, too, of the rages that alarmed his relatives and friends:

> But language –
> In thunder speaks the
> God.
> Often I have it, language
> anger, she said, was enough and approved by Apollo –
> If you have love enough, then, go on, rage out of love.
> Often I tried to sing, but they did not hear you. For
> that was holy Nature's will. For her you sang in your youth.
> Not singing
> You spoke to the deity,
> but what all of you have forgotten is that always the first-born belong
> not to mortals but to the gods.
> More common, more everyday
> the fruit must become, only then
> will mortals possess it.

Though far from becoming easier to grasp or to follow – the 'she' in the fifth line could be not a person but a noun feminine in German, like language itself – Hölderlin's language and imagery in the late poems did become more common, more everyday, often to the point of a colloquialism far removed from the sublime or abstract diction of his beginnings.

In July 1804 Sinclair took Hölderlin to Homburg, where he had obtained the hardly more than titular appointment of Court Librarian for his friend, paying the salary out of his own. In April the Sophocles book had appeared, with complimentary copies for Goethe, Hegel and Schelling, but not Schiller. Hölderlin's mother had resisted Sinclair's offer of the appointment, on the grounds that Hölderlin was unfit for it. In fact, Schelling and others thought that Hölderlin's condition had improved since the previous year, and Sinclair reported to Hölderlin's

mother that in his opinion many of Hölderlin's oddities had been deliber-
ately assumed. It was Hölderlin's failure to write to his mother at this
period that made her anxious. In January 1805 Hölderlin came close to
being implicated in the accusations raised against Sinclair, who was
denounced for a plot not against his immediate sovereign the Landgrave,
but against the Grand Duke of Württemberg. Hölderlin is reported to
have protested vociferously more than once in public that he was no
Jacobin – as indeed he had ceased to be, thanks to Napoleon's imperial
conquests. The Landgrave protected Hölderlin, but believed that he was
no longer capable of looking after himself. In new lodgings, in the absence
of his friend and patron Sinclair, he is reported to have 'strummed wildly
on his piano by day and by night'; but he was still capable of working
on his Pindar translation and commentary when Sinclair returned to
Homburg in July. In January 1806 Hölderlin's mother applied to the
Consistory for an annual bounty for her son from the royal purse – the
Grand Duke of Württemberg had assumed the title of King – on the
grounds of his illness and 'exhaustion of his patrimony'. The bounty was
awarded, although there is documentary evidence now that the substantial
fortune Hölderlin had inherited from his father and an aunt, far from
being 'exhausted', was withheld from him by his mother throughout his
life. Not even the interest on his capital had been spent by him or on
him when he died. In July of that year the Landgrave's territory was
merged in a new Grand Duchy, so that Hölderlin's titular appointment
was void.

In August Sinclair had to inform Hölderlin's mother that her son could
not remain in Homburg and would have to be taken into care elsewhere,
because he was in danger of being assaulted by the mob. In September
Hölderlin, who resisted vehemently, was removed by force to the lately
opened Autenrieth clinic in Tübingen. This was reputed to be the most
'advanced' mental home in Germany. There was drug treatment of a
sort, belladonna and digitalis, but also the notorious Autenrieth mask,
applied to stop patients from screaming, besides the straitjacket and long
forcible immersions in cold water inside a cage. One of Hölderlin's fellow
patients died of the treatment he received. Hölderlin was also treated for
a physical condition, scabies. In the summer of 1807 he was discharged
as an incurable case and given 'three years to live at the most'. He survived
for another 36 years – just about half his lifetime.

At the clinic he was visited by the carpenter Ernst Zimmer, who had
read *Hyperion*, and it was Zimmer who arranged with Autenrieth that
private care would be a better alternative for Hölderlin. It was in Zimmer's

house or 'tower' on the bank of the Neckar in Tübingen that Hölderlin was to spend the remainder of his life; and it was thanks to the kindness, understanding and care of the Zimmer family that this second half of Hölderlin's life was peaceful at least. Very soon Zimmer gave him not only the freedom of the house, but took him on those walks that were his consolation and the subject of verses not wholly void of personal responses and awareness, as the later ones became, when Hölderlin had ceased to exist as far as he was concerned, turning into 'Scardanelli, or something of the sort'.

The many reports by visitors in these later years, including those by the poet Wilhelm Waiblinger, who wrote a full account of his meetings, are of mainly pathological and sociological interest. I quote only Zimmer's account of the genesis of one little poem, 'The lines of life . . .', which shows that Hölderlin remained capable of at least one affection, though he kept most visitors at a distance with an excess of polite deference and forms of address like 'Your Highness' or 'Your Majesty'. In one of his periodic letters to Hölderlin's mother – who seems never to have visited her son in all the years up to her death in 1828 – the semi-literate carpenter informs her as follows of the writing of those lines: 'His poetic spirit still shows itself to be active, for instance in my house he saw the drawing of a temple. He told me to make one out of wood. I replied that I have to work for my living, that I am not so fortunate as to live in philosophic calm like him, immediately he replied, "Oh, I am a wretched creature", and in the same minute he wrote these verses on a wooden board with his pencil:

> The lines of life are various; they diverge and cease
> Like footpaths and the mountains' utmost ends.
> What here we are, elsewhere a God amends
> With harmonies, eternal recompense and peace.'

Almost all the later poems, usually on the seasons – with one or two exceptions in the years between 1823 and 1825 – were dashed off at the request of visitors, who wanted a memento or curio in exchange for little gifts of tobacco or the like. The poem 'Spring' ('When springtime from the depth . . .') is believed to have been written on Hölderlin's last birthday, in March 1843. He died suddenly of pulmonary congestion on 7 June of that year, at the age of 73.

It is useless to wonder what course Hölderlin's life might have taken if he had been granted some degree of financial independence at the age of 21, or even 25, but there can be little doubt that it would have been a rather less catastrophic one. At his death, in the absence of immediate heirs, his considerable inheritance passed to his sister and half-brother, without ever having been at his disposal. Even in the second half of his life, when there was no question of his earning a living, Zimmer had to make special appeals to Karl Gock, the half-brother, or to other legal guardians whenever Hölderlin's physical condition called for small additions to his frugal diet. Since Hölderlin's guardians also received the annual bounty for his maintenance out of royal funds, their treatment of him could not have been more callous or more mean. The piano that was Hölderlin's constant resort in those Tübingen years – he had come to prefer it to his first instrument, the flute – belonged not to him but to Zimmer, although Princess Auguste had given Hölderlin a piano in his Homburg years. It appears that, like most of his books, the piano was never moved into the room that was to be the nearest thing to a home ever occupied by him since his childhood.

In May or June 1807 Zimmer was also told to take away the loose-leaf folio manuscript sheaf in which Hölderlin had been drafting and rewriting his poems since the Homburg period, and deliver it to the family. The almost complete break in his work at this juncture may have a great deal to do with this confiscation of his work sheets – his only possible aid to continuity at the time. This is not to deny that there was a break and change in Hölderlin's personality both before and after his ordeal in the clinic. From his odes 'To the Fates' and 'The Course of Life' onwards he had predicted that his life would run an arc-shaped course, a sheer ascent and a sheer descent, a steep progression and a steep regression. In July 1799 he had written to his sister: 'And one day, when I am a grey-haired boy, may spring and the morning and the evening light rejuvenate me a little more each day, until I feel the last and sit down in the open air and from there go away, to eternal youth.'

Zimmer's comment on Hölderlin's 'madness' is as good as any: 'It's the too much he had in him that cracked his mind.' Another is by the poet Ernst Meister, one of a line of twentieth-century German poets, including Rilke, Trakl, Bobrowski and Celan, who were able to learn from Hölderlin in one way or another: 'Perhaps Hölderlin allowed himself to be "stricken" so as to make up for having missed the life of "ordinary" people, the provincial or parochial life, as it were, in the island's interior, against which the whole of being surges and breaks.'* According to

*Ernst Meister. *Prosa 1931 bis 1979* (Heidelberg. 1989).

Waiblinger's account, Hölderlin himself said: 'Only now do I understand human beings, now that I live far from them and in solitude.' In some of the later occasional verses there is such a degree of assent to the views and sentiments of 'ordinary' people that they read like mocking parodies of them, just as the letters Hölderlin was persuaded to write to his mother in those years read like mocking parodies of the filial sentiments he had long ceased to feel. That is why both contemporary and later commentators were able to suspect that his 'madness' was put on, that it served him as a means of deliberate non-communication. Other 'tower' poems, like 'The Walk' and 'The Merry Life', written out of a residual urge, rather than for casual visitors, hint at his own interpretation of his change of personality: peace at all costs, humble contentment, retraction as well as retirement, after unbearable endeavours, sufferings and defeats. Part of the cost, though, was loss of reality. Even the landscapes and townscapes of these poems have become scenery in more senses than one; they could be stage scenery, because there is nothing left in them of the breath, pulse and animation of Hölderlin's earlier responses to things seen, remembered or mythically evoked. What had gone out of them was conflict. 'Without Contraries there is no progression', Blake wrote. Hölderlin's last poems are poems of regression into a world ready-made for him and accepted, down to the tritest rhyming of one dead thing with another. Some of them do contain moments of unprecedented limpidity, just because the words used are impersonal and transparent. So in parts of the ode 'If from the distance . . .' in which Philippe Jaccottet found 'the most difficult and rarest thing of all, the moment when poetry, without seeming to do so, because it has been stripped of all brilliance, attains to what, to me, is the highest point'; but, in his *Paysages avec Figures Absentes* (1970), Jaccottet also found such moments in poems by Hölderlin written well before his years in the tower. In terms of Hölderlin's 'course of life' and its overall meaning, D. E. Sattler is not wrong in seeing 'childhood regained' in the best of the tower poems, but nor is David Constantine wrong in his judgement of these poems as a whole: 'Some of the Tübingen poems are beautiful and touching, and some have moments of the purest immanence such as the preceding poetry had always striven to achieve; but the inexorable trend is downwards and away.'

This selection now includes enough of the last verses for readers to judge for themselves – partly because I translated a batch of the Scardanelli poems for the first performance in England of Heinz Holliger's settings of them in his *Scardanelli Cycle* – one remarkable instance of the fascination the very unselfing in them can exercise. From his lifetime to its rediscovery and re-editing in this century, Hölderlin's work has given rise to so much disagreement, such diversity of judgement and interpretation, that I have tried hard here to confine myself to a sketching in of its background. It is in my selection and translations – reconsidered and enlarged over a period of fifty years – that my preferences are implicit; and though I have also tried hard not to rationalize the texts by ironing out their oddities, resolving their ambiguities and enigmas, texts like these cannot be translated at all without a modicum of interpretation. The controversies in the fifties about the newly discovered 'Friedensfeier', in which I took part briefly after identifying the manuscript in London, where it came to light, showed me that there could be no agreement even about the identity of the persons or powers invoked in the hymns, like the 'prince of the feast-day' in that poem, variously interpreted as Napoleon, as Christ, as a personification of peace itself, or as 'the genius of our people, . . . the long concealed "soul of the fatherland" '! Each of these interpretations was plausible and learnedly presented, each came to the conclusion most consonant with the interpreter's proclivities, beliefs and concerns. It became clear to me that what Hölderlin chose not to identify clearly in his poems – by circumscription, ambiguity or the withholding of names – should be left in suspense if at all possible. Nor, in Hölderlin's work, could a turn of speech or attribute in one poem necessarily serve as a key to its recurrence in another, because his progression was one through contraries, through conflicts strenuously fought out, and leaps into the unknown.

For Hölderlin, the need always to write in accordance with his latest insights and vision, even if these seemed to contradict earlier ones enacted with the same intensity, was more compelling still than the need for completeness and consistency. At the same time he believed in what, in an early letter, he called 'the aesthetic Church', demanding that everything done should come as close to artistic perfection as he could make it. That tension, as well as his precipitous career and the probable loss of many of his papers, goes far towards explaining the fragmentary state of much of his work. By producing later, much longer, versions of his brief Frankfurt odes, for instance, poems as artistically flawless as anything he produced, for himself he reduced these earlier odes to fragments, as it were, although the later, tragic or prophetic, elaborations of their themes made something quite different out of them, so that for his readers both versions are valid. On the other hand, for the last poems he sent out for periodical publication, he made poems of an unprecedented kind out of fragments.

Extreme antithesis and extreme synthesis make it hardly possible to separate aesthetic or stylistic considerations from religious and philosophical ones in Hölderlin's work, that of a poet who produced essentially classical work in a Romantic age. Yet one thing that is common to all of Hölderlin's work, not excluding the last poems, is what his coeval Wordsworth called 'natural piety'. It was in search of an all-pervading piety that Hölderlin turned to ancient Greece, away from a culture of which he wrote in *Hyperion*: 'Where you see nothing, there your gods dwell.' Because this ancient Greece could not be brought back, as Hölderlin came to acknowledge after daring plunges into its mysteries, the work up to his middle years is also distinguished by a powerful dynamic of aspiration – enacted not only by the enjambment of lines but the overflowing of whole strophes into the next – within strict forms and structures, a symmetry demanded by 'stillness of beauty'. (Even when he had abandoned the attempt to imitate the metrical correspondence in Pindar's odes, because the public function of their performance was missing, he kept to a basically triadic structure.) In the same way Hölderlin tried again and again to bridge what may well be unbridgeable antinomies between a pantheistic and polytheistic religion of nature and the 'solid letter' of Judaic–Christian monotheism, and to do so on the basis of his own epiphanies – up to the 'God of gods' of a late poem, a hierarchy that would embrace and justify the periodicity and alternation of divine revelation and retraction which he saw in successive eras. He himself was well aware that the language of his late hymns and fragments would be judged 'too unconventional' by contemporary readers, as his little preface to the 'Friedensfeier' attests. Some of the polysemies in such poems arose from his awareness that he was venturing on to forbidden ground, into mysteries that should be left unspoken; others from antinomies that he could not resolve, only bridge by a purely poetic structure and syntax or by images that are not metaphors reducible to a single meaning. One instance, not only 'too unconventional' but an affront to grammarians and logicians, if not to theologians, is the opening of his late 'Patmos' fragment:

> Voll Güt' ist; keiner aber fasset
> Allein Gott.

The syntactic preposterousness of those lines is heightened by an ambiguity which my translation could not render. Since the *allein* occurs in the second line, it could qualify either God or 'no one'; or both at once, just as 'God' is the elided subject of the first three words and the explicit object of the second clause. The lines could mean that no one can grasp God by himself, unaided, or that God cannot be grasped in Himself, alone; and the missing link in either case may or may not be the 'solid letter' of the earlier version of the poem, the tradition of scripture. It could also be the Trinity or unnamed agents of mediation. Poetically, though, these lines have the effect of a thunderclap and lightning flash – themselves the signs of the manifestation of God in antiquity and in Hölderlin's poems, and a physical phenomenon arising from the collision and fusion of disparate energies. This sentence explains why Ezra Pound liked to derive the German word *dichten*, to make poetry, from the adjective *dicht*, dense, so wresting a truth about poetry from an etymological error.

One way of dealing with such affronts offered by Hölderlin's poems is to ascribe them to his 'madness'. Yet already in his short ode of the Frankfurt years 'To the Sanctimonious Poets' – whose harshly sarcastic tone contrasts so starkly with that of his other poems of the period and makes it more like a satirical epigram – Hölderlin told the 'cold hypocrites' who were adorning their conventional poems with the names of Greek gods:

> You're rational! In Helios you don't believe,
> > Nor in the Thunderer or the Sea-God;
> > > Dead is our Earth, so what fool would thank her?

'Dead is our Earth'. As far as I know, these – ironically intended – words of Hölderlin have never been promoted to the kind of actuality accorded to a comparable assertion by Nietzsche about the death of God. Yet, in spite of my reluctance to extract messages, let alone slogans, from Hölderlin's texts, I see a distinctly topical relevance in his faith in the powers of nature, as embodied in the ancient gods – *the* constant theme in his work inseparable from its poetic radicalism, not dependent on the concerns of his interpreters and not amenable to their ideological use by the selection of this or that quotation. Because Hölderlin's faith in the powers and processes of nature was an absolute and religious one, he could dissolve works of his own, just as organic nature dissolves its phenomena, so that new growth can develop from the dissolution. Unlike Goethe, whose metamorphoses, entelechies and evolutions, up to the 'die and become' of a late poem, are akin to Hölderlin's, he did not allow self-preservation to set a limit to that quest: no less than his works, to him the producers of poems, too, were only vessels that could be broken when they had served their purpose. Goethe wanted to preserve his person, and therefore left his contraries to run along parallel lines, sometimes making a game of them. Hölderlin had to enact his to the point of self-destruction. The confrontation of the antinomies Nature and Art, timeless Saturn and time-bound, historic Jupiter, then the growing concern with historical persons and eras, even with the historicity of 'the Only One', Christ, and of Christendom – all this was too much for mere 'natural piety'. Yet even in his apology for his later, 'too unconventional' mode of singing, it was on nature that Hölderlin based his appeal: 'and Nature, whence it originates, will also receive it again'.

There is no need to point to the present relevance of a dead earth. Even the spiritual and secular guardians of our civilization have had to concede that there is something wrong with a technology and an ethos that give human beings the right not only to rule the earth, sea and sky, but to damage them irreparably. More consistently than Goethe's, Hölderlin's 'natural piety' insisted on bounds set to the human urge to know and to exploit knowledge. So in the tragic ode 'The Poet's Vocation':

> Too long now things divine have been cheaply used
> And all the powers of heaven, the kindly, spent
> In trifling waste by cold and cunning
> Men without thanks, who when he, the Highest,
>
> In person tills their field for them, think they know
> The daylight and the Thunderer, and indeed
> Their telescope may find them all, may
> Count and may name every star of heaven.
>
> Yet will the Father cover with holy night,
> That we may last on earth, our too knowing eyes.
> He loves no Titan! Never will our
> Free-ranging power coerce his heaven.
>
> Nor is it good to be all too wise . . .

Again, it would be idle to ask oneself whether Hölderlin could have preserved his faith that, ultimately, the universe cannot be 'coerced' or violated, if he had lived in this century. Every answer to that would be another profession of an interpreter's beliefs. I will only remark that the German text of the first of the strophes quoted does not run smoothly in metre, rhythm or grammar, so that, for once, the urgency of what Hölderlin had to say overruled his need for artistic perfection.

Hölderlin's 'love for Earth', which, in the fragment 'Home', is 'quenched' by picking berries, reached its fullest poetic enactment in poems he was unable to complete. It is in these fragments filled with immediate sensuous detail in which the phenomena of nature seem to be celebrated in their own right, rather than as symbols within a mythical, cosmological or eschatological system. So in 'For when the grape-vine's sap ...' or 'On fallow foliage ...'. These fragments are wholly unlike anything written by other European poets of Hölderlin's time. In a sense, they are also beyond interpretation, not so much because they are fragments whose larger context is missing as because anything read into them or out of them would so clearly fall short of doing justice to their immediacy. If there is anything to be regretted about the break that occurred in Hölderlin's middle years, it is that he did not salvage more of such fragments, completing them as short poems. Yet within a mere decade Hölderlin produced a poetic work so various, so rich in potentialities and possibilities for the 'future ages' in which he placed his hope, that regrets about it are out of place, as well as futile. Even his personal catastrophe is one that he foresaw at the start of that decade, willing to take the risk and pay the price; and, mad or not, even the verses he wrote in his decline, relapsing into generality and abstraction, can move us with faint echoes of his epiphanies, his verbal and visionary thunderclaps.

M.H.
Suffolk, October, 1989

BIBLIOGRAPHICAL NOTE

The German texts reproduced here, and the translations, are mainly based on Friedrich Beißner's edition, *Hölderlin: Sämtliche Werke* (Große Stuttgarter Ausgabe, Stuttgart, 1943–77), with a few emendations or variants taken from the facsimile editions of *Die Friedensfeier* by Wolfgang Binder and Alfred Kelletat (Tübingen, 1959) and of the *Homburger Folioheft* by D. E. Sattler and Emery E. George (Frankfurt, 1986), part of the current Frankfurt Edition of Hölderlin's works. The volume or volumes to be devoted to all the hymns and fragments in that edition had not appeared in time for my last revision of my work. Since for some of Hölderlin's poems there is no text that can be regarded as definitive, in one or two instances I have taken the liberty of producing a conflation of my own, so as to include those variants in the drafts that seemed most fully realized or most striking. Neither completeness in the presentation of variants nor elucidation could be attempted here. My notes are minimal and selective.

For the benefit of readers who wish to supplement the necessarily scanty material provided in my Introduction, I list a few publications in English that could prove helpful in different ways:

Marshall Montgomery: *Friedrich Hölderlin and the German Neo-Hellenic Movement*. Oxford, 1923
*E. M. Butler: *The Tyranny of Greece over Germany*. Cambridge, 1935
Ronald Peacock: *Hölderlin*. London, 1938
Agnes Stansfield: *Hölderlin*. Manchester, 1943
E. L. Stahl: *Hölderlin's Symbolism*. Oxford, 1945
*Edwin Muir: *Essays on Literature and Society*. London, 1949
L. S. Salzberger: *Hölderlin*. Cambridge, 1952
*C. M. Bowra: *Inspiration and Poetry*. London, 1955
*Michael Hamburger: *Reason and Energy*. Second Edition. London, 1970

Quarterly Review of Literature (Annandale-on-Hudson, N.Y.), Hölderlin
  Issue, Volume X, Numbers 1 & 2, 1959. (Contains essays by Martin
  Heidegger, Erich Heller, Norbert von Hellingrath and Anthony
  Thorlby; and excerpts from Hölderlin's *Hyperion* in English.)
M. B. Benn: *Hölderlin and Pindar*. The Hague, 1962
Richard Unger: *Hölderlin's Major Poetry*. Bloomington, Indiana and
  London, 1975
Eric L. Santer: *Friedrich Hölderlin. Narrative Vigilance and the Poetic
  Imagination*. New Brunswick and London, 1986
David Constantine: *Hölderlin*. Oxford, 1988

An English version by Willard R. Trask of Hölderlin's *Hyperion* was
published in 1965 by Signet Classics, New York and London.
A selection from Hölderlin's letters, translated by Christopher Middleton,
appeared in *The Poet's Vocation, Letters of Hölderlin, Rimbaud and Hart
Crane*, Austin, Texas, n.d. 1967 (?).

Translations of two of Hölderlin's essays on tragedy, by Jeremy Adler,
appeared in *Comparative Criticism*, Volume 7, Cambridge, 1985; his
translation of Hölderlin's notes on the *Oedipus* and *Antigone* of Sophocles
in Volume 6 of the same yearbook, 1983; and his versions of Hölderlin's
'Pindar Fragments' appeared in Volume 6 of that yearbook, in 1984.

*These books contain chapters on Hölderlin.

ODES AND EPIGRAMS
(1797–1799)

Epigrams (1797)

Guter Rath

Hast du Verstand und ein Herz, so zeige nur eines von beiden,
  Beides verdammen sie dir, zeigest du beides zugleich.

Die Beschreibende Poësie

Wißt! Apoll ist der Gott der Zeitungsschreiber geworden
  Und sein Mann ist, wer ihm treulich das Factum erzählt.

An Diotima

Schönes Leben! du lebst, wie die zarten Blüthen im Winter,
  In der gealterten Welt blühst du verschlossen, allein.
Liebend strebst du hinaus, dich zu sonnen am Lichte des Frühlings,
  Zu erwarmen an ihr suchst du die Jugend der Welt.
Deine Sonne, die schönere Zeit, ist untergegangen
  Und in frostiger Nacht zanken Orkane sich nun.

Diotima

Komm und besänftige mir, die du einst Elemente versöhntest
  Wonne der himmlischen Muse das Chaos der Zeit,
Ordne den tobenden Kampf mit Friedenstönen des Himmels
  Bis in der sterblichen Brust sich das entzweite vereint,
Bis der Menschen alte Natur die ruhige große,
  Aus der gährenden Zeit, mächtig und heiter sich hebt.
Kehr' in die dürftigen Herzen des Volks, lebendige Schönheit!
  Kehr an den gastlichen Tisch, kehr in die Tempel zurük!
Denn Diotima lebt, wie die zarten Blüthen im Winter,
  Reich an eigenem Geist sucht sie die Sonne doch auch.
Aber die Sonne des Geists, die schönere Welt ist hinunter
  Und in frostiger Nacht zanken Orkane sich nur.

Epigrams (1797)

Good Advice

You've a head *and* a heart? Reveal only one of them, I say;
  If you reveal both at once, doubly they'll damn you, for both.

Descriptive Poetry

Latest news: Apollo's become the god of journalists, press men,
  And his blue-eyed boy he who reports all the facts.

To Diotima

Beautiful being, you live as do delicate blossoms in winter,
  In a world that's grown old hidden you blossom, alone.
Lovingly outward you press to bask in the light of the springtime,
  To be warmed by it still, look for the youth of the world.
But your sun, the lovelier world, has gone down now,
  And the quarrelling gales rage in an icy bleak night.

Diotima

Bliss of the heavenly Muse who on elements once imposed order,
  Come, and for me now assuage the chaos come back in our time,
Temper the furious war with peace-giving, heavenly music
  Till in the mortal heart all that's divided unites,
Till the former nature of men, the calm, the majestic,
  From our turbulent age rises, restored to its prime.
Living beauty, return to the destitute hearts of the people,
  To the banqueting table return, enter the temples once more!
For Diotima lives as do delicate blossoms in winter,
  Blessed with a soul of her own, yet needing and seeking the sun.
But the lovelier world, the sun of the spirit is darkened,
  Only quarrelling gales rage in an icy bleak night.

Buonaparte

Heilige Gefäße sind die Dichter,
  Worinn des Lebens Wein, der Geist
    Der Helden sich aufbewahrt,

Aber der Geist dieses Jünglings
  Der schnelle, müßt' er es nicht zersprengen
    Wo es ihn fassen wollte, das Gefäß?

Der Dichter laß ihn unberührt wie den Geist der Natur,
  An solchem Stoffe wird zum Knaben der Meister.

Er kann im Gedichte nicht leben und bleiben,
  Er lebt und bleibt in der Welt.

Empedokles

Das Leben suchst du, suchst, und es quillt und glänzt
  Ein göttlich Feuer tief aus der Erde dir,
    Und du in schauderndem Verlangen
      Wirfst dich hinab, in des Aetna Flammen.

So schmelzt' im Weine Perlen der Übermuth
  Der Königin; und mochte sie doch! hättst du
    Nur deinen Reichtum nicht, o Dichter
      Hin in den gährenden Kelch geopfert!

Doch heilig bist du mir, wie der Erde Macht,
  Die dich hinwegnahm, kühner Getödteter!
    Und folgen möcht' ich in die Tiefe,
      Hielte die Liebe mich nicht, dem Helden.

Bonaparte

Poets are holy vessels
  In which the wine of life,
    The spirit of heroes is preserved;

But this young man's spirit,
  The quick – would it not burst
    Any vessel that tried to contain it?

Let the poet leave him untouched like the spirit of Nature,
  For both reduce to a bungling boy the masterly craftsman.

In the poem he cannot live and last;
  He lives and lasts in the world.

Empedocles

You look for life, you look and from deeps of Earth
  A fire, divinely gleaming wells up for you,
    And quick, aquiver with desire, you
      Hurl yourself down into Etna's furnace.

So did the Queen's exuberance once dissolve
  Rare pearls in wine; and why should she not? But you,
    If only you, O poet, had not
      Offered your wealth to the seething chalice!

Yet you are holy to me as is the power
  Of Earth that took you from us, the boldly killed!
    And gladly, did not love restrain me,
      Deep as the hero plunged down I'd follow.

An die Parzen

Nur Einen Sommer gönnt, ihr Gewaltigen!
  Und einen Herbst zu reifem Gesange mir,
    Daß williger mein Herz, vom süßen
      Spiele gesättiget, dann mir sterbe.

Die Seele, der im Leben ihr göttlich Recht
  Nicht ward, sie ruht auch drunten im Orkus nicht;
    Doch ist mir einst das Heil'ge, das am
      Herzen mir liegt, das Gedicht gelungen,

Willkommen dann, o Stille der Schattenwelt!
  Zufrieden bin ich, wenn auch mein Saitenspiel
    Mich nicht hinab geleitet; Einmal
      Lebt ich, wie Götter, und mehr bedarfs nicht.

Diotima

Du schweigst und duldest, und sie versteh'n dich nicht,
  Du heilig Leben! welkest hinweg und schweigst,
    Denn ach, vergebens bei Barbaren
      Suchst du die Deinen im Sonnenlichte,

Die zärtlichgroßen Seelen, die nimmer sind!
  Doch eilt die Zeit. Noch siehet mein sterblich Lied
    Den Tag, der, Diotima! nächst den
      Göttern mit Helden dich nennt, und dir gleicht.

To the Fates

One summer only grant me, you powerful Fates,
  And one more autumn only for mellow song,
    So that more willingly, replete with
      Music's late sweetness, my heart may die then.

The soul in life denied its god-given right
  Down there in Orcus also will find no peace;
    But when what's holy, dear to me, the
      Poem's accomplished, my art perfected,

Then welcome, silence, welcome cold world of shades!
  I'll be content, though here I must leave my lyre
    And songless travel down; for *once* I
      Lived like the gods, and no more is needed.

Diotima

You suffer and keep silent and, strange to them,
  You holy being, silently wilt away;
    For, ah, in vain among barbarians
      Here in the sunlight you seek your kindred,

The nobly tender spirits that are no more!
  Yet time speeds on. Though mortal, my song will live
    To see the day which next to gods, with
      Heroes will name you, itself be like you.

An Ihren Genius

Send' ihr Blumen und Frücht' aus nieversiegender Fülle,
  Send' ihr, freundlicher Geist, ewige Jugend herab!
Hüll' in deine Wonnen sie ein und laß sie die Zeit nicht
  Sehn, wo einsam und fremd sie, die Athenerin, lebt,
Bis sie im Lande der Seeligen einst die fröhlichen Schwestern,
  Die zu Phidias Zeit herrschten und liebten, umfängt.

Abbitte

Heilig Wesen! gestört hab' ich die goldene
  Götterruhe dir oft, und der geheimeren,
    Tiefern Schmerzen des Lebens
      Hast du manche gelernt von mir.

O vergiß es, vergieb! gleich dem Gewölke dort
  Vor dem friedlichen Mond, geh' ich dahin, und du
    Ruhst und glänzest in deiner
      Schöne wieder, du süßes Licht!

Ehmals und Jezt

In jüngern Tagen war ich des Morgens froh,
  Des Abends weint' ich; jezt, da ich älter bin,
    Beginn ich zweifelnd meinen Tag, doch
      Heilig und heiter ist mir sein Ende.

To Her Genius

Send her flowers and fruit from inexhaustible fulness,
   Send her, tutelar spirit, deathless youth from above!
Wrap her up in your joys and never let her experience
   Years when lonely, estranged, she, the Athenian, must live,
Till in the land of the blessed one day she fondly embraces
   Happy sisters who ruled, loved when Phidias was young.

Plea for Forgiveness

Holy being, I know, often I've troubled your
   Golden, godlike repose, so that you learned from me
      Much that might have been spared you,
         Life's more hidden, obscurer griefs.

O forgive me, forget! Look, as the clouds up there
   Veil with black the slow moon, I drift away, while you
      Stay and shine in your beauty,
         Gentle light, as you shone before.

Then and Now

In younger days each morning I rose with joy,
   To weep at nightfall; now, in my later years,
      Though doubting I begin my day, yet
         Always its end is serene and holy.

Lebenslauf

Hoch auf strebte mein Geist, aber die Liebe zog
   Schön ihn nieder; das Laid beugt ihn gewaltiger;
     So durchlauf ich des Lebens
       Bogen und kehre, woher ich kam.

Die Kürze

»Warum bist du so kurz? liebst du, wie vormals, denn
   »Nun nicht mehr den Gesang? fandst du, als Jüngling, doch,
     »In den Tagen der Hoffnung,
      »Wenn du sangest, das Ende nie!

Wie mein Glük, ist mein Lied. – Willst du im Abendroth
   Froh dich baden? hinweg ists! und die Erd' ist kalt,
     Und der Vogel der Nacht schwirrt
      Unbequem vor das Auge dir.

Menschenbeifall

Ist nicht heilig mein Herz, schöneren Lebens voll,
   Seit ich liebe? warum achtetet ihr mich mehr,
     Da ich stolzer und wilder,
      Wortereicher und leerer war?

Ach! der Menge gefällt, was auf den Marktplaz taugt,
   Und es ehret der Knecht nur den Gewaltsamen;
     An das Göttliche glauben
      Die allein, die es selber sind.

The Course of Life

High my spirit aspired, truly, however, love
   Pulled it earthward; and grief lower still bows it down.
      So I follow the arc of
         Life and return to my starting-place.

Brevity

'Why so brief now, so curt? Do you no longer, then,
   Love your art as you did? When in your younger days,
      Hopeful days, in your singing
         What you loathed was to make an end!'

Like my joy is my song. – Who in the sundown's red
   Glow would happily bathe? Gone it is, cold the earth,
      And the bird of the night whirs
         Down, so close that you shield your eyes.

Human Applause

Has love not hallowed, filled with new life my heart,
   With lovelier life? Then why did you prize me more
      When I was proud and wild and frantic,
         Lavish of words, yet in substance empty?

The crowd likes best what sells in the market-place,
   And loud-mouthed force alone wins a slave's respect.
      In gods and godhead only he can
         Truly believe who himself is godlike.

Die Heimath

Froh kehrt der Schiffer heim an den stillen Strom
   Von fernen Inseln, wo er geerndtet hat;
     Wohl möcht' auch ich zur Heimath wieder;
      Aber was hab' ich, wie Laid, geerndtet? –

Ihr holden Ufer, die ihr mich auferzogt,
   Stillt ihr der Liebe Laiden? ach! gebt ihr mir,
     Ihr Wälder meiner Kindheit, wann ich
      Komme, die Ruhe noch Einmal wieder?

Der Gute Glaube

Schönes Leben! du liegst krank, und das Herz ist mir
   Müd vom Weinen und schon dämmert die Furcht in mir,
     Doch, doch kann ich nicht glauben,
      Daß du sterbest, so lang du liebst.

Ihre Genesung

Deine Freundin, Natur! leidet und schläft und du
   Allbelebende, säumst? ach! und ihr heilt sie nicht,
     Mächt'ge Lüfte des Aethers,
      Nicht ihr Quellen des Sonnenlichts?

Alle Blumen der Erd', alle die fröhlichen,
   Schönen Früchte des Hains, heitern sie alle nicht
     Dieses Leben, ihr Götter!
      Das ihr selber in Lieb' erzogt? –

Ach! schon athmet und tönt heilige Lebenslust
   Ihr im reizenden Wort wieder wie sonst und schon
     Glänzt das Auge des Lieblings
      Freundlichoffen, Natur! dich an.

Home

Content the boatman turns to the river's calm
   From distant isles, his harvest all gathered in;
     I too would gladly now turn homeward,
       Only, what harvest but pain have I reaped?

Kind river-banks that tended and brought me up,
   Can you allay love's sufferings, give me back,
     You forests of my childhood, should I
       Come to you now, the same peace as ever?

Good Faith

Dearest one, you lie sick, so that with weeping my
   Heart is weary, and fear almost takes root in me;
     Yet I cannot believe that
       You could die when you still can love.

Her Recovery

Nature, she who's your friend drowses and ails, and you
   Dally, giver of life? Cannot you heal her, then,
     Potent breezes of Aether,
       Sunlight's well-springs, will you not help?

All the flowers of the earth, all the good ripening
   Happy fruits of the grove, how can it be that all
     Fail to cheer this one life which,
       Gods, yourselves you raised up with love?

Ah, already restored, holy desire to live
   Breathes and sounds in her talk, charming as ever, and
     Fondly, Nature, your darling
       Open-eyed to your beam responds.

Das Unverzeihliche.

Wenn ihr Freunde vergeßt, wenn ihr den Künstler höhnt,
Und den tieferen Geist klein und gemein versteht,
    Gott vergiebt es, doch stört nur
      Nie den Frieden der Liebenden.

An die Jungen Dichter

Lieben Brüder! es reift unsere Kunst vielleicht,
    Da, dem Jünglinge gleich, lange sie schon gegährt,
      Bald zur Stille der Schönheit;
        Seid nur fromm, wie der Grieche war!

Liebt die Götter und denkt freundlich der Sterblichen!
    Haßt den Rausch, wie den Frost! lehrt und beschreibet nicht!
      Wenn der Meister euch ängstigt,
        Fragt die große Natur um Rath.

An die Deutschen

Spottet ja nicht des Kinds, wenn es mit Peitsch' und Sporn
    Auf dem Rosse von Holz muthig und groß sich dünkt,
      Denn, ihr Deutschen, auch ihr seyd
        Thatenarm und gedankenvoll.

Oder kömmt, wie der Stral aus dem Gewölke kömmt,
    Aus Gedanken die That? Leben die Bücher bald?
      O ihr Lieben, so nimmt mich,
        Daß ich büße die Lästerung.

The Unpardonable

If you drop an old friend, laugh at the artist and
   Meanly, vulgarly judge, wronging the deeper mind,
      God forgives you; but never
         Break the quiet that lovers know.

To the Young Poets

Quite soon, dear brothers, perhaps our art,
   So long in youth-like ferment, will now mature
      To beauty's plenitude, to stillness;
         Only be pious, like Grecian poets!

Of mortal men think kindly, but love the gods!
   Loathe drunkenness like frost! Don't describe or teach!
      And if you fear your master's bluntness,
         Go to great Nature, let her advise you!

To the Germans

Do not laugh at the child when with his whip and spurs
   Brave and mighty he feels up on his rocking-horse,
      For, you Germans, you too are
         Poor in deeds though you've thoughts enough!

Or, as lightning from clouds, out of mere thoughts will deeds,
   Potent, come leaping out? Books now begin to live?
      O, my dear ones, then seize me,
         Make me pay for my slanderous words.

Die Scheinheiligen Dichter

Ihr kalten Heuchler, sprecht von den Göttern nicht!
  Ihr habt Verstand! ihr glaubt nicht an Helios,
    Noch an den Donnerer und Meergott;
      Todt ist die Erde, wer mag ihr danken? –

Getrost ihr Götter! zieret ihr doch das Lied,
  Wenn schon aus euren Nahmen die Seele schwand,
    Und ist ein großes Wort vonnöthen,
      Mutter Natur! so gedenkt man deiner.

Sonnenuntergang

Wo bist du? trunken dämmert die Seele mir
  Von aller deiner Wonne; denn eben ist's,
    Daß ich gelauscht, wie, goldner Töne
      Voll der entzükende Sonnenjüngling

Sein Abendlied auf himmlischer Leyer spielt';
  Es tönten rings die Wälder und Hügel nach.
    Doch fern ist er zu frommen Völkern,
      Die ihn noch ehren, hinweggegangen.

An Unsere Grossen Dichter

Des Ganges Ufer hörten des Freudengotts
  Triumph, als allerobernd vom Indus her
    Der junge Bacchus kam, mit heilgem
      Weine vom Schlafe die Völker wekend.

O wekt, ihr Dichter! wekt sie vom Schlummer auch,
  Die jezt noch schlafen, gebt die Geseze, gebt
    Uns Leben, siegt, Heroën! ihr nur
      Habt der Eroberung Recht, wie Bacchus.

The Sanctimonious Poets

Cold hypocrites, of gods do not dare to speak!
  You're rational! In Helios you don't believe,
    Nor in the Thunderer or the Sea-God;
      Dead is our Earth, so what fool would thank her? –

Take comfort, gods! For yet you adorn their verse
  Though now the soul's gone out of your pilfered names;
    And if some high-flown word is needed,
      You, Mother Nature, they still remember.

Sunset

Where are you? Dazzled, drunken my soul grows faint
  And dark with so much gladness; for even now
    I listened while, too rich in golden
      Sounds, the enrapturing youth, the sun-god

Intoned his evening hymn on a heavenly lyre;
  All round the hills and forests re-echoed it,
    Though far from here – to pious nations
      Who still revere him – by now he's journeyed.

To Our Great Poets

The banks of Ganges heard how the god of joy
  Was hailed when conquering all from far Indus came
    The youthful Bacchus, and with holy
      Wine from their drowsiness woke the peoples.

You also, poets, rouse them, awaken those
  Who still are sleepy, give us the laws, and give
    Us life! Make known your triumph! Only
      You, like that god, have the right to conquer.

Sokrates und Alcibiades

»Warum huldigest du, heiliger Sokrates,
    »Diesem Jünglinge stets? kennest du Größers nicht?
        »Warum siehet mit Liebe,
            »Wie auf Götter, dein Aug' auf ihn?

Wer das Tiefste gedacht, liebt das Lebendigste,
    Hohe Jugend versteht, wer in die Welt geblikt
        Und es neigen die Weisen
            Oft am Ende zu Schönem sich.

Epigrams (1799)

Sophokles
Viele versuchten umsonst das Freudigste freudig zu sagen
    Hier spricht endlich es mir, hier in der Trauer sich aus.

Der Zürnende Dichter
Fürchtet den Dichter nicht, wenn er edel zürnet, sein Buchstab
    Tödtet, aber es macht Geister lebendig der Geist.

Wurzel Alles Übels
Einig zu seyn, ist göttlich und gut; woher ist die Sucht denn
    Unter den Menschen, daß nur Einer und Eines nur sei?

Socrates and Alcibiades

'Holy Socrates, why always with deference
  Do you treat this young man? Don't you know greater things?
    Why so lovingly, raptly,
      As on gods, do you gaze on him?

Who the deepest has thought loves what is most alive,
  Wide experience may well turn to what's best in youth,
    And the wise in the end will
      Often bow to the beautiful.

Epigrams (1799)

Sophocles

Many have tried, but in vain, with joy to express the most joyful;
  Here at last, in grave sadness, wholly I find it expressed.

The Angry Poet

Never fear the poet when nobly he rages; his letter
  Kills, but his spirit to spirits gives new vigour, new life.

The Root of All Evil

Being at one is godlike and good, but human, too human, the mania
  Which insists there is only the One, one country, one truth and one
      way.

THE LATER ODES
(1798–1803)

Der Mensch

Kaum sproßten aus den Wassern, o Erde, dir
  Der jungen Berge Gipfel und dufteten
    Lustathmend, immergrüner Haine
      Voll, in des Oceans grauer Wildniß

Die ersten holden Inseln; und freudig sah
  Des Sonnengottes Auge die Neulinge
    Die Pflanzen, seiner ew'gen Jugend
      Lächelnde Kinder, aus dir geboren.

Da auf der Inseln schönster, wo immerhin
  Den Hain in zarter Ruhe die Luft umfloß,
    Lag unter Trauben einst, nach lauer
      Nacht, in der dämmernden Morgenstunde

Geboren, Mutter Erde! dein schönstes Kind; –
  Und auf zum Vater Helios sieht bekannt
    Der Knab', und wacht und wählt die süßen
      Beere versuchend, die heil'ge Rebe

Zur Amme sich; und bald ist er groß; ihn scheun
  Die Thiere, denn ein anderer ist, wie sie
    Der Mensch; nicht dir und nicht dem Vater
      Gleicht er, denn kühn ist in ihm und einzig

Des Vaters hohe Seele mit deiner Lust,
  O Erd'! und deiner Trauer von je vereint;
    Der Göttermutter, der Natur, der
      Allesumfassenden möcht' er gleichen!

Ach! darum treibt ihn, Erde! vom Herzen dir
  Sein Übermuth, und deine Geschenke sind
    Umsonst und deine zarten Bande;
      Sucht er ein Besseres doch, der Wilde!

Man

When scarcely from the waters, O Earth, for you
  Young mountain peaks had sprouted and, breathing joy,
    The first delightful islands, full of
      Evergreen copses, gave out their fragrance.

Amid the sea's grey desert; and glad of them
  The Sun-God's eye looked down at the newly raised,
    The plants, the smiling children of his
      Weariless youth, and of you, their mother –

Then on the loveliest island where delicate
  And calm the air flowed ceaselessly round the copse,
    One morning, born in early half-light
      After a temperate night, and bedded

Beneath the clustered grapes, lay your loveliest child; –
  And up to Father Helios now the boy
    Turns eyes that know him, wakes and, tasting
      Berries for sweetness, as nurse he chooses

The holy vine; and soon is grown up. He's shunned
  By animals, for different from them is Man.
    Not you, his mother, nor his father
      Does he resemble, for in him, boldly

Uniquely blended, live both his father's soul
  And, Earth, your joy, your sadness, inveterate;
    He longs to be like her, like Nature,
      Mother of gods and the all-embracing!

O that is why his arrogance drives him far
  From your safe-keeping, Earth, and in vain are all
    Your gifts and all your gentle fetters –
      Little to him, who wants more, the wild one!

Von seines Ufers duftender Wiese muß
  Ins blüthenlose Wasser hinaus der Mensch,
    Und glänzt auch, wie die Sternenacht, von
      Goldenen Früchten sein Hain, doch gräbt er

Sich Höhlen in den Bergen und späht im Schacht
  Von seines Vaters heiterem Lichte fern.
    Den Sonnengott auch ungetreu, der
      Knechte nicht liebt und der Sorge spottet.

Denn freier athmen Vögel des Walds, wenn schon
  Des Menschen Brust sich herrlicher hebt, und der
    Die dunkle Zukunft sieht, er muß auch
      Sehen den Tod und allein ihn fürchten.

Und Waffen wider alle, die athmen, trägt
  In ewigbangem Stolze der Mensch; im Zwist
    Verzehrt er sich und seines Friedens
      Blume, die zärtliche, blüht nicht lange.

Ist er von allen Lebensgenossen nicht
  Der seeligste? Doch tiefer und reißender
    Ergreift das Schiksaal, allausgleichend,
      Auch die entzündbare Brust dem Starken.

Hyperions Schiksaalslied

Ihr wandelt droben im Licht
  Auf weichem Boden, seelige Genien!
    Glänzende Götterlüfte
      Rühren euch leicht,
        Wie die Finger der Künstlerin
          Heilige Saiten.

Beyond his fragrant river-side meadows, out
   Into the flowerless water is Man impelled
     And though with golden fruit his orchard
       Gleams like the star-jewelled night, yet caves for

Himself he digs in mountains and scans the shaft,
   Remote from his great father's untroubled light,
     Disloyal also to the Sun-God,
       Scorner of cares never fond of drudges.

For woodland birds more freely draw breath, and though
   Man's breast more grandly, proudly expands, his gaze
     Can penetrate the future's darkness,
       Death he sees too and alone must fear it.

And arms against all creatures that live and stir
   In pride for ever anxious he bears; consumes
     Himself in discord; and not long the
       Delicate bloom of his peace contents him.

Is Man not blessed, not blissful compared to all
   His fellow creatures? Yet with a tighter hold,
     More deeply Fate, all-levelling, grips the
       Strong one's inflammable heart to wrench it.

Hyperion's Song of Fate

You walk above in the light,
   Weightless tread a soft floor, blessed genii!
     Radiant the gods' mild breezes
       Gently play on you
         As the girl artist's fingers
           On holy strings.

Schiksaallos, wie der schlafende
  Säugling, athmen die Himmlischen;
    Keusch bewahrt
      In bescheidener Knospe,
        Blühet ewig
          Ihnen der Geist,
            Und die seeligen Augen
              Bliken in stiller
                Ewiger Klarheit.

Doch uns ist gegeben,
  Auf keiner Stätte zu ruhn,
    Es schwinden, es fallen
      Die leidenden Menschen
        Blindlings von einer
          Stunde zur andern,
            Wie Wasser von Klippe
              Zu Klippe geworfen,
                Jahr lang ins Ungewisse hinab.

Da Ich ein Knabe War . . .

Da ich ein Knabe war,
  Rettet' ein Gott mich oft
    Vom Geschrei und der Ruthe der Menschen,
      Da spielt' ich sicher und gut
        Mit den Blumen des Hains,
          Und die Lüftchen des Himmels
            Spielten mit mir.

Und wie du das Herz
Der Pflanzen erfreust,
Wenn sie entgegen dir
Die zarten Arme streken,

Fateless the Heavenly breathe
   Like an unweaned infant asleep;
     Chastely preserved
       In modest bud
         For ever their minds
          Are in flower
            And their blissful eyes
               Eternally tranquil gaze,
               Eternally clear.

But we are fated
   To find no foothold, no rest,
     And suffering mortals
       Dwindle and fall
         Headlong from one
          Hour to the next,
            Hurled like water
              From ledge to ledge
               Downward for years to the vague abyss.

In my boyhood days . . .

In my boyhood days
   Often a god would save me
     From the shouts and the rod of men;
       Safe and good then I played
         With the orchard flowers
          And the breezes of heaven
           Played with me.

And as you make glad
The hearts of the plants
When toward you they stretch
Their delicate arms,

So hast du mein Herz erfreut
Vater Helios! und, wie Endymion,
War ich dein Liebling,
Heilige Luna!

O all ihr treuen
Freundlichen Götter!
Daß ihr wüßtet,
Wie euch meine Seele geliebt!

Zwar damals rieff ich noch nicht
Euch mit Nahmen, auch ihr
Nanntet mich nie, wie die Menschen sich nennen
Als kennten sie sich.

Doch kannt' ich euch besser,
Als ich je die Menschen gekannt,
Ich verstand die Stille des Aethers
Der Menschen Worte verstand ich nie.

Mich erzog der Wohllaut
Des säuselnden Hains
Und lieben lernt' ich
Unter den Blumen.

Im Arme der Götter wuchs ich groß.

Der Zeitgeist

Zu lang schon waltest über dem Haupte mir
  Du in der dunkeln Wolke, du Gott der Zeit!
    Zu wild, zu bang ist's ringsum, und es
      Trümmert und wankt ja, wohin ich blike.

Ach! wie ein Knabe, seh' ich zu Boden oft,
  Such' in der Höhle Rettung von dir, und möcht'
    Ich Blöder, eine Stelle finden,
      Alleserschütt'rer! wo du nicht wärest.

So you made glad my heart,
Father Helios, and like Endymion
I was your darling,
Holy Luna.

O all you loyal,
Kindly gods!
Would that you knew how
My soul loved you then.

True, at that time I did not
Evoke you by name yet, and you
Never named me, as men use names,
As though they knew one another.

Yet I knew you better
Than ever I have known men,
I understood the silence of Aether,
But human words I've never understood.

I was reared by the euphony
Of the rustling copse
And learned to love
Amid the flowers.

I grew up in the arms of the gods.

The Spirit of the Age

Too long above my head you have governed there,
  Wrapped in the thunder cloud, you the God of Time!
    Too desolate and awed the land lies,
      All that I look at breaks up and totters.

O like a boy at times I cast down my eyes,
  Seek refuge from you in some deep cave, and search,
    Poor craven, for a single place where
      You, the all-shattering, might be absent.

Lass' endlich, Vater! offenen Aug's mich dir
     Begegnen! hast denn du nicht zuerst den Geist
          Mit deinem Stral aus mir gewekt? mich
               Herrlich an's Leben gebracht, o Vater! –

Wohl keimt aus jungen Reben uns heil'ge Kraft;
     In milder Luft begegnet den Sterblichen,
          Und wenn sie still im Haine wandeln,
               Heiternd ein Gott; doch allmächt'ger wekst du

Die reine Seele Jünglingen auf, und lehrst
     Die Alten weise Künste; der Schlimme nur
          Wird schlimmer, daß er bälder ende,
               Wenn du, Erschütterer! ihn ergreiffest.

Abendphantasie

Vor seiner Hütte ruhig im Schatten sizt
     Der Pflüger, dem Genügsamen raucht sein Heerd.
          Gastfreundlich tönt dem Wanderer im
               Friedlichen Dorfe die Abendgloke.

Wohl kehren izt die Schiffer zum Hafen auch,
     In fernen Städten, fröhlich verrauscht des Markts
          Geschäfft'ger Lärm; in stiller Laube
               Glänzt das gesellige Mahl den Freunden.

Wohin denn ich? Es leben die Sterblichen
     Von Lohn und Arbeit; wechselnd in Müh' und Ruh'
          Ist alles freudig; warum schläft denn
               Nimmer nur mir in der Brust der Stachel?

Am Abendhimmel blühet ein Frühling auf;
     Unzählig blühn die Rosen und ruhig scheint
          Die goldne Welt; o dorthin nimmt mich
               Purpurne Wolken! und möge droben

But, Father, open-eyed let me meet at last
   Your face! Was it not you with your beam who first
      Drew out the mind in me, awakened,
         Gloriously brought me to life, O Father? –

True, from young vines we gather a holy strength;
   In mild spring air, or when they are wandering
      In orchards calmly, men will meet a
         Brightening god; yet with powers more far-flung

You rouse the souls of youths, and to older men
   Impart wise arts; the bad man alone grows worse,
      So that his end will come the sooner,
         When with your world-shaking might you seize him.

Evening Fantasy

At peace the ploughman sits in the shade outside
   His cottage; smoke curls up from his modest hearth.
      A traveller hears the bell for vespers
         Welcome him in to a quiet village.

Now too the boatmen make for the harbour pool,
   In distant towns the market's gay noise and throng
      Subside; a glittering meal awaits the
         Friends in the garden's most hidden arbour.

But where shall I go? Does not a mortal live
   By work and wages? Balancing toil with rest
      All makes him glad. Must I alone then
         Find no relief from the thorn that goads me?

A springtime buds high up in the evening sky,
   There countless roses bloom, and the golden world
      Seems calm, fulfilled; O there now take me,
         Crimson-edged clouds, and up there at last let

In Licht und Luft zerrinnen mir Lieb' und Laid! –
  Doch, wie verscheucht von thöriger Bitte, flieht
    Der Zauber; dunkel wirds und einsam
      Unter dem Himmel, wie immer, bin ich –

Komm du nun, sanfter Schlummer! zu viel begehrt
  Das Herz; doch endlich, Jugend! verglühst du ja,
    Du ruhelose, träumerische!
      Friedlich und heiter ist dann das Alter.

Des Morgens

Vom Thaue glänzt der Rasen; beweglicher
  Eilt schon die wache Quelle; die Buche neigt
    Ihr schwankes Haupt und im Geblätter
      Rauscht es und schimmert; und um die grauen

Gewölke streifen röthliche Flammen dort,
  Verkündende, sie wallen geräuschlos auf;
    Wie Fluthen am Gestade, woogen
      Höher und höher die Wandelbaren.

Komm nun, o komm, und eile mir nicht zu schnell,
  Du goldner Tag, zum Gipfel des Himmels fort!
    Denn offner fliegt, vertrauter dir mein
      Auge, du Freudiger! zu, so lang du

In deiner Schöne jugendlich blikst und noch
  Zu herrlich nicht, zu stolz mir geworden bist;
    Du möchtest immer eilen, könnt ich,
      Göttlicher Wandrer, mit dir! – doch lächelst

Des frohen übermüthigen du, daß er
  Dir gleichen möchte; seegne mir lieber dann
    Mein sterblich Thun und heitre wieder
      Gütiger! heute den stillen Pfad mir.

My love and sorrow melt into light and air! –
    As if that foolish plea had dispersed it, though,
        The spell breaks; darkness falls, and lonely
            Under the heavens I stand as always. –

Now you come, gentle sleep! For the heart demands
    Too much; but youth at last, you the dreamy, wild,
        Unquiet, will burn out, and leave me
            All my late years for serene contentment.

In the Morning

With dew the lawn is glistening; more nimbly now,
    Awake, the stream speeds onward; the beech inclines
        Her limber head and in the leaves a
            Rustle, a glitter begins; and round the

Grey cloud-banks there a flicker of reddish flames,
    Prophetic ones, flares up and in silence plays;
        Like breakers by the shore they billow
            Higher and higher, the ever-changing.

Now come, O come, and not too impatiently,
    You golden day, speed on to the peaks of heaven!
        For more familiar and more open,
            Glad one, my vision flies up towards you

While youthful in your beauty you gaze and have
    Not grown too glorious, dazzling and proud for me;
        Speed as you will, I'd say, if only
            I could go with you, divinely ranging!

But at my happy arrogance now you smile,
    That would be like you; rather, then, rambler, bless
        My mortal acts, and this day also,
            Kindly one, brighten my quiet pathway.

Der Main

Wohl manches Land der lebenden Erde möcht'
  Ich sehn, und öfters über die Berg' enteilt
    Das Herz mir, und die Wünsche wandern
      Über das Meer, zu den Ufern, die mir

Vor andern, so ich kenne, gepriesen sind;
  Doch lieb ist in der Ferne nicht Eines mir,
    Wie jenes, wo die Göttersöhne
      Schlafen, das trauernde Land der Griechen.

Ach! einmal dort an Suniums Küste möcht'
  Ich landen, deine Säulen, Olympion!
    Erfragen, dort, noch eh der Nordsturm
      Hin in den Schutt der Athenertempel

Und ihrer Götterbilder auch dich begräbt;
  Denn lang schon einsam stehst du, o Stolz der Welt,
    Die nicht mehr ist! – und o ihr schönen
      Inseln Ioniens, wo die Lüfte

Vom Meere kühl an warme Gestade wehn,
  Wenn unter kräft'ger Sonne die Traube reift,
    Ach! wo ein goldner Herbst dem armen
      Volk in Gesänge die Seufzer wandelt,

Wenn die Betrübten izt ihr Limonenwald
  Und ihr Granatbaum, purpurner Äpfel voll
    Und süßer Wein und Pauk' und Zithar
      Zum labyrintischen Tanze ladet –

Zu euch vieleicht, ihr Inseln! geräth noch einst
  Ein heimathloser Sänger; denn wandern muß
    Von Fremden er zu Fremden, und die
      Erde, die freie, sie muß ja leider!

The River Main

True, on this living earth there are many lands
   I long to see, and over the hills at times
      My heart runs off, my wishes wander
         Seaward, and on to those shores which more than

All others that I know have been glorified;
   But far away not one is as dear to me
      As that where now the sons of gods lie
         Sleeping, the mournful, the Hellenes' country.

O once I long to land there, on Sunium's coast,
   Once ask my way to your columns, Olympion,
      And soon, before the northern gale can
         Bury you too in the scattered rubble

Of temples Athens raised, and their imaged gods;
   For long now desolate you have stood, O pride
      Of worlds that are no more! And O you
         Lovely Ionian isles, where breezes

Waft coolness to warm shores from the open sea
   While under potent sunbeams the grape matures,
      And, oh, where still a golden autumn
         Turns into songs the poor people's sighing,

Now that their lemon grove, their pomegranate tree
   That bends with purple fruit, and sweet wine and drum
      And zither to the labyrinthine
         Dance have allured them, however troubled –

To you, perhaps, you islands, yet one day shall
   A homeless singer come; for he's driven on
      From stranger still to stranger, and the
         Earth, the unbounded, alas, must serve him.

Statt Vaterlands ihm dienen, so lang er lebt,
  Und wenn er stirbt – doch nimmer vergeß ich dich,
    So fern ich wandre, schöner Main! und
      Deine Gestade, die vielbeglükten.

Gastfreundlich nahmst du Stolzer! bei dir mich auf
  Und heitertest das Auge dem Fremdlinge,
    Und still hingleitende Gesänge
      Lehrtest du mich und geräuschlos Leben.

O ruhig mit den Sternen, du Glüklicher!
  Wallst du von deinem Morgen zum Abend fort,
    Dem Bruder zu, dem Rhein; und dann mit
      Ihm in den Ocean freudig nieder!

Mein Eigentum

In seiner Fülle ruhet der Herbsttag nun,
  Geläutert ist die Traub und der Hain ist roth
    Vom Obst, wenn schon der holden Blüthen
      Manche der Erde zum Danke fielen.

Und rings im Felde, wo ich den Pfad hinaus
  Den stillen wandle, ist den Zufriedenen
    Ihr Gut gereift und viel der frohen
      Mühe gewähret der Reichtum ihnen.

Vom Himmel bliket zu den Geschäfftigen
  Durch ihre Bäume milde das Licht herab,
    Die Freude theilend, denn es wuchs durch
      Hände der Menschen allein die Frucht nicht.

Und leuchtest du, o Goldnes, auch mir, und wehst
  Auch du mir wieder, Lüftchen, als seegnetest
    Du eine Freude mir, wie einst, und
      Irrst, wie um Glükliche, mir am Busen?

In place of home and nation his whole life long,
    And when he dies – but never, delightful Main,
        Shall I forget you or your banks, the
            Variously blessed, on my farthest travels.

Hospitably, though proud, you admitted me,
    And, smoothly flowing, brightened the stranger's eye
        And taught me gently gliding songs, and
            Taught me the strength that's alive in silence.

O calmly as the stars move, you happy one,
    You travel from your morning to evening,
        Towards your brother, Rhine; then, with him,
            Joyfully down to the greater ocean.

My Possessions

At rest in fulness, calm lies the autumn day,
    The mellow grape is clear and the orchard red
        With fruit, though many treasured blossoms
            Long ago fell to the Earth in tribute.

And all around where now by the quiet path
    I cross the field, for satisfied men their crops
        Have ripened, and their riches grant them
            Hour after hour of rewarding labour.

From heaven through leafy boughs on the busy ones
    A light subdued and temperate glances down
        To share their pleasure; for not human
            Hands by themselves made the cornfield prosper.

And, golden light, for me will you also shine,
    And, breeze, once more for me will you waft, as though
        To bless a joy, and still around me
            Flutter and play, as for happy mortals?

Einst war ichs, doch wie Rosen, vergänglich war
  Das fromme Leben, ach! und es mahnen noch,
    Die blühend mir geblieben sind, die
      Holden Gestirne zu oft mich dessen.

Beglükt, wer, ruhig liebend ein frommes Weib,
  Am eignen Heerd in rühmlicher Heimath lebt,
    Es leuchtet über vestem Boden
      Schöner dem sicheren Mann sein Himmel.

Denn, wie die Pflanze, wurzelt auf eignem Grund
  Sie nicht, verglüht die Seele des Sterblichen,
    Der mit dem Tageslichte nur, ein
      Armer, auf heiliger Erde wandelt.

Zu mächtig ach! ihr himmlischen Höhen zieht
  Ihr mich empor, bei Stürmen, am heitern Tag
    Fühl ich verzehrend euch im Busen
      Wechseln, ihr wandelnden Götterkräfte.

Doch heute laß mich stille den trauten Pfad
  Zum Haine gehn, dem golden die Wipfel schmükt
    Sein sterbend Laub, und kränzt auch mir die
      Stirne, ihr holden Erinnerungen!

Und daß mir auch zu retten mein sterblich Herz,
  Wie andern eine bleibende Stätte sei,
    Und heimathlos die Seele mir nicht
      Über das Leben hinweg sich sehne,

Sei du, Gesang, mein freundlich Asyl! sei du
  Beglükender! mit sorgender Liebe mir
    Gepflegt, der Garten, wo ich, wandelnd
      Unter den Blüthen, den immerjungen,

In sichrer Einfalt wohne, wenn draußen mir
  Mit ihren Wellen allen die mächtge Zeit
    Die Wandelbare fern rauscht und die
      Stillere Sonne mein Wirken fördert.

I too was one, but brief as the full-blown rose
   My good life passed, and they that alone are left
      In flower for me, the constellations,
         Often, too often, remind me of it.

Blessed he who calmly loving a gentle wife
   Can call a worthy homeland and hearth his own;
      Above firm ground more brightly for the
         Settled man shines his own sky's effulgence.

For like the plant that fails to take root within
   Its native ground, the soul of that mortal wilts
      Who with the daylight only roams, a
         Pauper astray on our Earth, the hallowed.

Too strongly always, heavenly heights, you pull
   Me upward; gales that rage on a sunny day
      Bring home to me your clashing powers,
         Mutable gods, and they rend, destroy me.

Today, though, let me walk the familiar path
   In silence to the copse that is crowned with gold
      Of dying leaves; and my brow also
         Garland with gold now, dear recollections!

And that my mortal heart nonetheless may last,
   A quiet, sure retreat, as are other men's,
      And that my soul may not outfly this
         Life in its longing, for ever homeless.

You be my gracious refuge now, song, and you,
   Joy-giver, now be tended with loving care,
      The garden where intently walking
         Under the blossoms that do not wither,

I live in safe ingenuousness while outside
   With all its waves the changeable, mighty Time,
      Roars far away, and to my labours
         Only the quieter sun contributes.

Ihr seegnet gütig über den Sterblichen
  Ihr Himmelskräfte! jedem sein Eigentum,
    O seegnet meines auch und daß zu
      Frühe die Parze den Traum nicht ende.

Der Prinzessin Auguste von Homburg
DEN 28TEN NOV. 1799

Noch freundlichzögernd scheidet vom Auge dir
  Das Jahr, und in hesperischer Milde glänzt
    Der Winterhimmel über deinen
      Gärten, den dichtrischen, immergrünen.

Und da ich deines Festes gedacht' und sann,
  Was ich dir dankend reichte, da weilten noch
    Am Pfade Blumen, daß sie dir zur
      Blühenden Krone, du Edle, würden.

Doch Andres beut dir, Größeres, hoher Geist!
  Die festlichere Zeit, denn es hallt hinab
    Am Berge das Gewitter, sieh! und
      Klar, wie die ruhigen Sterne, gehen

Aus langem Zweifel reine Gestalten auf;
  So dünkt es mir; und einsam, o Fürstin! ist
    Das Herz der Freigebornen wohl nicht
      Länger im eigenen Glük; denn würdig

Gesellt im Lorbeer ihm der Heroë sich,
  Der schöngereifte, ächte; die Weisen auch,
    Die Unsern sind es werth; sie bliken
      Still aus der Höhe des Lebens, die ernsten Alten.

Geringe dünkt der träumende Sänger sich,
  Und Kindern gleich am müßigen Saitenspiel,
    Wenn ihn der Edlen Glük, wenn ihn die
      That und der Ernst der Gewalt'gen aufwekt.

Above us mortals, heavenly powers, you bless
  Each man's possessions, kindly disposed to all;
    O bless mine also, lest too soon the
      Fate put an end to my earthly dreaming.

To Princess Augusta of Homburg
28 NOVEMBER 1799

Still kindly lingering the year from your eye departs,
  And in hesperian mildness now faintly gleams
    The winter sky above your gardens,
      Evergreen arbours, poetic orchards.

And as I pondered here on your birthday, thought
  What, thankful, I might offer, there still remained
    Late flowers beside the pathway, fit to
      Make you a crown that's alive, Augusta.

Yet, lofty spirit, other and greater things
  A time more festive yields you; the thunder rolls
    Away down mountain-sides and, look, as
      Tranquil and clear as the constellations

Pure shapes, pure signs arise from protracted doubt;
  So now it seems to me; and no longer shall
    The hearts of free-born men be lonely
      In their own triumph, Princess; for worthy,

The hero in his laurel consorts with them,
  The well-matured, the true one; and wise men too,
    Our own, deserve to join them; calmly
      Down from life's summit they gaze, those grave ones.

How small the dreaming singer must think himself,
  How like a child who randomly plucks the strings,
    When roused by triumph of the noble,
      Deeds, and decisions of mighty rulers.

Doch herrlicht mir dein Nahme das Lied; dein Fest
  Augusta! durft' ich feiern; Beruf ist mirs,
    Zu rühmen Höhers, darum gab die
      Sprache der Gott und den Dank ins Herz mir.

O daß von diesem freudigen Tage mir
  Auch meine Zeit beginne, daß endlich auch
    Mir ein Gesang in deinen Hainen,
      Edle! gedeihe, der deiner werth sei.

Geh unter, schöne Sonne . . .

Geh unter, schöne Sonne, sie achteten
  Nur wenig dein, sie kannten dich, Heilge, nicht,
    Denn mühelos und stille bist du
      Über den mühsamen aufgegangen.

Mir gehst du freundlich unter und auf, o Licht!
  Und wohl erkennt mein Auge dich, herrliches!
    Denn göttlich stille ehren lernt' ich
      Da Diotima den Sinn mir heilte.

O du des Himmels Botin! wie lausch ich dir!
  Dir, Diotima! Liebe! wie sah von dir
    Zum goldnen Tage dieses Auge
      Glänzend und dankend empor. Da rauschten

Lebendiger die Quellen, es athmeten
  Der dunkeln Erde Blüthen mich liebend an,
    Und lächelnd über Silberwolken
      Neigte sich seegnend herab der Aether.

Yet by your name my song is enhanced for me;
    Allowed to mark your day, my own call I serve,
        To praise what's higher: for this the
            God gave me speech and a heart that's grateful.

O that this joyful day would initiate
    For me a new time also, one song of mine
        Within your groves at last would prosper,
            Noble as you are and worthy of you.

Go down, then, lovely sun . . .

Go down, then, lovely sun, for but little they
    Regarded you, nor, holy one, knew your worth,
        Since without toil you rose, and quiet,
            Over a people for ever toiling.

To me, however, kindly you rise and set,
    O glorious light, and brightly my eyes respond,
        For godly, silent reverence I
            Learned when Diótima soothed my frenzy.

O how I listened, Heaven's own messenger,
    To you, my teacher! Love! How to the golden day
        These eyes transfused with thanks looked up from
            Gazing at you. And at once more living

The brooks began to murmur, more lovingly
    The blossoms of dark Earth breathed their scent at me
        And through the silver clouds a smiling
            Aether bowed down to bestow his blessing.

An die Deutschen

Spottet nimmer des Kinds, wenn noch das albernne
  Auf dem Rosse von Holz herrlich und viel sich dünkt,
    O ihr Guten! auch wir sind
      Thatenarm und gedankenvoll!

Aber kommt, wie der Stral aus dem Gewölke kommt,
  Aus Gedanken vieleicht, geistig und reif die That?
    Folgt die Frucht, wie des Haines
      Dunklem Blatte, der stillen Schrift?

Und das Schweigen im Volk, ist es die Feier schon
  Vor dem Feste? die Furcht, welche den Gott ansagt?
    O dann nimmt mich, ihr Lieben!
      Daß ich büße die Lästerung.

Schon zu lange, zu lang irr ich, dem Laien gleich,
  In des bildenden Geists werdender Werkstatt hier,
    Nur was blühet, erkenn ich,
      Was er sinnet, erkenn ich nicht.

Und zu ahnen ist süß, aber ein Leiden auch,
  Und schon Jahre genug leb'ich in sterblicher
    Unverständiger Liebe
      Zweifelnd, immer bewegt vor ihm,

Der das stetige Werk immer aus liebender
  Seele näher mir bringt, lächelnd dem Sterblichen
    Wo ich zage, des Lebens
      Reine Tiefe zu Reife bringt.

Schöpferischer, o wann, Genius unsers Volks,
  Wann erscheinest du ganz, Seele des Vaterlands,
    Daß ich tiefer mich beuge,
      Daß die leiseste Saite selbst

To the Germans

Never laugh at the child, seeing the silly one
  Feel important and great up on his rocking-horse;
    O my brothers, we too are
      Poor in deeds though we've thoughts enough!

But as lightning from clouds, out of mere thoughts perhaps
  Will the deed in the end, lucid, mature, leap out?
    As from dark orchard leaves, from
      Quiet scripts does the fruit ensue?

And this hush in the crowd, is it the joy before
  Joy's occasion? The awe marking the god's approach?
    O then seize me, my dear ones,
      Make me pay for my slanderous words.

Far too long now, too long like a poor layman I
  In the shaping Spirit's workshop have roamed perplexed;
    Things half-grown I can see there,
      What he schemes I can not make out.

Sweet it is to divine, but an affliction too,
  And enough years I've spent loving as mortals do,
    Doubting, uncomprehending,
      Ever moved in his presence who

Ever closer to me out of his loving soul
  Brings the constant great work, smiles at the mortal man
    Where I falter, and to its
      Ripeness brings the pure depth of life.

O creative one, when, genius innate in us,
  Wholly will you appear, soul of our fatherland?
    So that lower I bow then,
      Of my strings the most muted then

Mir verstumme vor dir, daß ich beschämt
  Eine Blume der Nacht, himmlischer Tag, vor dir
    Enden möge mit Freuden,
      Wenn sie alle, mit denen ich

Vormals trauerte, wenn unsere Städte nun
  Hell und offen und wach, reineren Feuers voll
    Und die Berge des deutschen
      Landes Berge der Musen sind,

Wie die herrlichen einst, Pindos und Helikon,
  Und Parnassos, und rings unter des Vaterlands
    Goldnem Himmel die freie,
      Klare, geistige Freude glänzt.

Wohl ist enge begränzt unsere Lebenszeit,
  Unserer Jahre Zahl sehen und zählen wir,
    Doch die Jahre der Völker,
      Sah ein sterbliches Auge sie?

Wenn die Seele dir auch über die eigne Zeit
  Sich die sehnende schwingt, trauernd verweilest du
    Dann am kalten Gestade
      Bei den Deinen und kennst sie nie,

Und die Künftigen auch, sie, die Verheißenen
  Wo, wo siehest du sie, daß du an Freundeshand
    Einmal wieder erwarmest,
      Einer Seele vernehmlich seist?

Klanglos,   ists in der Halle längst,
  Armer Seher! bei dir, sehnend verlischt dein Aug
    Und du schlummerst hinunter
      Ohne Namen und unbeweint.

Dare not sound, and ashamed, dumb before you I droop
  Like a flower of the night, heavenly day, and long
    But to wither with gladness,
      When all those in whose midst I could

Only mourn – when our towns, brightened now, are awake,
  Open and communal, full of a purer fire,
    And the mountains of German
      Lands are mountains the Muses haunt

Like those glorious ones then, Pindos and Helicon
  And Parnassus, and here under the fatherland's
    Golden sky the pellucid,
      Free and enlightened gladness gleams.

True, the span of our lives briefly extends; we can
  See and count the few years granted to us on earth,
    But the years of the peoples,
      These what mortal man's eye has seen?

Though your soul roams away, winged with its yearning soars
  Far beyond your own time, mournful you linger here,
    Cold on desolate shores, with
      Your own kind, but estranged from them;

And those others to come, those for whose advent we wait,
  Where, O where can you see them, that once more you'll be
    Warmed by one hand that's friendly,
      Audible to one living soul?

Without resonance, long empty for you it's been
  In your hall, poor seer, now; yearning your eye grows dim,
    And you drowse away, vanish
      Never noticed, unnamed, unwept.

Rousseau

Wie eng begränzt ist unsere Tageszeit.
    Du warst und sahst und stauntest, schon Abend ists,
        Nun schlafe, wo unendlich ferne
            Ziehen vorüber der Völker Jahre.

Und mancher siehet über die eigne Zeit
    Ihm zeigt ein Gott ins Freie, doch sehnend stehst
        Am Ufer du, ein Ärgerniß den
            Deinen, ein Schatten, und liebst sie nimmer.

Und jene, die du nennst, die Verheißenen,
    Wo sind die Neuen, daß du an Freundeshand
        Erwarmst, wo nahn sie, daß du einmal
            Einsame Rede, vernehmlich seiest?

Klanglos ists, armer Mann, in der Halle dir,
    Und gleich den Unbegrabenen, irrest du
        Unstät und suchest Ruh und niemand
            Weiß den beschiedenen Weg zu weisen.

Sei denn zufrieden!   der Baum entwächst
    Dem heimatlichen Boden, aber es sinken ihm
        Die liebenden, die jugendlichen
            Arme, und trauernd neigt er sein Haupt.

Des Lebens Überfluß, das Unendliche,
    Das um ihn   und dämmert, er faßt es nie.
        Doch lebts in ihm und gegenwärtig,
            Wärmend und wirkend, die Frucht entquillt ihm.

Du hast gelebt!   auch dir, auch dir
    Erfreuet die ferne Sonne dein Haupt,
        Und Stralen aus der schönern Zeit. Es
            Haben die Boten dein Herz gefunden.

Rousseau

How narrowly confined is our day-time here.
　　You were and saw and wondered, and darkness falls;
　　　　Now sleep, where infinitely far the
　　　　　　Years of the peoples go drifting past you.

And some there are whose vision outflies their time;
　　Abroad a god directs them, but, yearning, you
　　　　Must haunt the shore, a shade, an outcast
　　　　　　Cursed by your kin, and no longer love them,

And those you name, whose coming is promised us,
　　Where are those new ones, that by a friendly hand
　　　　You may be warmed, where drawing near, that
　　　　　　Audibly, you, lonely speech, may sound then?

The hall yields no response to your voice, poor man;
　　And like the unburied dead you must roam about
　　　　Unquiet, seeking rest, and no one
　　　　　　To the allotted way can direct you.

So be content!　　　　the tree outgrows
　　His native soil, but soon will his branching arms
　　　　The loving, youthful, then begin to
　　　　　　Droop, and his head he will bow in sadness.

Life's superfluity, the immensely rich
　　That teems and glimmers round him, he'll never grasp.
　　　　And yet it lives in him, and present,
　　　　　　Warming, effective, his fruit contains it.

You lived! and *your* crest too, though but once, yours too
　　Is gladdened by the light of a distant sun,
　　　　The radiance of a better age. The
　　　　　　Heralds who looked for your heart have found it.

Vernommen hast du sie, verstanden die Sprache der Fremdlinge,
    Gedeutet ihre Seele! Dem Sehnenden war
        Der Wink genug, und Winke sind
            Von Alters her die Sprache der Götter.

Und wunderbar, als hätte von Anbeginn
    Des Menschen Geist das Werden und Wirken all,
        Des Lebens Weise schon erfahren

Kennt er im ersten Zeichen Vollendetes schon,
    Und fliegt, der kühne Geist, wie Adler den
        Gewittern, weissagend seinen
            Kommenden Göttern voraus,

Heidelberg

Lange lieb' ich dich schon, möchte dich, mir zur Lust,
    Mutter nennen, und dir schenken ein kunstlos Lied,
        Du, der Vaterlandsstädte
            Ländlichschönste, so viel ich sah.

Wie der Vogel des Walds über die Gipfel fliegt,
    Schwingt sich über den Strom, wo er vorbei dir glänzt,
        Leicht und kräftig die Brüke,
            Die von Wagen und Menschen tönt.

Wie von Göttern gesandt, fesselt' ein Zauber einst
    Auf die Brüke mich an, da ich vorüber gieng,
        Und herein in die Berge
            Mir die reizende Ferne schien,

Und der Jüngling, der Strom, fort in die Ebne zog,
    Traurigfroh, wie das Herz, wenn es, sich selbst zu schön,
        Liebend unterzugehen,
            In die Fluthen der Zeit sich wirft.

You've heard and comprehended the strangers' tongue,
    Interpreted their soul! For the yearning man
        The hint sufficed, because in hints from
            Time immemorial the gods have spoken.

And marvellous, as though from the very first
    The human mind had known all that grows and moves,
        Foreknown life's melody and rhythm,

In seed grains he can measure the full-grown plant;
    And flies, bold spirit, flies as the eagles do
        Ahead of thunder-storms, preceding
            Gods, his own gods, to announce their coming,

Heidelberg
ALCAIC VERSION

Long I have loved you, and now for my own delight
    Would call you Mother, offer an artless song
        To you, of all the homeland cities
            Which I have seen the most lapped in beauty.

As over hilltops birds of the forest fly,
    Across the river gleaming past you the bridge
        Vaults over, sturdily and lightly,
            Loud with the traffic of feet and coachwheels.

As though divinely sent, an enchantment once
    Transfixed me on the bridge as I walked that way
        And right into the hills there came the
            Radiance and lure of far-distant places

And he, the youth, the river sought out the plains
    As sadly glad as hearts that, too full for ease,
        To perish out of love's abundance
            Hurl themselves down into time's quick torrents.

Quellen hattest du ihm, hattest dem Flüchtigen
    Kühle Schatten geschenkt, und die Gestade sahn
        All' ihm nach, und es bebte
            Aus den Wellen ihr lieblich Bild.

Aber schwer in das Thal hieng die gigantische,
    Schiksaalskundige Burg nieder bis auf den Grund,
        Von den Wettern zerrissen;
            Doch die ewige Sonne goß

Ihr verjüngendes Licht über das alternde
    Riesenbild, und umher grünte lebendiger
        Epheu; freundliche Wälder
            Rauschten über die Burg herab.

Sträuche blühten herab, bis wo im heitern Thal,
    An den Hügel gelehnt, oder dem Ufer hold,
        Deine fröhlichen Gassen
            Unter duftenden Gärten ruhn.

Der Nekar

In deinen Thälern wachte mein Herz mir auf
    Zum Leben, deine Wellen umspielten mich,
        Und all der holden Hügel, die dich
            Wanderer! kennen, ist keiner fremd mir.

Auf ihren Gipfeln löste des Himmels Luft
    Mir oft der Knechtschaft Schmerzen; und aus dem Thal,
        Wie Leben aus dem Freudebecher,
            Glänzte die bläuliche Silberwelle.

Der Berge Quellen eilten hinab zu dir,
    Mit ihnen auch mein Herz und du nahmst uns mit,
        Zum stillerhabnen Rhein, zu seinen
            Städten hinunter und lustgen Inseln.

To him, the fleeting, well-springs you'd given, and
    Cool shade enough, and after him all the banks
        Now gazed, and from the rippled water
            Quivered their beautiful mirror image.

But heavy, hulking into the valley hung
    The fate-acquainted castle, the vast, all torn
        And battered down to its foundations;
            Nevertheless even there the sun now

Poured out renewing, youth-giving light upon
    That aging bastion's bulk, and around it bloomed
        The living ivy; kindly forests
            Breathed their soft murmur on brittle stonework.

Shrubs blossomed down to where in the valley's calm,
    Close to the hillside, leaning or fondly pressed
        Against the river-bank, your cheerful
            Streets are at rest beneath fragrant gardens.

The Neckar

Your banks and dells awakened my heart to life,
    Your wavelets played, their rippling my music then;
        Of all the lovely hills that know you,
            Rambler, not one is unknown to me there.

Up on their tops quite often the heavens' air
    Allayed the pangs of servitude; from the vale,
        As from the wine-cup life and gladness,
            Glittered the bluish and silver wavelet.

The mountain brooks came hurrying down to you,
    And with them came my heart, and you carried us
        To calm, exalted Rhine, conveyed us
            Down to his cities and pleasant islets.

Noch dünkt die Welt mir schön, und das Aug entflieht
  Verlangend nach den Reizen der Erde mir,
    Zum goldenen Paktol, zu Smirnas
      Ufer, zu Ilions Wald. Auch möcht ich

Bei Sunium oft landen, den stummen Pfad
  Nach deinen Säulen fragen, Olympion!
    Noch eh der Sturmwind und das Alter
      Hin in den Schutt der Athenertempel

Und ihrer Gottesbilder auch dich begräbt,
  Denn lang schon einsam stehst du, o Stolz der Welt,
    Die nicht mehr ist. Und o ihr schönen
      Inseln Ioniens! wo die Meerluft

Die heißen Ufer kühlt und den Lorbeerwald
  Durchsäuselt, wenn die Sonne den Weinstok wärmt,
    Ach! wo ein goldner Herbst dem armen
      Volk in Gesänge die Seufzer wandelt,

Wenn sein Granatbaum reift, wenn aus grüner Nacht
  Die Pomeranze blinkt, und der Mastyxbaum
    Von Harze träuft und Pauk und Cymbel
      Zum labyrintischen Tanze klingen.

Zu euch, ihr Inseln! bringt mich vielleicht, zu euch
  Mein Schuzgott einst; doch weicht mir aus treuem Sinn
    Auch da mein Nekar nicht mit seinen
      Lieblichen Wiesen und Uferweiden.

Die Heimath

Froh kehrt der Schiffer heim an den stillen Strom,
  Von Inseln fernher, wenn er geerndtet hat;
    So käm' auch ich zur Heimath, hätt' ich
      Güter so viele, wie Laid, geerndtet.

The world seems lovely still, and my vision flees
   From me, allured by Earth and her various charms,
      To golden Pactolus, to Smyrna's
         Coast or to Ilium's woods. And often

I long to land at Sunium and ask the path,
   The dumb, where are your pillars, Olympion,
      And soon, before the gales and age can
         Bury you too in the scattered rubble

Of temples Athens raised, and her imaged gods,
   For long now desolate you have stood, O pride
      Of worlds that are no more. And O you
         Lovely Ionian isles where the sea breeze

Wafts coolness on hot shores and runs rustling through
   The laurel wood, when sunbeams caress the vine,
      And oh, where still a golden autumn
         Turns into songs the poor people's sighing,

When their pomegranate ripens, the orange glints
   In a green night and richly the resin drips
      From mastic trees and drum and cymbal
         Beat to the wild labyrinthine dances.

To you, perhaps, you islands, my guardian god
   One day will take me; yet even then I should
      Recall my Neckar, loyal to his
         Amiable meadows and bankside willows.

Home

Content the boatman turns to the river's calm
   From distant isles, his harvest all gathered in;
      So too would I go home now, had I
         Reaped as much wealth as I've gathered sorrow.

Ihr theuern Ufer, die mich erzogen einst,
   Stillt ihr der Liebe Leiden, versprecht ihr mir,
     Ihr Wälder meiner Jugend, wenn ich
       Komme, die Ruhe noch einmal wieder?

Am kühlen Bache, wo ich der Wellen Spiel,
   Am Strome, wo ich gleiten die Schiffe sah,
     Dort bin ich bald; euch traute Berge,
       Die mich behüteten einst, der Heimath

Verehrte sichre Grenzen, der Mutter Haus
   Und liebender Geschwister Umarmungen
     Begrüß' ich bald und ihr umschließt mich,
       Daß, wie in Banden, das Herz mir heile,

Ihr treugebliebnen! aber ich weiß, ich weiß,
   Der Liebe Laid, diß heilet so bald mir nicht,
     Diß singt kein Wiegensang, den tröstend
       Sterbliche singen, mir aus dem Busen.

Denn sie, die uns das himmlische Feuer leihn,
   Die Götter schenken heiliges Laid uns auch,
     Drum bleibe diß. Ein Sohn der Erde
       Schein' ich; zu lieben gemacht, zu leiden.

Die Liebe

Wenn ihr Freunde vergeßt, wenn ihr die Euern all,
   O ihr Dankbaren, sie, euere Dichter schmäht,
     Gott vergeb' es, doch ehret
       Nur die Seele der Liebenden.

Denn o saget, wo lebt menschliches Leben sonst,
   Da die knechtische jezt alles, die Sorge zwingt?
     Darum wandelt der Gott auch
       Sorglos über dem Haupt uns längst.

Dear river-banks that reared me and taught me once,
   Do you allay love's sufferings, promise me
      You forests of my childhood, should I
         Come to you now, the same peace as ever?

Where by the stream, the cool, I saw wavelets play
   And on the river's meadow watched boats glide past,
      There soon I'll be; you long-loved mountains,
         Once my protectors, and still the homeland's

Revered and certain frontiers, my mother's house,
   Embrace of loving brother and sister there
      I'll welcome soon, and you'll enclose me,
         Healing my heart like a gentle bandage,

You ever loyal ones; but I know, I know,
   This grief, the grief of love, will be slow to heal,
      Of this no lullaby that mortals
         Chant to give comfort will now relieve me.

For they who lend us heavenly light and fire,
   The gods, with holy sorrow endow us too.
      So be it, then. A son of Earth I
         Seem; and was fashioned to love, to suffer.

Love

If you drop an old friend, if, O you grateful ones,
   Your own poets you slight, slander and cheapen, may
      God forgive you, but always
         Honour lovers, respect their soul.

For, I ask you, where else humanly do men live
   Now that slavish one, Care, rules and compels us all?
      Therefore too has the God long
         Moved uncaring above our heads.

Doch, wie immer das Jahr kalt und gesanglos ist
    Zur beschiedenen Zeit, aber aus weißem Feld
        Grüne Halme doch sprossen,
            Oft ein einsamer Vogel singt,

Wenn sich mälig der Wald dehnet, der Strom sich regt,
    Schon die mildere Luft leise von Mittag weht
        Zur erlesenen Stunde,
            So ein Zeichen der schönern Zeit,

Die wir glauben, erwächst einziggenügsam noch,
    Einzig edel und fromm über dem ehernen,
        Wilden Boden die Liebe,
            Gottes Tochter, von ihm allein.

Sei geseegnet, o sei, himmlische Pflanze, mir
    Mit Gesange gepflegt, wenn des ätherischen
        Nektars Kräfte dich nähren,
            Und der schöpfrische Stral dich reift.

Wachs und werde zum Wald! eine beseeltere,
    Vollentblühende Welt! Sprache der Liebenden
        Sei die Sprache des Landes,
            Ihre Seele der Laut des Volks!

Lebenslauf

Größers wolltest auch du, aber die Liebe zwingt
    All uns nieder, das Laid beuget gewaltiger,
        Doch es kehret umsonst nicht
            Unser Bogen, woher er kommt.

Aufwärts oder hinab! herrschet in heil'ger Nacht,
    Wo die stumme Natur werdende Tage sinnt,
        Herrscht im schiefesten Orkus
            Nicht ein Grades, ein Recht noch auch?

Yet no matter how cold, songless the year may be,
   When the season is due still from the field all white
      New green blades will be sprouting,
         Often one lonely small bird will sing,

When the woods all expand, slowly, the river stirs
   Milder breezes at last tenderly blow from the south,
      At the hour pre-elected,
         So, a sign of the better age

We believe in, unique thanks to her self-content,
   Noble, pious, on soil hard as iron and waste,
      Love, the daughter of God, comes,
         Only his and from him alone.

You, then, heavenly plant, now let me bless, and be
   Ever tended with song, when the aetherial
      Nectar's energies feed you,
         Ripened by the creative ray.

Grow and be a whole wood! Be a more soul-inspired,
   Fully blossoming world! Language of lovers now
      Be the language our land speaks,
         And their soul be the people's lilt!

The Course of Life

More you also desired, but every one of us
   Love draws earthward, and grief bends with still greater power;
      Yet our arc not for nothing
         Brings us back to our starting-place.

Whether upward or down – does not in holy night
   Where mute Nature thinks out days that are still to come,
      Though in crookedest Orcus,
         Yet a straightness, a law prevail?

Diß erfuhr ich. Denn nie, sterblichen Meistern gleich,
   Habt ihr Himmlischen, ihr Alleserhaltenden,
      Daß ich wüßte, mit Vorsicht
         Mich des ebenen Pfads geführt.

Alles prüfe der Mensch, sagen die Himmlischen,
   Daß er, kräftig genährt, danken für Alles lern',
      Und verstehe die Freiheit,
         Aufzubrechen, wohin er will.

Ihre Genesung

Sieh! dein Liebstes, Natur, leidet und schläft und du
   Allesheilende, säumst? oder ihr seids nicht mehr,
      Zarte Lüfte des Aethers,
         Und ihr Quellen des Morgenlichts?

Alle Blumen der Erd, alle die goldenen
   Frohen Früchte des Hains, alle sie heilen nicht
      Dieses Leben, ihr Götter,
         Das ihr selber doch euch erzogt?

Ach! schon athmet und tönt heilige Lebenslust
   Ihr im reizenden Wort wieder, wie sonst und schon
      Glänzt in zärtlicher Jugend
         Deine Blume, wie sonst, dich an,

Heilge Natur, o du, welche zu oft, zu oft,
   Wenn ich trauernd versank, lächelnd das zweifelnde
      Haupt mit Gaaben umkränzte,
         Jugendliche, nun auch, wie sonst!

Wenn ich altre dereinst, siehe so geb ich dir,
   Die mich täglich verjüngt, Allesverwandelnde,
      Deiner Flamme die Schlaken,
         Und ein anderer leb ich auf.

This I learned. For not once, as mortal masters do,
    Did you heavenly ones, wise preservers of all,
        To my knowledge, with foresight
            Lead me on by a level path.

All a man shall try out, thus say the heavenly,
    So that strongly sustained he shall give thanks for all,
        Learn to grasp his own freedom
            To be gone where he's moved to go.

Her Recovery

Nature, look, your most loved drowses and ails, and you
    Dally, healer of all? Have you grown weak, then, tired,
        Gentle breezes of Aether,
            Limpid sources of morning light?

All the flowers of the earth, all the deep golden-hued
    Happy fruits of the grove, how can it be that all
        Fail to cure this one life which,
            Gods, you raised for your own delight?

Ah, already restored, holy desire to live
    Breathes and sounds in her talk, charming as ever, and
        Tenderly youthful your flower
            Gleams at you as she did before,

Holy Nature, the same who all too often when
    Sadness made me sink down, smiling would garland my
        Head with gifts, with your riches,
            Youthful Nature, now too restored!

Look, one day when I'm old, you that transmute all things,
    And now daily renew youth in me, I will give
        To your flame the dead cinders
            And revive as a different man.

Der Abschied
ZWEITE FASSUNG

Trennen wollten wir uns? wähnten es gut und klug?
  Da wirs thaten, warum schrökte, wie Mord, die That?
    Ach! wir kennen uns wenig,
      Denn es waltet ein Gott in uns.

Den verrathen? ach ihn, welcher uns alles erst,
  Sinn und Leben erschuff, ihn, den beseelenden
    Schuzgott unserer Liebe,
      Diß, diß Eine vermag ich nicht.

Aber anderen Fehl denket der Weltsinn sich,
  Andern ehernen Dienst übt er und anders Recht,
    Und es listet die Seele
      Tag für Tag der Gebrauch uns ab.

Wohl! ich wußt' es zuvor. Seit die gewurzelte
  Ungestalte die Furcht Götter und Menschen trennt,
    Muß, mit Blut sie zu sühnen,
      Muß der Liebenden Herz vergehn.

Laß mich schweigen! o laß nimmer von nun an mich
  Dieses Tödtliche sehn, daß ich im Frieden doch
    Hin ins Einsame ziehe,
      Und noch unser der Abschied sei!

Reich die Schaale mir selbst, daß ich des rettenden
  Heilgen Giftes genug, daß ich des Lethetranks
    Mit dir trinke, daß alles
      Haß und Liebe vergessen sei!

Hingehn will ich. Vieleicht seh' ich in langer Zeit
  Diotima! dich hier. Aber verblutet ist
    Dann das Wünschen und friedlich
      Gleich den Seeligen, fremde gehn

The Farewell
SECOND VERSION

So we wanted to part? Thought it both good and wise?
　　Why, then, why did the act shock us as murder would?
　　　Ah, ourselves we know little,
　　　　For within us a god commands.

Wrong that god? And betray him who created for us
　　Meaning, life, all we had, him who inspired and moved,
　　　Who protected our loving,
　　　　This, this one thing I cannot do.

But a different wrong, different slavery
　　Now the world's mind invents, threatens with other laws,
　　　And, by cunning, convention
　　　　Day by day steals away our souls.

Oh, I knew it before. Ever since deep-rooted Fear,
　　Ugly, crippled, estranged mortals from heaven's gods
　　　To appease them with bloodshed
　　　　Lovers' hearts must be sacrificed.

Silent now let me be! Never henceforth let me know
　　This, my deadly disgrace, so that in peace I may
　　　Hide myself where it's lonely
　　　　And the parting at least be ours.

Pass the cup, then, yourself, that of the rescuing,
　　Holy poison enough, that of the lethal draught
　　　I may drink with you, all things,
　　　　Hate and love be forgotten then.

To be gone is my wish. Later perhaps one day,
　　Diotima, we'll meet – here, but desire by then
　　　Will have bled away, peaceful
　　　　Like the blessed, and like strangers we'll

Wir umher, ein Gespräch führet uns ab und auf,
  Sinnend, zögernd, doch izt mahnt die Vergessenen
    Hier die Stelle des Abschieds,
      Es erwarmet ein Herz in uns,

Staunend seh' ich dich an, Stimmen und süßen Sang,
  Wie aus voriger Zeit hör' ich und Saitenspiel,
    Und die Lilie duftet
      Golden über dem Bach uns auf.

Diotima

Du schweigst und duldest, denn sie verstehn dich nicht,
  Du edles Leben! siehest zur Erd' und schweigst
    Am schönen Tag, denn ach! umsonst nur
      Suchst du die Deinen im Sonnenlichte,

Die Königlichen, welche, wie Brüder doch,
  Wie eines Hains gesellige Gipfel sonst
    Der Lieb' und Heimath sich und ihres
      Immerumfangenden Himmels freuten,

Des Ursprungs noch in tönender Brust gedenk;
  Die Dankbarn, sie, sie mein' ich, die einzigtreu
    Bis in den Tartarus hinab die Freude
      Brachten, die Freien, die Göttermenschen,

Die zärtlichgroßen Seelen, die nimmer sind;
  Denn sie beweint, so lange das Trauerjahr
    Schon dauert, von den vor'gen Sternen
      Täglich gemahnet, das Herz noch immer

Und diese Todtenklage, sie ruht nicht aus.
  Die Zeit doch heilt. Die Himmlischen sind jezt stark,
    Sind schnell. Nimmt denn nicht schon ihr altes
      Freudiges Recht die Natur sich wieder?

Walk about, as our talk leads us now here, now there,
    Musing, hesitant, but then the oblivious ones
        See the place where they parted,
            And a heart newly warms in us,

Wondering I look at you, voices and lovely song
    As from distant times, music of strings, I hear
        And the lily unfolds her
            Fragrance, golden above the brook.

Diotima

You suffer and keep silent, unknown to them,
    You noble being, silently earthward gaze
        At brightest noon, for it's in vain that
            Here in the sunlight you seek your kindred,

Those regal ones who truly like brothers once,
    Like crests of one companionable grove were glad
        Of love and of their homeland and the
            Heaven that ever enfolded, blessed them,

Their tuneful bosoms true to their origin;
    Those grateful ones, I mean, who unmatched in faith
        As far as deepest Tartarus proffered
            Gladness, untrammelled as gods, though human,

Those tender noble spirits that are no more;
    For these, though long already our time of loss
        Has lasted, by the former planets
            Daily reminded, the heart still weeps, and

This keening for the dead does not flag or rest.
    Yet time heals all. The Heavenly now are strong,
        Are quick. Already does not Nature
            Claim her old joy-giving rights, reclaim them?

Sieh! eh noch unser Hügel, o Liebe, sinkt,
  Geschiehts, und ja! noch siehet mein sterblich Lied
    Den Tag, der, Diotima! nächst den
      Göttern mit Helden dich nennt, und dir gleicht.

Rükkehr in die Heimath

Ihr milden Lüfte! Boten Italiens!
  Und du mit deinen Pappeln, geliebter Strom!
    Ihr woogenden Gebirg! o all ihr
      Sonnigen Gipfel, so seid ihrs wieder?

Du stiller Ort! in Träumen erschienst du fern
  Nach hoffnungslosem Tage dem Sehnenden,
    Und du mein Haus, und ihr Gespielen,
      Bäume des Hügels, ihr wohlbekannten!

Wie lang ists, o wie lange! des Kindes Ruh
  Ist hin, und hin ist Jugend und Lieb' und Lust;
    Doch du, mein Vaterland! du heilig
      Duldendes! siehe, du bist geblieben.

Und darum, daß sie dulden mit dir, mit dir
  Sich freun, erziehst du, theures! die Deinen auch
    Und mahnst in Träumen, wenn sie ferne
      Schweifen und irren, die Ungetreuen.

Und wenn im heißen Busen dem Jünglinge
  Die eigenmächt'gen Wünsche besänftiget
    Und stille vor dem Schiksaal sind, dann
      Giebt der Geläuterte dir sich lieber.

Lebt wohl dann, Jugendtage, du Rosenpfad
  Der Lieb', und all' ihr Pfade des Wanderers,
    Lebt wohl! und nimm und seegne du mein
      Leben, o Himmel der Heimath, wieder!

Look, Diotima, dear one, before our mound
  Subsides that age will come, and my mortal song
    Yet see the day which next to gods, with
      Heroes will name you, itself be like you.

Return to the Homeland

You gentle breezes, heralds of Italy,
  And you with all your poplars, dear river-banks,
    You billowing mountain range, and sunny
      Peaks – can it be, is it really you, then?

You quiet place, in dreams after hopeless days
  You taunted me, the homesick, but stayed remote,
    And you, my house, and you, my playmates,
      Trees of the hillside, my old companions!

How long ago, how long! Now the child's calm trust
  Is gone, and gone are youth and delight and love;
    But you, the suffering, the holy,
      Look, you alone have remained, my homeland.

And it's for that, to suffer with you, with you
  To share their joys that, dear one, you raise your sons,
    And when, unfaithful, far from you they
      Wander astray, in their dreams remind them.

And when at last the youth in his fervid heart
  Feels autocratic wishes abate, grow still
    In face of destiny, to you more
      Readily too will the mellowed yield then.

Good-bye, then, days of youth, and you rose-lined path
  Of love, and all you paths of the roaming man,
    Good-bye! And you, my homeland's heaven,
      Take back this life that was yours, and bless it.

Das Ahnenbild
NE VIRTUS ULLA PEREAT!

Alter Vater! Du blikst immer, wie ehmals, noch,
  Da du gerne gelebt unter den Sterblichen,
    Aber ruhiger nur, und
      Wie die Seeligen, heiterer

In die Wohnung, wo doch, Vater! das Söhnlein nennt,
  Wo es lächelnd vor dir spielt und den Muthwill übt,
    Wie die Lämmer im Feld', auf
      Grünem Teppiche, den zur Lust

Ihm die Mutter gegönnt. Ferne sich haltend, sieht
  Ihm die Liebende zu, wundert der Sprache sich
    Und des jungen Verstandes
      Und des blühenden Auges schon.

Und an andere Zeit mahnt sie der Mann, dein Sohn;
  An die Lüfte des Mais, da er geseufzt um sie,
    An die Bräutigamstage,
      Da der Stolze die Demuth lernt.

Doch es wandte sich bald: Sicherer, denn er war,
  Ist er, herrlicher ist unter den Seinigen
    Nun der Zweifachgeliebte,
      Und ihm gehet sein Tagewerk.

Stiller Vater! auch du lebtest und liebtest so:
  Darum wohnest du nun, als ein Unsterblicher,
    Bei den Kindern, und Leben,
      Wie vom schweigenden Aether, kommt

Öfters über das Haus, ruhiger Mann! von dir,
  Und es mehrt sich, es reift, edler von Jahr zu Jahr,
    In bescheidenem Glüke,
      Was mit Hofnungen du gepflanzt.

The Ancestral Portrait
NE VIRTUS ULLA PEREAT!*

Aged father, you gaze now as you did before
   When it pleased you to live here among mortal kin,
      Yet more quietly now and,
         Like the blessed, more serenely too,

On the room where a boy, father, still speaks your name,
   Where he smiles as he plays, frolics in front of you
      Like the lambs in the field, on
         His green carpet, laid out for him

By his mother, for joy. Keeping her distance, she
   Raptly loving, looks on, marvels at words he tries,
      At his young comprehension,
         At the light that shines from his eyes.

And her husband, your son, turns her fond musing back:
   May-time breezes in which only for her he sighed,
      Testing days of his courtship,
         When the proud one must learn to bow.

But quite soon that was changed: surer than once he'd been
   He has grown, more secure, lordly amid his own,
      Now the doubly belovèd,
         And his labour goes well for him.

Tranquil father, so too you once would live and love;
   That is why you can dwell, now an immortal, here
      With your children, a life like
         That of Aether, the silent, comes

To the house at times, calm of your calm, from you
   And, more noble each year, all that your hopes could plant
      Thrives, matures and increases
         In their modest, their frugal bliss.

*'That no virtue be lost!'

Die du liebend erzogst, siehe! sie grünen dir,
  Deine Bäume, wie sonst, breiten ums Haus den Arm,
    Voll von dankenden Gaaben;
      Sichrer stehen die Stämme schon;

Und am Hügel hinab, wo du den sonnigen
  Boden ihnen gebaut, neigen und schwingen sich
    Deine freudigen Reben,
      Trunken, purpurner Trauben voll.

Aber unten im Haus ruhet, besorgt von dir,
  Der gekelterte Wein. Theuer ist der dem Sohn',
    Und er sparet zum Fest das
      Alte, lautere Feuer sich.

Dann beim nächtlichen Mahl, wenn er, in Lust und Ernst,
  Von Vergangenem viel, vieles von Künftigem
    Mit den Freunden gesprochen,
      Und der lezte Gesang noch hallt,

Hält er höher den Kelch, siehet dein Bild und spricht:
  Deiner denken wir nun, dein, und so werd' und bleib'
    Ihre Ehre des Haußes
      Guten Genien, hier und sonst!

Und es tönen zum Dank hell die Krystalle dir;
  Und die Mutter, sie reicht, heute zum erstenmal,
    Daß es wisse vom Feste,
      Auch dem Kinde von deinem Trank.

Die Entschlafenen

Einen vergänglichen Tag lebt' ich und wuchs mit den Meinen,
  Eins um's andere schon schläft mir und fliehet dahin.
Doch ihr Schlafenden wacht am Herzen mir, in verwandter
  Seele ruhet von euch mir das entfliehende Bild.
Und lebendiger lebt ihr dort, wo de göttlichen Geistes
  Freude die Alternden all, alle die Todten verjüngt.

Those that loving you reared, look! they grow green for you,
   These your trees, as before, spreading around the house
      Grateful gifts by the armful;
         Firmer, stronger their trunks have grown;

On the slope of this hill, where you had cut for them
   Sunny tracts, now there sway, bend in the autumn winds
      Happy grapevines you planted,
         Drunken, laden with purple fruit.

Down below, in the house, thanks to your work and care,
   Lies the wine that you pressed. Dear it is to your son,
      And he saves for the feast-day
         Yours, the older, more mellow fire.

Then, at table by night, when, at once glad and grave,
   Much of days that have passed, much of the days to come
      With his friends he has spoken,
         And the last of their songs subsides,

High he raises his glass, looks at your portrait, says:
   Now our thought be of you, yours be the name that guards
      This our household, its honour,
         Now and ever, within, without!

And for you, giving thanks, brightly the crystals clink;
   And the mother for once, so that he too may share,
      Know the festive occasion,
         Lets the child even taste your wine.

The Departed

With my own kind I lived and could grow for a day that was fleeting,
   One by one they depart, gone from me into their sleep.
Yet you sleepers within me are wakeful, and in my related
   Soul an image of each, fugitive, lingers and rests.
And more living there you live on where the god-given spirit's
   Joy rejuvenates all, all who have aged, and the dead.

Ermunterung
ZWEITE FASSUNG

Echo des Himmels! heiliges Herz! warum,
  Warum verstummst du unter den Lebenden,
    Schläfst, freies! von den Götterlosen
      Ewig hinab in die Nacht verwiesen?

Wacht denn, wie vormals, nimmer des Aethers Licht?
  Und blüht die alte Mutter, die Erde nicht?
    Und übt der Geist nicht da und dort, nicht
      Lächelnd die Liebe das Recht noch immer?

Nur du nicht mehr! doch mahnen die Himmlischen,
  Und stillebildend weht, wie ein kahl Gefild,
    Der Othem der Natur dich an, der
      Alleserheiternde, seelenvolle.

O Hoffnung! bald, bald singen die Haine nicht
  Des Lebens Lob allein, denn es ist die Zeit,
    Daß aus der Menschen Munde sie, die
      Schönere Seele sich neuverkündet,

Dann liebender im Bunde mit Sterblichen
  Das Element sich bildet, und dann erst reich,
    Bei frommer Kinder Dank, der Erde
      Brust, die unendliche, sich entfaltet

Und unesre Tage wieder, wie Blumen, sind,
  Wo sie, des Himmels Sonne sich ausgetheilt
    Im stillen Wechsel sieht und wieder
      Froh in den Frohen das Licht sich findet,

Und er, der sprachlos waltet und unbekannt
  Zukünftiges bereitet, der Gott, der Geist
    Im Menschenwort, am schönen Tage
      Kommenden Jahren, wie einst, sich ausspricht.

Exhortation
SECOND VERSION

Echo of Heaven, heart that is hallowed, why,
   Why do you now fall silent, though living still,
      And sleep, you free one, by the godless
         Banished for ever to Night's deep dungeons?

Does not the light of Aether, as always, wake?
   And Earth, our ancient mother, still thrive and flower?
      And here and there does not the spirit,
         Love, with a smile wield her laws as ever?

You only fail! Yet heavenly powers exhort,
   And silently at work, like a stubble field,
      The breath of Nature blows upon you,
         She the all-brightening, soul-inspiring.

O hope, now soon, now soon not the groves alone
   Shall sing life's praise, for almost the time is come
      When through the mouths of mortals, this, the
         Lovelier soul will make known her coming.

Allied with men more lovingly then once more
   The element will form, and not rich or full
      But when her pious children thank her,
         Endless the breast of our Earth unfold then,

And once again like blossoms our days will be
   Where heavenly Helios sees his own light shared out
      In quiet alternation, finding
         Joy in the joy of those mortal mirrors,

And he who silent rules and in secret plans
   Things yet to come, the Godhead, the Spirit housed
      In human words, once more, at noontide,
         Clearly will speak to the future ages.

Natur und Kunst
ODER
Saturn und Jupiter

Du waltest hoch am Tag' und es blühet dein
   Gesez, du hältst die Waage, Saturnus Sohn!
      Und theilst die Loos' und ruhest froh im
         Ruhm der unsterblichen Herrscherkünste.

Doch in den Abgrund, sagen die Sänger sich,
   Habst du den heil'gen Vater, den eignen, einst
      Verwiesen und es jammre drunten,
         Da, wo die Wilden vor dir mit Recht sind,

Schuldlos der Gott der goldenen Zeit schon längst:
   Einst mühelos, und größer, wie du, wenn schon
      Er kein Gebot aussprach und ihn der
         Sterblichen keiner mit Nahmen nannte.

Herab denn! oder schäme des Danks dich nicht!
   Und willst du bleiben, diene dem Älteren,
      Und gönn' es ihm, daß ihn vor Allen,
         Göttern und Menschen, der Sänger nenne!

Denn, wie aus dem Gewölke dein Bliz, so kömmt
   Von ihm, was dein ist, siehe! so zeugt von ihm,
      Was du gebeutst, und aus Saturnus
         Frieden ist jegliche Macht erwachsen.

Und hab' ich erst am Herzen Lebendiges
   Gefühlt und dämmert, was du gestaltetest
      Und war in ihrer Wiege mir in
         Wonne die wechselnde Zeit entschlummert:

Dann kenn' ich dich, Kronion! dann hör' ich dich,
   Den weisen Meister, welcher, wie wir, ein Sohn
      Der Zeit, Geseze giebt und, was die
         Heilige Dämmerung birgt, verkündet.

Nature and Art
OR
Saturn and Jupiter

High up in day you govern, your law prevails,
   You hold the scales of judgement, O Saturn's son,
      Hand out our lots and well-contented
         Rest on the fame of immortal kingship.

Yet, singers know it, down the abyss you hurled
   The holy father once, your own parent, who
      Long now has lain lamenting where the
         Wild ones before you more justly languish,

Quite guiltless he, the god of the golden age:
   Once effortless and greater than you, although
      He uttered no commandment, and no
         Mortal on earth ever named his presence.

So down with you! Or cease to withhold your thanks!
   And if you'll stay, defer to the older god
      And grant him that above all others,
         Gods and great mortals, the singer name him!

For as from clouds your lightning, from him has come
   What you call yours. And, look, the commands you speak
      To him bear witness, and from Saturn's
         Primitive peace every power developed.

And once my heart can feel and contain that life
   Most living, his, and things that you shaped grow dim,
      And in his cradle changing Time has
         Fallen asleep and sweet quiet lulls me –

I'll know you then, Kronion, and hear you then,
   The one wise master who, like ourselves, a son
      Of Time, gives laws to us, uncovers
         That which lies hidden in holy twilight.

Unter den Alpen gesungen

Heilige Unschuld, du der Menschen und der
Götter liebste vertrauteste! du magst im
Hauße oder draußen ihnen zu Füßen
        Sizen, den Alten,

Immerzufriedner Weisheit voll; denn manches
Gute kennet der Mann, doch staunet er, dem
Wild gleich, oft zum Himmel, aber wie rein ist
        Reine, dir alles!

Siehe! das rauhe Thier des Feldes, gerne
Dient und trauet es dir, der stumme Wald spricht
Wie vor Alters, seine Sprüche zu dir, es
        Lehren die Berge

Heil'ge Geseze dich, und was noch jezt uns
Vielerfahrenen offenbar der große
Vater werden heißt, du darfst es allein uns
        Helle verkünden.

So mit den Himmlischen allein zu seyn, und
Geht vorüber das Licht, und Strom und Wind, und
Zeit eilt hin zum Ort, vor ihnen ein stetes
        Auge zu haben,

Seeliger weiß und wünsch' ich nichts, so lange
Nicht auch mich, wie die Weide, fort die Fluth nimmt,
Daß wohl aufgehoben, schlafend dahin ich
        Muß in den Woogen;

Aber es bleibt daheim gern, wer in treuem
Busen Göttliches hält, und frei will ich, so
Lang ich darf, euch all', ihr Sprachen des Himmels!
        Deuten und singen.

Sung beneath the Alps

Innocence, you the holy, dearest and nearest
Both to men and to gods! In the house or
Out of doors alike to sit at the ancients'
                    Feet it behoves you,

Ever contented wisdom yours; for men know
Much that's good, yet like animals often
Scan the heavens perplexed; to you, though, how pure are
                    All things, you pure one!

Look, the rough grassland beast is glad to serve and
Trust you; mute though it be, yet the forest
Now as ever yields its oracles up, the
                    Mountains still teach you

God-hallowed laws, and that which even now the
Mighty Father desires to make known to
Us the much experienced, you, and you only
                    Clearly may tell us.

Being alone with heavenly powers, and when the
Light begins to pass by, and swiftly river,
Wind and time seek out the place, with a constant
                    Eye then to face them –

Nothing more blessed I know, nor want, as long as
Not like willows me too the flood sweeps on, and
Well looked after, sleeping, down I must travel,
                    Waves for my bedding;

Gladly, though, he will stay at home who harbours
Things divine in his heart; and you, all Heaven's
Languages, freely, as long as I may, I'll
                    Sing and interpret.

Dichterberuf

Des Ganges Ufer hörten des Freudengotts
  Triumph, als alleroberud vom Indus her
    Der junge Bacchus kam, mit heilgem
      Weine vom Schlafe die Völker wekend.

Und du, des Tages Engel! erwekst sie nicht,
  Die jezt noch schlafen? gieb die Geseze, gieb
    Uns Leben, siege, Meister, du nur
      Hast der Eroberung Recht, wie Bacchus.

Nicht, was wohl sonst des Menschen Geschik und Sorg'
  Im Haus und unter offenem Himmel ist,
    Wenn edler, denn das Wild, der Mann sich
      Wehret und nährt! denn es gilt ein anders,

Zu Sorg' und Dienst den Dichtenden anvertraut!
  Der Höchste, der ists, dem wir geeignet sind,
    Daß näher, immerneu besungen
      Ihn die befreundete Brust vernehme.

Und dennoch, o ihr Himmlischen all, und all
  Ihr Quellen und ihr Ufer und Hain' und Höhn,
    Wo wunderbar zuerst, als du die
      Loken ergriffen, und unvergeßlich

Der unverhoffte Genius über uns
  Der schöpferische, göttliche kam, daß stumm
    Der Sinn uns ward und, wie vom
      Strale gerührt das Gebein erbebte,

Ihr ruhelosen Thaten in weiter Welt!
  Ihr Schiksaalstag', ihr reißenden, wenn der Gott
    Stillsinnend lenkt, wohin zorntrunken
      Ihn die gigantischen Rosse bringen,

The Poet's Vocation

The banks of Ganges heard how the god of joy
　　Was hailed when conquering all from far Indus came
　　　　The youthful Bacchus, and with holy
　　　　　　Wine from their drowsiness woke the peoples.

And you, our own day's angel, do not awake
　　Those drowsing still? O give us the laws, and give
　　　　Us life. You, Master, triumph! Only
　　　　　　You, like that god, have the right to conquer.

Not that which else is human kind's care and skill
　　Both in the house and under the open sky
　　　　When, nobler than wild beasts, men work to
　　　　　　Fend, to provide for themselves – to poets

A different task and calling have been assigned.
　　The Highest, he it is whom alone we serve,
　　　　So that more closely, ever newly
　　　　　　Sung, he will meet with a friendly echo.

And yet, you heavenly powers, you all, and all
　　You fountains, all you banks and you groves and peaks
　　　　Where marvellous at first when by the
　　　　　　Forelock you seized us, and unforeseen the

Divine, creative Genius came over us,
　　Dumbfounding mind and sense, unforgettably,
　　　　And left us as though struck by lightning
　　　　　　Down to our bones that were still aquiver,

You restless deeds at large in a boundless world!
　　You fateful days, you sweeping ones, when the God
　　　　Drives calmly pondering where, drunk with
　　　　　　Rage, the gigantic horses take him –

Euch sollten wir verschweigen, und wenn in uns
  Vom stetigstillen Jahre der Wohllaut tönt,
    So sollt' es klingen, gleich als hätte
      Muthig und müßig ein Kind des Meisters

Geweihte, reine Saiten im Scherz gerührt?
  Und darum hast du, Dichter! des Orients
    Propheten und den Griechensang und
      Neulich die Donner gehört, damit du

Den Geist zu Diensten brauchst und die Gegenwart
  Des Guten übereilest, in Spott, und den Albernen
    Verläugnest, herzlos, und zum Spiele
      Feil, wie gefangenes Wild, ihn treibest?

Bis aufgereizt vom Stachel im Grimme der
  Des Ursprungs sich erinnert und ruft, daß selbst
    Der Meister kommt, dann unter heißen
      Todesgeschossen entseelt dich lässet.

Zu lang ist alles Göttliche dienstbar schon
  Und alle Himmelskräfte verscherzt, verbraucht
    Die Gütigen, zur Lust, danklos, ein
      Schlaues Geschlecht und zu kennen wähnt es,

Wenn ihnen der Erhabne den Aker baut,
  Das Tagslicht und den Donnerer, und es späht
    Das Sehrohr wohl sie all und zählt und
      Nennet mit Nahmen des Himmels Sterne.

Der Vater aber deket mit heilger Nacht,
  Damit wir bleiben mögen, die Augen zu.
    Nicht liebt er Wildes! Doch es zwinget
      Nimmer die weite Gewalt den Himmel.

Noch ists auch gut, zu weise zu seyn. Ihn kennt
  Der Dank. Doch nicht behält er es leicht allein,
    Und gern gesellt, damit verstehn sie
      Helfen, zu anderen sich ein Dichter.

Of you should we keep silent, and when in us
   Euphonious peals the constant, the quiet year,
      Then should it sound as though capricious,
         Curious, a child had been idly twanging

The Master's lyre, the hallowed, the pure, in jest?
   And for that only, poet, you heard the East's
      Great prophets, heard Greek song, and lately
         Heard divine thunder ring out – to make a

Vile trade of it, exploiting the Spirit, presume
   On his kind presence, mocking him, heartlessly
      Deny the simple one and drive him
         Round like a captured wild beast for pennies?

Till by that prodding roused in fierce anger he
   Recalls his origin and cries out, so that
      The Master comes himself, to leave you
         Lifeless and seared by his lethal missiles.

Too long now things divine have been cheaply used
   And all the powers of heaven, the kindly, spent
      In trifling waste by cold and cunning
         Men without thanks, who when he, the Highest,

In person tills their field for them, think they know
   The daylight and the Thunderer, and indeed
      Their telescope may find them all, may
         Count and may name every star of heaven.

Yet will the Father cover with holy night,
   That we may last on earth, our too knowing eyes.
      He loves no Titan! Never will our
         Free-ranging power coerce his heaven.

Nor is it good to be all too wise. Our thanks
   Know God. Yet never gladly the poet keeps
      His lore unshared, but likes to join with
         Others who help him to understand it.

Furchtlos bleibt aber, so er es muß, der Mann
   Einsam vor Gott, es schüzet die Einfalt ihn,
      Und keiner Waffen brauchts und keiner
         Listen, so lange, bis Gottes Fehl hilft.

Stimme des Volks
ZWEITE FASSUNG

Du seiest Gottes Stimme, so glaubt' ich sonst
   In heil'ger Jugend; ja, und ich sag' es noch!
      Um unsre Weisheit unbekümmert
         Rauschen die Ströme doch auch, und dennoch,

Wer liebt sie nicht? und immer bewegen sie
   Das Herz mir, hör' ich ferne die Schwindenden,
      Die Ahnungsvollen meine Bahn nicht,
         Aber gewisser ins Meer hin eilen.

Denn selbstvergessen, allzubereit den Wunsch
   Der Götter zu erfüllen, ergreift zu gern
      Was sterblich ist, wenn offnen Augs auf
         Eigenen Pfaden es einmal wandelt,

Ins All zurük die kürzeste Bahn; so stürzt
   Der Strom hinab, er suchet die Ruh, es reißt,
      Es ziehet wider Willen ihn, von
         Klippe zu Klippe den Steuerlosen

Das wunderbare Sehnen dem Abgrund zu;
   Das Ungebundne reizet und Völker auch
      Ergreifft die Todeslust und kühne
         Städte, nachdem sie versucht das Beste,

Von Jahr zu Jahr forttreibend das Werk, sie hat
   Ein heilig Ende troffen; die Erde grünt
      Und stille vor den Sternen liegt, den
         Betenden gleich, in den Sand geworfen

But, if he must, undaunted the man remains
  Alone with God – ingenuousness keeps him safe –
    And needs no weapon and no wile till
      God's being missed in the end will help him.

Voice of the People
SECOND VERSION

The voice of God I called you and thought you once,
  In holy youth; and still I do not recant!
    No less indifferent to our wisdom
      Likewise the rivers rush on, but who does

Not love them? Always too my own heart is moved
  When far away I hear those foreknowing ones,
    The fleeting, by a route not mine but
      Surer than mine, and more swift, roar seaward,

For once they travel down their allotted paths
  With open eyes, self-oblivious, too ready to
    Comply with what the gods have wished them,
      Only too gladly will mortal beings

Speed back into the All by the shortest way;
  So rivers plunge – not movement, but rest they seek –
    Drawn on, pulled down against their will from
      Boulder to boulder – abandoned, helmless –

By that mysterious yearning toward the chasm;
  Chaotic deeps attract, and whole peoples too
    May come to long for death, and valiant
      Towns that have striven to do the best thing,

Year in, year out pursuing their task – these too
  A holy end has stricken; the earth grows green,
    And there beneath the stars, like mortals
      Deep in their prayers, quite still, prostrated

Freiwillig überwunden die lange Kunst
  Vor jenen Unnachahmbaren da; er selbst,
    Der Mensch, mit eigner Hand zerbrach, die
      Hohen zu ehren, sein Werk der Künstler.

Doch minder nicht sind jene den Menschen hold,
  Sie lieben wieder, so wie geliebt sie sind,
    Und hemmen öfters, daß er lang im
      Lichte sich freue, die Bahn des Menschen.

Und, nicht des Adlers Jungen allein, sie wirft
  Der Vater aus dem Neste, damit sie nicht
    Zu lang' ihm bleiben, uns auch treibt mit
      Richtigem Stachel hinaus der Herrscher.

Wohl jenen, die zur Ruhe gegangen sind,
  Und vor der Zeit gefallen, auch die, auch die
    Geopfert, gleich den Erstlingen der
      Erndte, sie haben ein Theil gefunden.

Am Xanthos lag, in griechischer Zeit, die Stadt,
  Jezt aber, gleich den größeren die dort ruhn
    Ist durch ein Schiksaal sie dem heilgen
      Lichte des Tages hinweggekommen.

Sie kamen aber nicht in der offnen Schlacht
  Durch eigne Hand um. Fürchterlich ist davon,
    Was dort geschehn, die wunderbare
      Sage von Osten zu uns gelanget.

Es reizte sie die Güte von Brutus. Denn
  Als Feuer ausgegangen, so bot er sich
    Zu helfen ihnen, ob er gleich, als Feldherr,
      Stand in Belagerung vor den Thoren.

Doch von den Mauern warfen die Diener sie
  Die er gesandt. Lebendiger ward darauf
    Das Feuer und sie freuten sich und ihnen
      Streket' entgegen die Hände Brutus

On sand, outgrown, and willingly, lies long art
   Flung down before the Matchless; and he himself,
      The man, the artist with his own two
         Hands broke his work for their sake, in homage.

Yet they, the Heavenly, to men remain well-disposed,
   As we love them so they will return our love
      And lest too briefly he enjoy the
         Light, will obstruct a man's course to ruin.

And not the eagle's fledglings alone their sire
   Throws out of eyries, knowing that else too long
      They'd idle – us the Ruler also
         Goads into flight with a prong that's fitting.

Those men I praise who early lay down to rest,
   Who fell before their time, and those also, those
      Like first-fruits of the harvest offered
         Up – they were granted a part, a portion.

By Xanthos once, in Grecian times, there stood
   The town, but now, like greater ones resting there,
      Because a destiny ordained it
         Xanthos is lost to our holy daylight.

But not in open battle, by their own hands
   Her people perished. Dreadful and marvellous
      The legend of that town's destruction,
         Travelling on from the East, has reached us.

The kindliness of Brutus provoked them. For
   When fire broke out, most nobly he offered them
      His help, although he led those troops which
         Stood at their gates to besiege the township.

Yet from the walls they threw all the servants down
   Whom he had sent. Much livelier then at once
      The fire flared up, and they rejoiced, and
         Brutus extended his arms towards them,

Und alle waren außer sich selbst. Geschrei
  Entstand und Jauchzen. Drauf in die Flamme warf
    Sich Mann und Weib, von Knaben stürzt' auch
      Der von dem Dach, in der Väter Schwerdt der.

Nicht räthlich ist es, Helden zu trozen. Längst
  Wars aber vorbereitet. Die Väter auch
    Da sie ergriffen waren, einst, und
      Heftig die persischen Feinde drängten,

Entzündeten, ergreiffend des Stromes Rohr,
  Daß sie das Freie fänden, die Stadt. Und Haus
    Und Tempel nahm, zum heilgen Aether
      Fliegend, und Menschen hinweg die Flamme.

So hatten es die Kinder gehört, und wohl
  Sind gut die Sagen, denn ein Gedächtniß sind
    Dem Höchsten sie, doch auch bedarf es
      Eines, die heiligen auszulegen.

Der Blinde Sänger

ἔλυσεν αἰνὸν ἄχος ἀπ' ὀμμάτων Ἀρης – SOPHOKLES

Wo bist du, Jugendliches! das immer mich
  Zur Stunde wekt des Morgens, wo bist du, Licht!
    Das Herz ist wach, doch bannt und hält in
      Heiligem Zauber die Nacht mich immer.

Sonst lauscht' ich um die Dämmerung gern, sonst harrt'
  Ich gerne dein am Hügel, und nie umsonst!
    Nie täuschten mich, du Holdes, deine
      Boten, die Lüfte, denn immer kamst du,

All were beside themselves. And great crying there,
  Great jubilation sounded. Then into flames
    Leapt man and woman; boys came hurtling
      Down from the roofs or their fathers stabbed them.

It is not wise to fight against heroes. But
  Events long past prepared it. Their ancestors
    When they were quite encircled once and
      Strongly the Persian forces pressed them,

Took rushes from the rivers and, that their foes
  Might find a desert there, set ablaze their town;
    And house and temple – breathed to holy
      Aether – and men did the flame carry off there.

So their descendants heard, and no doubt such lore
  Is good, because it serves to remind us of
    The Highest; yet there's also need of
      One to interpret these holy legends.

The Blind Singer
ἔλυσεν αἰνὸν ἄχος ἀπ' ὀμμάτων Ἄρης – SOPHOCLES*

Where are you, youthful herald who always once
  Would waken me at daybreak, where are you, light?
    The heart's awake, but always Night now
      Holds me and binds me with holy magic.

Once towards dawn I'd listen, was glad to wait
  For you upon your hillside, and never in vain!
    Nor ever did your messengers, the
      Breezes, deceive me, for always, dear one,

---

*'Cruel woe has Ares lifted from our eyes'.

Sophocles, *Ajax*, 706

Kamst allbeseeligend den gewohnten Pfad
  Herein in deiner Schöne, wo bist du, Licht!
    Das Herz ist wieder wach, doch bannt und
      Hemmt die unendliche Nacht mich immer.

Mir grünten sonst die Lauben; es leuchteten
  Die Blumen, wie die eigenen Augen, mir;
    Nicht ferne war das Angesicht der
      Meinen und leuchtete mir und droben

Und um die Wälder sah ich die Fittige
  Des Himmels wandern, da ich ein Jüngling war;
    Nun siz ich still allein, von einer
      Stunde zur anderen und Gestalten

Aus Lieb und Laid der helleren Tage schafft
  Zur eignen Freude nun mein Gedanke sich,
    Und ferne lausch' ich hin, ob nicht ein
      Freundlicher Retter vieleicht mir komme.

Dann hör ich oft die Stimme des Donnerers
  Am Mittag, wenn der eherne nahe kommt,
    Wenn ihm das Haus bebt und der Boden
      Unter ihm dröhnt und der Berg es nachhallt.

Den Retter hör' ich dann in der Nacht, ich hör'
  Ihn tödtend, den Befreier, belebend ihn,
    Den Donnerer vom Untergang zum
      Orient eilen und ihm nach tönt ihr,

Ihm nach, ihr meine Saiten! es lebt mit ihm
  Mein Lied und wie die Quelle dem Strome folgt,
    Wohin er denkt, so muß ich fort und
      Folge dem Sicheren auf der Irrbahn.

Wohin? wohin? ich höre dich da und dort
  Du Herrlicher! und rings um die Erde tönts.
    Wo endest du? und was, was ist es
      Über den Wolken und o wie wird mir?

You came, delighting all, in your loveliness,
   Came down the usual pathway; where are you, light?
      The heart's awake once more, but always
         Infinite Night now constricts me, binds me.

Once green the bowers would beckon to me; the flowers
   Would shine for me, would gleam like my own two eyes;
      Not distant from me were my loved ones'
         Faces and shone for me, up above me

And round the woods I saw, as they travelled on,
   The wings of heaven – then, in the time of youth;
      Now here I sit alone in silence
         Hour after hour and for only comfort

My mind devises shapes for itself, made up
   Of love and grief remembered from brighter days,
      And far I strain my hearing lest a
         Kindly deliverer perhaps is coming.

Then often I can hear the great Thunderer's voice,
   At noon when he, the brazen one, draws most near,
      When his own house quakes, the foundations
         Under him boom and the hill repeats it.

The saviour then I hear in the night, I hear
   Him kill, the liberator, and give new life,
      From West to East I hear the Thunderer
         Quickly sweep on, and it's him you echo,

My strings! With him, with him does my poem live,
   And as the stream must follow the river's course,
      Where his thought goes I'm drawn, impelled to
         Follow the sure one through devious orbits.

Where to? where to? I hear you now here now there,
   You glorious one! And all round the earth it sounds.
      Where do you end? And what, what is it
         Lurks above clouds there, and what befalls me?

Tag! Tag! du über stürzenden Wolken! sei
  Willkommen mir! es blühet mein Auge dir.
    O Jugendlicht! o Glük! das alte
      Wieder! doch geistiger rinnst du nieder

Du goldner Quell aus heiligem Kelch! und du,
  Du grüner Boden, friedliche Wieg'! und du,
    Haus meiner Väter! und ihr Lieben,
      Die mir begegneten einst, o nahet,

O kommt, daß euer, euer die Freude sei,
  Ihr alle, daß euch seegne der Sehende!
    O nimmt, daß ichs ertrage, mir das
      Leben, das Göttliche mir vom Herzen.

Chiron

Wo bist du, Nachdenkliches! das immer muß
  Zur Seite gehn, zu Zeiten, wo bist du, Licht?
    Wohl ist das Herz wach, doch mir zürnt, mich
      Hemmt die erstaunende Nacht nun immer.

Sonst nemlich folgt' ich Kräutern des Walds und lauscht'
  Ein waiches Wild am Hügel; und nie umsonst.
    Nie täuschten, auch nicht einmal deine
      Vögel; denn allzubereit fast kamst du,

So Füllen oder Garten dir labend ward,
  Rathschlagend, Herzens wegen; wo bist du, Licht?
    Das Herz ist wieder wach, doch herzlos
      Zieht die gewaltige Nacht mich immer.

Ich war's wohl. Und von Krokus und Thymian
  Und Korn gab mir die Erde den ersten Straus.
    Und bei der Sterne Kühle lernt' ich,
      Aber das Nennbare nur. Und bei mir

Day! Day! Above the tottering clouds, it's you
 I welcome back! My eyes are in flower for you.
  O light of youth! And joy, the same as
   Once! Yet more spiritual now you pour from

A holy chalice, pure golden source! And you,
 You verdant earth, our cradle of peace, and you,
  Ancestral house, and all you dear ones
   Met in the past, O draw near, assemble,

O come that yours, that yours be the joy, return
 And all receive the seeing man's blessing now!
  O take, that I may bear it, take this
   Life, the divine, from my heart too burdened.

Chiron

Where are you, thought-infusing, which at this time
 Must always move beside me, where are you, light?
  Indeed the heart's awake, but, wrathful,
   Always astonishing Night constricts me.

For then I'd look for herbs of the wood, and on
 The hillside hear soft game; and never in vain.
  And never once your birds deceived me,
   Never; but almost too promptly then you

Would come, when foal or garden contented you,
 Advising, for the heart's sake; where are you, light?
  The heart's awake once more, but, heartless,
   Always most powerful Night allures me.

That one was I, it seems. And of crocus, thyme
 And corn then Earth would pick the first bunch for me.
  And in the cool of stars I learned, but
   Only the nameable. Disenchanting

Das wilde Feld entzaubernd, das traur'ge, zog
  Der Halbgott, Zevs Knecht, ein, der gerade Mann;
    Nun siz' ich still allein, von einer
      Stunde zur anderen, und Gestalten

Aus frischer Erd' und Wolken der Liebe schafft,
  Weil Gift ist zwischen uns, mein Gedanke nun;
    Und ferne lausch' ich hin, ob nicht ein
      Freundlicher Retter vieleicht mir komme.

Dann hör' ich oft den Wagen des Donnerers
  Am Mittag, wenn er naht, der bekannteste,
    Wenn ihm das Haus bebt und der Boden
      Reiniget sich, und die Quaal Echo wird.

Den Retter hör' ich dann in der Nacht, ich hör'
  Ihn tödtend, den Befreier, und drunten voll
    Von üpp'gem Kraut, als in Gesichten
      Schau ich die Erd', ein gewaltig Feuer;

Die Tage aber wechseln, wenn einer dann
  Zusiehet denen, lieblich und bös', ein Schmerz,
    Wenn einer zweigestalt ist, und es
      Kennet kein einziger nicht das Beste;

Das aber ist der Stachel des Gottes; nie
  Kann einer lieben göttliches Unrecht sonst.
    Einheimisch aber ist der Gott dann
      Angesichts da, und die Erd' ist anders.

Tag! Tag! Nun wieder athmet ihr recht; nun trinkt,
  Ihr meiner Bäche Weiden! ein Augenlicht,
    Und rechte Stapfen gehn, und als ein
      Herrscher, mit Sporen, und bei dir selber

Örtlich, Irrstern des Tages, erscheinest du,
  Du auch, o Erde, friedliche Wieg', und du,
    Haus meiner Väter, die unstädtisch
      Sind, in den Wolken des Wilds, gegangen.

That wild, sad open meadow the demigod,
 Zeus' servant came, the straight man, to lodge with me;
  Now here I sit alone in silence
   Hour after hour, and my mind devises

Shapes for itself – since poison divides us now –
 Made up of love's new earth and the clouds of love;
  And far I strain my hearing lest a
   Kindly deliverer perhaps is coming.

Then often I can hear the great Thunderer's voice
 At noon when he, the best-known of all, draws near,
  When his own house quakes, the foundations,
   Shaken, are cleansed and my torment echoes.

The Saviour then I hear in the night, I hear
 Him kill, the liberator, and down below,
  As if in visions, full of luscious
   Weeds I see Earth, a tremendous fire;

But days go by, both lovely and bad, when one
 Observes their changes, suffering pain because
  Of twofold nature, and when none can
   Ever be sure what is best and fittest;

But that's the very sting of the god; and else
 Divine injustice never could claim men's love.
  But native then, at home, the god is
   Visibly present, and Earth is different.

Day! Day! Once more you can breathe, now drink,
 You willows of my streams, an illumined sight,
  And sure, true footsteps go, and as a
   Ruler, with spurs, and located in your

Own orbit you, the planet of day, appear,
 And you, O Earth, our cradle of peace, and you,
  House of my forebears who unurban
   Travelled in clouds with the woodland creatures.

Nimm nun ein Roß, und harnische dich und nimm
  Den leichten Speer, o Knabe! Die Wahrsagung
    Zerreißt nicht, und umsonst nicht wartet,
      Bis sie erscheinet, Herakles Rükkehr.

Thränen

Himmlische Liebe! zärtliche! wenn ich dein
  Vergäße, wenn ich, o ihr geschiklichen,
    Ihr feur'gen, die voll Asche sind und
      Wüst und vereinsamet ohnediß schon,

Ihr lieben Inseln, Augen der Wunderwelt!
  Ihr nemlich geht nun einzig allein mich an,
    Ihr Ufer, wo die abgöttische
      Büßet, doch Himmlischen nur, die Liebe.

Denn allzudankbar haben die Heiligen
  Gedienet dort in Tagen der Schönheit und
    Die zorn'gen Helden; und viel Bäume
      Sind, und die Städte daselbst gestanden,

Sichtbar, gleich einem sinnigen Mann; izt sind
  Die Helden todt, die Inseln der Liebe sind
    Entstellt fast. So muß übervortheilt,
      Albern doch überall seyn die Liebe.

Ihr waichen Thränen, löschet das Augenlicht
  Mir aber nicht ganz aus; ein Gedächtniß doch,
    Damit ich edel sterbe, laßt ihr
      Trügrischen, Diebischen, mir nachleben.

Now take a horse and armour and lastly, boy,
   Take up the slender spear! For the prophecy
      Will not be torn, and not for nothing
         Heracles' promised return awaits it.

Tears

O heavenly love, the tender, if you I should
   Forget, if you, the site that a fate has marked,
      The fiery that are full of ash and
         Even before that were wild, deserted,

Dear islands, you, the eyes of the wondrous world!
   Since only you concern me and matter now,
      You banks where the idolatrous, where
         Love, but to heaven alone, does penance.

For too devoutly almost, too gratefully
   In days of beauty there did the holy serve,
      And furious heroes; and no lack of
         Trees, and the cities at one time stood there,

Visible, like a pondering man; now dead
   Those heroes are, the islands of love defaced,
      Disfigured nearly. So for ever
         Love is outwitted, for ever silly.

And yet, soft tears, not utterly now put out
   For me the light of vision; a memory,
      To make my dying noble, still, you
         Thievish, deceitful ones, let outlast me.

An die Hofnung

O Hofnung! holde! gütiggeschäfftige!
  Die du das Haus der Trauernden nicht verschmähst,
    Und gerne dienend, Edle! zwischen
      Sterblichen waltest und Himmelsmächten,

Wo bist du? wenig lebt' ich; doch athmet kalt
  Mein Abend schon. Und stille, den Schatten gleich,
    Bin ich schon hier; und schon gesanglos
      Schlummert das schaudernde Herz im Busen.

Im grünen Thale, dort, wo der frische Quell
  Vom Berge täglich rauscht, und die liebliche
    Zeitlose mir am Herbsttag aufblüht,
      Dort, in der Stille, du Holde, will ich

Dich suchen, oder wenn in der Mitternacht
  Das unsichtbare Leben im Haine wallt,
    Und über mir die immerfrohen
      Blumen, die blühenden Sterne, glänzen,

O du des Aethers Tochter! erscheine dann
  Aus deines Vaters Gärten, und darfst du nicht
    Ein Geist der Erde, kommen, schrök', o
      Schröke mit anderem nur das Herz mir.

Vulkan

Jezt komm und hülle, freundlicher Feuergeist,
  Den zarten Sinn der Frauen in Wolken ein,
    In goldne Träum' und schüze sie, die
      Blühende Ruhe der Immerguten.

To Hope

O hope, benignly active one, dear to men,
    Who do not scorn the house of the sorrowing
        And, noble, love to serve, to fashion
            Links between mortals and heavenly powers,

Where are you? Little yet I have lived; but cold
    My evening breathes. And silent already, like
        The shades, I walk here while within me
            Songless my shuddering heart is drowsing.

That vale so green where down from the mountain purls
    The spring's cool water daily, and now for me
        The lovely autumn crocus opens,
            There in the stillness I'll wait and, dear one,

Look out for you, or when in the rustling grove
    At midnight wild, invisible creatures teem
        And when, above, the ever-joyful
            Blossoms, the flowering stars, are gleaming,

Then come, O Aether's daughter, appear to me
    Out of your father's gardens; and if you may
        Not wear the shape of earthly spirits,
            Frighten my heart with a different aspect.

Vulcan

You come now, friendly spirit of fire, and wrap
    The women's delicate minds in a veil of clouds,
        In golden dreams, and there keep safe the
            Blossoming peace of the ever-kindly.

Dem Manne laß sein Sinnen, und sein Geschäfft,
  Und seiner Kerze Schein, und den künftgen Tag
    Gefallen, laß des Unmuths ihm, der
      Häßlichen Sorge zu viel nicht werden,

Wenn jezt der immerzürnende Boreas,
  Mein Erbfeind, über Nacht mit dem Frost das Land
    Befällt, und spät, zur Schlummerstunde,
      Spottend der Menschen, sein schröklich Lied singt,

Und unsrer Städte Mauren und unsern Zaun,
  Den fleißig wir gesezt, und den stillen Hain
    Zerreißt, und selber im Gesang die
      Seele mir störet, der Allverderber,

Und rastlos tobend über den sanften Strom
  Sein schwarz Gewölk ausschüttet, daß weit umher
    Das Thal gährt, und, wie fallend Laub, vom
      Berstenden Hügel herab der Fels fällt.

Wohl frömmer ist, denn andre Lebendige,
  Der Mensch; doch zürnt es draußen, gehöret der
    Auch eigner sich, und sinnt und ruht in
      Sicherer Hütte, der Freigeborne.

Und immer wohnt der freundlichen Genien
  Noch Einer gerne seegnend mit ihm, und wenn
    Sie zürnten all', die ungelehrgen
      Geniuskräfte, doch liebt die Liebe.

Dichtermuth
ERSTE FASSUNG

Sind denn dir nicht verwandt alle Lebendigen?
  Nährt zum Dienste denn nicht selber die Parze dich?
    Drum! so wandle nur wehrlos
      Fort durch's Leben und sorge nicht!

The man leave still content with his pondering,
   His work, his candle's gleam and the day to come,
      And not too many vexing tangles,
         Ugly small cares let impose upon him.

When now the ever-raging one, Boreas,
   My enemy from birth, overnight assails
      The land with frost, and late, past midnight,
         Jeering at men, sings his dreadful war-song,

And blasts our city walls and tears down the fence
   That in long toil we built, and the quiet grove,
      And even interrupts my soul in
         Making its music, for all provokes him,

And wild with fury over the gentle stream
   Pours out his black cloud-bundles, till far and wide
      The valley seethes, like falling foliage
         Down come great rocks from the bursting hillside.

More godly, true, than all that shares life with him
   Is Man. Yet, faced with fury outside, he too
      Is more himself and rests and ponders
         Safe in his cottage, the free-born mortal.

And one at least, one spirit friendly to Man,
   Still, blessing, gladly dwells with him there, and though
      All others, fierce untutored spirit
         Powers, were to rage, will Love be loving.

The Poet's Courage
FIRST VERSION

Is not all that's alive close and akin to you,
   Does the Fate not herself keep you to serve her ends?
      Well, then, travel defenceless
         On through life, and fear nothing there!

Was geschiehet, es sei alles geseegnet dir,
  Sei zur Freude gewandt! oder was könnte denn
    Dich belaidigen. Herz! was
      Da begegnen, wohin du sollst?

Denn, wie still am Gestad, oder in silberner
  Fernhintönender Fluth, oder auf schweigenden
    Wassertiefen der leichte
      Schwimmer wandelt, so sind auch wir.

Wir, die Dichter des Volks, gerne, wo Lebendes
  Um uns athmet und wallt, freudig, und jedem hold,
    Jedem trauend; wie sängen
      Sonst wir jedem den eignen Gott?

Wenn die Wooge denn auch einen der Muthigen,
  Wo er treulich getraut, schmeichlend hinunterzieht,
    Und die Stimme des Sängers
      Nun in blauender Halle schweigt;

Freudig starb er und noch klagen die Einsamen,
  Seine Haine, den Fall ihres Geliebtesten;
    Öfters tönet der Jungfrau
      Vom Gezweige sein freundlich Lied.

Wenn des Abends vorbei Einer der Unsern kömmt,
  Wo der Bruder ihm sank, denket er manches wohl
    An der warnenden Stelle,
      Schweigt und gehet gerüsteter.

Blödigkeit

Sind denn dir nicht bekannt viele Lebendigen?
  Geht auf Wahrem dein Fuß nicht, wie auf Teppichen?
    Drum, mein Genius! tritt nur
      Baar in's Leben, und sorge nicht!

All that happens there be welcome, be blessed to you,
 Be an adept in joy, or is there anything
  That could harm you there, heart, that
   Could offend you, where you must go?

For, as quiet near shores, or in the silvery
 Flood resounding afar, or over silent deep
  Water travels the flimsy
   Swimmer, likewise we love to be

Where around us there breathe, teem those alive, our kin,
 We, their poets; and glad, friendly to every man,
  Trusting all. And how else for
   Each of them could we sing his god?

Though the wave will at times, flattering, drag below
 One such brave man where, true, trusting he makes his way,
  And the voice of that singer
   Now falls mute as the hall turns blue;

Glad he died there, and still lonely his groves lament
 Him whom most they had loved, lost, though with joy he drowned;
  Often a virgin will hear his
   Kindly song in the distant boughs.

When at nightfall a man like him, of our kind, comes
 Past the place where he sank, many a thought he'll give
  To the site and the warning,
   Then in silence, more armed, walk on.

Timidness

Of the living are not many well-known to you?
 On the truth don't your feet walk as they would on rugs?
  Boldly, therefore, my genius,
   Step right into the thick of life!

Was geschiehet, es sei alles gelegen dir!
  Sei zur Freude gereimt, oder was könnte denn
    Dich belaidigen, Herz, was
      Da begegnen, wohin du sollst?

Denn, seit Himmlischen gleich Menschen, ein einsam Wild
  Und die Himmlischen selbst führet, der Einkehr zu,
    Der Gesang und der Fürsten
      Chor, nach Arten, so waren auch

Wir, die Zungen des Volks, gerne bei Lebenden,
  Wo sich vieles gesellt, freudig und jedem gleich,
    Jedem offen, so ist ja
      Unser Vater, des Himmels Gott,

Der den denkenden Tag Armen und Reichen gönnt,
  Der, zur Wende der Zeit, uns die Entschlafenden
    Aufgerichtet an goldnen
      Gängelbanden, wie Kinder, hält.

Gut auch sind und geschikt einem zu etwas wir,
  Wenn wir kommen, mit Kunst, und von den Himmlischen
    Einen bringen. Doch selber
      Bringen schikliche Hände wir.

Der Gefesselte Strom

Was schläfst und träumst du, Jüngling, gehüllt in dich,
  Und säumst am kalten Ufer, Geduldiger,
    Und achtest nicht des Ursprungs, du, des
      Oceans Sohn, des Titanenfreundes!

Die Liebesboten, welche der Vater schikt,
  Kennst du die lebenathmenden Lüfte nicht?
    Und trift das Wort dich nicht, das hell von
      Oben der wachende Gott dir sendet?

All that happens there be welcome, a boon to you!
  Be disposed to feel joy, or is there anything
    That could harm you there, heart, that
      Could affront you, where you must go?

For since gods grew like men, lonely as woodland beasts,
  And since, each in its way, song and the princely choir
    Brought the Heavenly in person
      Back to earth, so we too, the tongues

Of the people, have liked living men's company,
  Where all kinds are conjoined, equal and open to
    Everyone, full of joy – for
      So our Father is, Heaven's God,

Who to rich men and poor offers the thinking day,
  At the turning of Time holds us, the sleepy ones,
    Upright still with his golden
      Leading-strings, as one holds a child.

Someone, some way, we too serve, are of use, are sent
  When we come, with our art, and of the heavenly powers
    Bring one with us. But fitting,
      Skilful hands we ourselves provide.

The Fettered River

Why do you sleep and dream, in yourself wrapped up,
  And by the cold bank linger, too patient youth,
    And do not heed your origin, you
      Son of great Ocean, the friend of Titans!

Those messengers of love whom your father sends,
  Do you not know those winds breathing life at you?
    Does not that word strike home which, bright, the
      Vigilant god from above dispatches?

Schon tönt, schon tönt es ihm in der Brust, es quillt,
   Wie, da er noch im Schoose der Felsen spielt',
      Ihm auf, und nun gedenkt er seiner
         Kraft, der Gewaltige, nun, nun eilt er,

Der Zauderer, er spottet der Fesseln nun,
   Und nimmt und bricht und wirft die Zerbrochenen
      Im Zorne, spielend, da und dort zum
         Schallenden Ufer und an der Stimme

Des Göttersohns erwachen die Berge rings,
   Es regen sich die Wälder, es hört die Kluft
      Den Herold fern und schaudernd regt im
         Busen der Erde sich Freude wieder.

Der Frühling kommt; es dämmert das neue Grün;
   Er aber wandelt hin zu Unsterblichen;
      Denn nirgend darf er bleiben, als wo
         Ihn in die Arme der Vater aufnimmt.

Ganymed

Was schläfst du, Bergsohn, liegest in Unmuth, schief,
   Und frierst am kahlen Ufer, Gedultiger!
      Denkst nicht der Gnade du, wenn's an den
         Tischen die Himmlischen sonst gedürstet?

Kennst drunten du vom Vater die Boten nicht,
   Nicht in der Kluft der Lüfte geschärfter Spiel?
      Trift nicht das Wort dich, das voll alten
         Geists ein gewanderter Mann dir sendet?

Schon tönet's aber ihm in der Brust. Tief quillt's,
   Wie damals, als hoch oben im Fels er schlief,
      Ihm auf. Im Zorne reinigt aber
         Sich der Gefesselte nun, nun eilt er

Yet now, already now it resounds in him,
   Wells up for him as when in the lap of rocks
      He played, and he recalls his strength, the
         Power of his youth now, and now he hurries,

The loiterer, and laughs at his fetters now
   And takes and tears and throws the torn fetters down
      In fury, playing, here and there on
         Banks that re-echo, and at the voice of

That son of gods the mountains all round awake,
   The woods begin to stir, the ravine can hear
      The distant herald, roused within the
         Bosom of Earth with a shudder joy stirs.

Spring comes; new verdure glistens, a dawn of leaves;
   But he far off departs, to immortal kin;
      For nowhere he may rest, but where the
         Arms of his father once more receive him.

Ganymede

Why do you sleep, lie crooked, ill-humoured here,
   And freeze on banks all bare, you the mountains' son?
      Too patient, do not think of grace, when
         Once there was thirst at the heavenly tables?

Nor know your father's messengers now, down there,
   In the ravine the breezes' more whetted play?
      Does not that word strike home which now a
         Travelled man sends you, its ancient meaning?

But now it sounds in him, as deeply wells up
   And when before high up on the rock he slept.
      And in his anger now the fettered
         Cleanses himself, and now he hurries,

Der Linkische; der spottet der Schlaken nun,
  Und nimmt und bricht und wirft die Zerbrochenen
    Zorntrunken, spielend, dort und da zum
      Schauenden Ufer und bei des Fremdlings

Besondrer Stimme stehen die Heerden auf,
  Es regen sich die Wälder, es hört tief Land
    Den Stromgeist fern, und schaudernd regt im
      Nabel der Erde der Geist sich wieder.

Der Frühling kömmt. Und jedes, in seiner Art,
  Blüht. Der ist aber ferne; nicht mehr dabei.
    Irr gieng er nun; denn allzugut sind
      Genien; himmlisch Gespräch ist sein nun.

The clumsy one; he laughs at his fetters now,
　　And takes and tears and throws the torn fetters down,
　　　　Wrath-drunken, playing, here and there on
　　　　　　Banks that observe him, and at the stranger's

Peculiar voice, the herds that were resting rise,
　　The woods awake, far down all the land can hear
　　　　The river-god, and roused within the
　　　　　　Navel of Earth now the spirit shivers.

Spring comes. And everything, in its way and kind,
　　Blossoms. But he's far off; is no longer there.
　　　　Has gone astray; for all too good are
　　　　　　Genii; heavenly talk is his now.

HEXAMETERS AND ELEGIES
(1800–1801)

Der Archipelagus

Kehren die Kraniche wieder zu dir, und suchen zu deinen
Ufern wieder die Schiffe den Lauf? umathmen erwünschte
Lüfte dir die beruhigte Fluth, und sonnet der Delphin,
Aus der Tiefe gelokt, am neuen Lichte den Rüken?

Blüht Ionien? ists die Zeit? denn immer im Frühling,
Wenn den Lebenden sich das Herz erneut und die erste
Liebe den Menschen erwacht und goldner Zeiten Erinnrung,
Komm' ich zu dir und grüß' in deiner Stille dich, Alter!

Immer, Gewaltiger! lebst du noch und ruhest im Schatten
Deiner Berge, wie sonst; mit Jünglingsarmen umfängst du
Noch dein liebliches Land, und deiner Töchter, o Vater!

Deiner Inseln ist noch, der blühenden, keine verloren.
Kreta steht und Salamis grünt, umdämmert von Lorbeern,
Rings von Stralen umblüht, erhebt zur Stunde des Aufgangs
Delos ihr begeistertes Haupt, und Tenos und Chios
Haben der purpurnen Früchte genug, von trunkenen Hügeln
Quillt der Cypriertrank, und von Kalauria fallen
Silberne Bäche, wie einst, in die alten Wasser des Vaters.
Alle leben sie noch, die Heroënmütter, die Inseln,
Blühend von Jahr zu Jahr, und wenn zu Zeiten, vom Abgrund
Losgelassen, die Flamme der Nacht, das untre Gewitter,
Eine der holden ergriff, und die Sterbende dir in den Schoos sank,
Göttlicher! du, du dauertest aus, denn über den dunkeln
Tiefen ist manches schon dir auf und untergegangen.

Auch die Himmlischen, sie, die Kräfte der Höhe, die stillen,
Die den heiteren Tag und süßen Schlummer und Ahnung
Fernher bringen über das Haupt der fühlenden Menschen
Aus der Fülle der Macht, auch sie, die alten Gespielen,
Wohnen, wie einst, mit dir, und oft am dämmernden Abend,
Wenn von Asiens Bergen herein das heilige Mondlicht
Kömmt und die Sterne sich in deiner Wooge begegnen,

The Archipelago

Are the cranes returning to you, and the mercantile vessels
Making again for your shores? Do breezes longed for and prayed for
Blow for you round the quieter flood and, lured from beneath it,
Does the dolphin now warm his back in a new year's gathering
      radiance?
Is Ionia in flower? Is it the season? For always in springtime
When the hearts of the living renew themselves, the first love of
Human kind, reawakened, stirs and the golden age is remembered,
You, old Sea-God, I visit and you I greet in your stillness.

Even now you live on and, mighty as ever, untroubled
Rest in the shade of your mountains; with arms ever youthful
Still embrace your beautiful land, and still of your daughters, O
      Father,
Of your islands, the flowering, not one has been taken.
Crete remains, and Salamis lies in a dark-green twilight of laurels,
In a ring of blossoming beams even now at the hour of sunrise
Delos lifts her ecstatic head, and Tenos and Chios
Still have plenty of purple fruit, and the Cyprian liquor
Gushes from drunken hillsides while from Calauria the silver
Brooks cascade, as before, into the Father's old vastness.
Every one of them lives, those mothers of heroes, the islands,
Flowering year after year, and if at times the subterranean
Thunder, the flame of Night, let loose from the primal abysses,
Seized on one of the dear isles and, dying, she sank in your waters,
You, divine one, endured, for much already has risen,
Much gone down for you here above your deeper foundations.

And the heavenly, too, the powers up above us, the silent,
Who from afar bring the cloudless day, delicious sleep and forebodings
Down to the heads of sentient mortals, bestowing
Gifts in their fullness and might, they too, your playmates as ever,
Dwell with you as before, and often in evening's glimmer
When from Asia's mountains the holy moonlight comes drifting
In and the stars commingle and meet in your billows,

Leuchtest du von himmlischem Glanz, und so, wie sie wandeln,
Wechseln die Wasser dir, es tönt die Weise der Brüder

Droben, ihr Nachtgesang, im liebenden Busen dir wieder.
Wenn die allverklärende dann, die Sonne des Tages,
Sie, des Orients Kind, die Wunderthätige, da ist,
Dann die Lebenden all' im goldenen Traume beginnen,
Den die Dichtende stets des Morgens ihnen bereitet,
Dir, dem trauernden Gott, dir sendet sie froheren Zauber,

Und ihr eigen freundliches Licht ist selber so schön nicht
Denn das Liebeszeichen, der Kranz, den immer, wie vormals,
Deiner gedenk, doch sie um die graue Loke dir windet.
Und umfängt der Aether dich nicht, und kehren die Wolken,
Deine Boten, von ihm mit dem Göttergeschenke, dem Strale
Aus der Höhe dir nicht? dann sendest du über das Land sie,
Daß am heißen Gestad die gewittertrunkenen Wälder

Rauschen und woogen mit dir, daß bald, dem wandernden Sohn
      gleich,
Wenn der Vater ihn ruft, mit den tausend Bächen Mäander
Seinen Irren enteilt und aus der Ebne Kayster
Dir entgegenfrohlokt, und der Erstgeborne, der Alte,
Der zu lange sich barg, dein majestätischer Nil izt
Hochherschreitend aus fernem Gebirg, wie im Klange der Waffen,
Siegreich kömmt, und die offenen Arme der sehnende reichet.

Dennoch einsam dünkest du dir; in schweigender Nacht hört
Deine Weheklage der Fels, und öfters entflieht dir
Zürnend von Sterblichen weg die geflügelte Wooge zum Himmel.
Denn es leben mit dir die edlen Lieblinge nimmer,
Die dich geehrt, die einst mit den schönen Tempeln und Städten
Deine Gestade bekränzt, und immer suchen und missen,
Immer bedürfen ja, wie Heroën den Kranz, die geweihten
Elemente zum Ruhme das Herz der fühlenden Menschen.

Sage, wo ist Athen? ist über den Urnen der Meister
Deine Stadt, die geliebteste dir, an den heiligen Ufern,

With a heavenly brightness you shine, and just as they circle
So do your waters turn, and the theme of your brothers, their night
    song
Vibrant up there, re-echoes lovingly here in your bosom.
When the all-transfiguring, then, she, the child of the Orient,
Miracle-worker, the sun of our day-time, is present,
All that's alive in a golden dream recommences,
Golden dream the poetic one grants us anew every morning,
Then to you, the sorrowing god, she will send a still gladder
    enchantment,
And her own beneficent light is not equal in beauty
To the token of love, the wreath, which even now and as ever
Mindful of you, she winds round your locks that are greying.
Does not Aether enfold you, too, and your heralds, the clouds, do
They not return to you with his gift, the divine, with the rays that
Come from above? And then you scatter them over the country
So that drunken with thunder-storms woods on the sweltering
    coastline
Heave and roar as you do, and soon like a boy playing truant,

Hearing his father call out, with his thousand sources Meander
Hurries back from his wanderings and from his lowlands Kayster
Cheering rushes towards you, and even the first-born, that old one
Who too long lay hidden, your Nile, the imperious, majestic,
Haughtily striding down from the distant peaks, as though armed with
Clanging weapons, victorious arrives, and longs to enfold you.

Yet you think yourself lonely; at night in the silence the rock hears
Your repeated lament, and often, winged in their anger,
Up to heaven away from mortals your waves will escape you.
For no longer they live beside you, these noble beloved ones
Who revered you, who once with beautiful temples and cities
Wreathed your shores; and always they seek it and miss it,
Always, as heroes need garlands, the hallowed elements likewise
Need the hearts of us men to feel and to mirror their glory.

Tell me, where now is Athens? Over the urns of the masters
Here, on your shores, on the holy, sorrowing god, has your city

Trauernder Gott! dir ganz in Asche zusammengesunken,
Oder ist noch ein Zeichen von ihr, daß etwa der Schiffer,
Wenn er vorüberkommt, sie nenn' und ihrer gedenke?
Stiegen dort die Säulen empor und leuchteten dort nicht
Sonst vom Dache der Burg herab die Göttergestalten?
Rauschte dort die Stimme des Volks, die stürmischbewegte,
Aus der Agora nicht her, und eilten aus freudigen Pforten
Dort die Gassen dir nicht zu geseegnetem Hafen herunter?

Siehe! da löste sein Schiff der fernhinsinnende Kaufmann,
Froh, denn es wehet' auch ihm die beflügelnde Luft und die Götter
Liebten so, wie den Dichter, auch ihn, dieweil er die guten
Gaaben der Erd' ausglich und Fernes Nahem vereinte.
Fern nach Cypros ziehet er hin und ferne nach Tyros,
Strebt nach Kolchis hinauf und hinab zum alten Aegyptos,
Daß er Purpur und Wein und Korn und Vließe gewinne
Für die eigene Stadt, und öfters über des kühnen
Herkules Säulen hinaus, zu neuen seeligen Inseln
Tragen die Hoffnungen ihn und des Schiffes Flügel, indessen
Anders bewegt, am Gestade der Stadt ein einsamer Jüngling
Weilt und die Wooge belauscht, und Großes ahndet der Ernste,
Wenn er zu Füßen so des erderschütternden Meisters
Lauschet und sizt, und nicht umsonst erzog ihn der Meergott.

    Denn des Genius Feind, der vielgebietende Perse,
Jahrlang zählt' er sie schon, der Waffen Menge, der Knechte,

Spottend des griechischen Lands und seiner wenigen Inseln,
Und sie deuchten dem Herrscher ein Spiel, und noch, wie ein Traum,
        war
Ihm das innige Volk, vom Göttergeiste gerüstet.
Leicht aus spricht er das Wort und schnell, wie der flammende
        Bergquell,
Wenn er furchtbar umher vom gährenden Aetna gegossen,
Städte begräbt in der purpurnen Fluth und blühende Gärten,
Bis der brennende Strom im heiligen Meere sich kühlet,
So mit dem Könige nun, versengend, städteverwüstend,
Stürzt von Ekbatana daher sein prächtig Getümmel;
Weh! und Athene, die herrliche, fällt; wohl schauen und ringen

Dearest of all to you perished, utterly crumbled to ashes,
Or does a token, a trace remain, just so much that a sailor
Passing by will mention her name, will notice the site and recall her?
There did not columns rise high, and there on the citadel roof-top
Did not shining figures of gods once gaze down at the people?
And the voice of the people, did it not roar like a wind-lashed
Forest from the Agora, and there, to a prosperous harbour
From the joyful gates did the streets not come hurrying down to meet
    you?
Look, the distantly scheming merchant unmoored his good ship there,
Glad, since the winged breeze blew for his sake no less and him also,
Like their poets, the gods could love for his service in sharing
Out the good gifts of Earth and linking far countries to near ones.
Far away to Cyprus he sails and still farther to Tyros,
Makes his way up to Colchis and down to the ancient Aegyptos,
Bringing the purple dye and the wine and the corn and the fleeces
Back to his native town and even at times well beyond the
Pillars of daring Hercules, to the new, to the fortunate islands
Widely ranging hope and his vessel's taut wings will convey him,
While, quite differently moved, a lonely young man on the shore will
Long sit listening, and much that's great from the waves he will gather
Sitting there at the feet of him, the world-battering master,
Listening to waves; and not in vain was he reared by the Sea-God.

For the foe of genius, the vastly, far-governing Persian,
Now for years has been counting the strength of his weapons and
    soldiers,
Laughing at Greece, full of scorn at her handful of minuscule islands,
Less than a trifle to him, and still like a dream to that ruler

Seemed the fervent people of Greece, the divinely defended.
Lightly he speaks the command and fast as the flames of the torrent

Horribly spurted and poured from Etna's ebullient crater
Buries towns in its purple flood, and blossoming gardens,
Till the glowing effusion cools in the holy sea's waters –
So with that King now: a fire destroying, devouring the cities,
Down from Ekbatana his gaudily flashing wild hordes rush;
Oh, and glorious Athene falls; though high up in their mountain

Vom Gebirg, wo das Wild ihr Geschrei hört, fliehende Greise
Nach den Wohnungen dort zurük und den rauchenden Tempeln;
Aber es wekt der Söhne Gebet die heilige Asche
Nun nicht mehr, im Thal ist der Tod, und die Wolke des Brandes
Schwindet am Himmel dahin, und weiter im Lande zu erndten,
Zieht, vom Frevel erhizt, mit der Beute der Perse vorüber.

   Aber an Salamis Ufern, o Tag an Salamis Ufern!
Harrend des Endes stehn die Athenerinnen, die Jungfraun,
Stehn die Mütter, wiegend im Arm das gerettete Söhnlein,

Aber den Horchenden schallt von Tiefen die Stimme des Meergotts

Heilweissagend herauf, es schauen die Götter des Himmels
Wägend und richtend herab, denn dort an den bebenden Ufern
Wankt seit Tagesbeginn, wie langsamwandelnd Gewitter,
Dort auf schäumenden Wassern die Schlacht, und es glühet der
        Mittag,
Unbemerket im Zorn, schon über dem Haupte den Kämpfern.
Aber die Männer des Volks, die Heroënenkel, sie walten
Helleren Auges jezt, die Götterlieblinge denken
Des beschiedenen Glüks, es zähmen die Kinder Athenes
Ihren Genius, ihn, den todverachtenden, jezt nicht.
Denn wie aus rauchendem Blut das Wild der Wüste noch einmal
Sich zulezt verwandelt erhebt, der edleren Kraft gleich,
Und den Jäger erschrökt; kehrt jezt im Glanze der Waffen,
Bei der Herrscher Gebot, furchtbargesammelt den Wilden,
Mitten im Untergang die ermattete Seele noch einmal.
Und entbrandter beginnts; wie Paare ringender Männer
Fassen die Schiffe sich an, in die Wooge taumelt das Steuer,
Unter den Streitern bricht der Boden, und Schiffer und Schiff sinkt.

   Aber in schwindelnden Traum vom Liede des Tages gesungen,

Rollt der König den Blik; irrlächelnd über den Ausgang
Droht er, und fleht, und frohlokt, und sendet, wie Blize, die Boten.
Doch er sendet umsonst, es kehret keiner ihm wieder.
Blutige Boten, Erschlagne des Heers, und berstende Schiffe,

Refuge where animals hear their outcry, old men do their utmost
Even now to press back to their dwellings and smouldering temples,
Yet no prayer of their sons will awaken those ashes, the holy,
Now that death is let loose in the valley, the cloud of destruction
Drifts away in the sky, and whetted by one crime the Persian
Passes by with his booty and on to more plentiful harvest.

But by the shores of Salamis – O day by the shores of Salamis! –
Waiting there for the end, the Athenian virgins and mothers
Stand and rock in their arms small daughters and sons who were
        rescued;
As they strain their ears, from the depths now the voice of the
        Sea-God
Rises, predicting salvation; weighing and judging, the eyes of
Heaven's gods now gaze down, for there by the shores which repeated
Tremors rock, on the waves all foaming, like slow-moving thunder
Ever since dawn a battle has hung in the balance, and noon now

Glows on the combatants' heads, unnoticed by them in their fury.
But the Grecian men, the grandsons of heroes, with brighter
Eyes give battle now; beloved of the gods, they grow mindful
Of the triumph allotted to them; and no longer Athene's
Children suppress their genius, the reckless and death-deprecating.
As, in the end, from its steaming blood the wild beast of the desert
Rises once more, transformed, restored to his prowess, his pride, and
Startling the huntsman, turns; so now, with their weapons aglitter,
At their rulers' command, to the terribly straining, ferocious,
In the midst of defeat their once flagging spirit returns now.
And the battle flares up, like pairs of interlocked wrestlers
Triremes engage and grapple, the rudder's ripped off and adrift the
Floating battlefield cracks, and down go both trireme and sailors.

Yet lulled off into dizzying dream by the song which that day
        crooned,
Now the King rolls his eyes; and, smiling askew at the outcome,
Threatens, beseeches, exults and sends away runners like lightning.
But he sends them in vain: not one will return with a message.
Runners all covered in blood, and corpses of soldiers and wrecks of

Wirft die Rächerin ihm zahllos, die donnernde Wooge,
Vor den Thron, wo er sizt am bebenden Ufer, der Arme,
Schauend die Flucht, und fort in die fliehende Menge gerissen,
Eilt er, ihn treibt der Gott, es treibt sein irrend Geschwader
Über die Fluthen der Gott, der spottend sein eitel Geschmeid ihm
Endlich zerschlug und den Schwachen erreicht' in der drohenden
    Rüstung.

    Aber liebend zurük zum einsamharrenden Strome
Kommt der Athener Volk und von den Bergen der Heimath

Woogen, freudig gemischt, die glänzenden Schaaren herunter
Ins verlassene Thal, ach! gleich der gealterten Mutter,
Wenn nach Jahren das Kind, das verlorengeachtete, wieder
Lebend ihr an die Brüste kehrt, ein erwachsener Jüngling,
Aber im Gram ist ihr die Seele gewelkt und die Freude
Kommt der hoffnungsmüden zu spät und mühsam vernimmt sie,
Was der liebende Sohn in seinem Danke geredet;
So erscheint den Kommenden dort der Boden der Heimath.
Denn es fragen umsonst nach ihren Hainen die Frommen,
Und die Sieger empfängt die freundliche Pforte nicht wieder,
Wie den Wanderer sonst sie empfieng, wenn er froh von den Inseln
Wiederkehrt' und die seelige Burg der Mutter Athene
Über sehnendem Haupt ihm fernherglänzend heraufgieng.
Aber wohl sind ihnen bekannt die verödeten Gassen
Und die trauernden Gärten umher und auf der Agora,
Wo des Portikus Säulen gestürzt und die göttlichen Bilder
Liegen, da reicht in der Seele bewegt, und der Treue sich freuend,
Jezt das liebende Volk zum Bunde die Hände sich wieder.
Bald auch suchet und sieht den Ort des eigenen Haußes
Unter dem Schutt der Mann; ihm weint am Halse, der trauten
Schlummerstäte gedenk, sein Weib, es fragen die Kindlein
Nach dem Tische, wo sonst in lieblicher Reihe sie saßen,
Von den Vätern gesehn, den lächelnden Göttern des Haußes.
Aber Gezelte bauet das Volk, es schließen die alten
Nachbarn wieder sich an, und nach des Herzens Gewohnheit
Ordnen die luftigen Wohnungen sich umher an den Hügeln.
So indessen wohnen sie nun, wie die Freien, die Alten,
Die, der Stärke gewiß und dem kommenden Tage vertrauend,

Ships that have split, the thundering wave, the avenger,
Hurls at the poor man's throne where quaking he sits on the shore and
Watches his hordes in retreat; till, himself swept up by the fleeing,
Off he hurries, spurred on by the god, his squadrons all scattered
Driven to sea by the god, who, laughing at last at the weakling,
Smashed his vain baubles and reached him under his threatening
    armour.

   But now lovingly back to the river that, lonely, awaits them
Come the Athenians, and down from their homeland's neighbourly
    mountains,
Joyfully mingled, they surge, a colourful, shining procession
Into the desolate valley – but oh, like a time-ravaged mother
When the child long ago given up for lost after years comes
Back alive to her breast, no child but a fully grown youth now,
But with grieving her soul has withered, and joy comes too late for
Her, exhausted with hoping, and hardly she hears and can follow
What her loving son in gratitude hastens to tell her;
So to the people come back now seemed the old soil of their homeland.
For in vain after grove and garden the pious enquire now
And no friendly old door is waiting to welcome the victors
As it used to do once when, happy, a man voyaged homeward
From the islands and, blessed, the fortress of Mother Athene,
Distantly gleaming, appeared to eyes uplifted in longing.
Yet familiar enough, though stripped and deserted, the streets are,
All the gardens that mourn within and beyond the Agora,
Where the portico's pillars and limbs of the gods lie in pieces,
There, stirred up in their souls and rejoicing in faith, now the people
Lovingly link their hands in token of newly pledged union.
Soon the man, too, will seek and find the old site of his dwelling
Under the rubble; his wife, recalling the look of their bedroom,
Weeps and embraces him; the children excitedly ask him
For the table at which they'd sit in a circle at mealtimes
Watched by ancestors, by benevolent gods of the household.
But the people raise tents, and neighbours renew their old friendships,
Choosing familiar sites, and true to the heart and its habits
Airy new habitations fall into place on the hillsides.
Meanwhile, however, they live as did their forefathers, the free ones,
Who, assured of their strength and trusting the day and its morrow

Wandernden Vögeln gleich, mit Gesange von Berge zu Berg' einst
Zogen, die Fürsten des Forsts und des weitumirrenden Stromes.
Doch umfängt noch, wie sonst, die Muttererde, die treue,
Wieder ihr edel Volk, und unter heiligem Himmel
Ruhen sie sanft, wenn milde, wie sonst, die Lüfte der Jugend
Um die Schlafenden wehn, und aus Platanen Ilissus
Ihnen herüberrauscht, und neue Tage verkündend,

Lokend zu neuen Thaten, bei Nacht die Wooge des Meergotts

Fernher tönt und fröhliche Träume den Lieblingen sendet.
Schon auch sprossen und blühn die Blumen mälig, die goldnen,
Auf zertretenem Feld, von frommen Händen gewartet,
Grünet der Ölbaum auf, und auf Kolonos Gefilden
Nähren friedlich, wie sonst, die Athenischen Rosse sich wieder.

    Aber der Muttererd' und dem Gott der Wooge zu Ehren
Blühet die Stadt izt auf, ein herrlich Gebild, dem Gestirn gleich
Sichergegründet, des Genius Werk, denn Fesseln der Liebe
Schafft er gerne sich so, so hält in großen Gestalten,
Die er selbst sich erbaut, der immerrege sich bleibend.
Sieh! und dem Schaffenden dienet der Wald, ihm reicht mit den
        andern
Bergen nahe zur Hand der Pentele Marmor und Erze,
Aber lebend, wie er, und froh und herrlich entquillt es
Seinen Händen, und leicht, wie der Sonne, gedeiht das Geschäfft ihm.

Brunnen steigen empor und über die Hügel in reinen
Bahnen gelenkt, ereilt der Quell das glänzende Beken;
Und umher an ihnen erglänzt, gleich festlichen Helden
Am gemeinsamen Kelch, die Reihe der Wohnungen, hoch ragt
Der Prytanen Gemach, es stehn Gymnasien offen,
Göttertempel entstehn, ein heiligkühner Gedanke
Steigt, Unsterblichen nah, das Olympion auf in den Aether
Aus dem seeligen Hain; noch manche der himmlischen Hallen!
Mutter Athene, dir auch, dir wuchs dein herrlicher Hügel
Stolzer aus der Trauer empor und blühte noch lange,
Gott der Woogen und dir, und deine Lieblinge sangen
Frohversammelt noch oft am Vorgebirge den Dank dir.

As do migrant birds, from mountain to mountain once travelled
Singing, the princes of woods and of far-meandering rivers.
Yet their maternal earth, the faithful, as ever enfolds her
Noble people once more, and under a heaven still holy
Gently they sleep, while mild as ever the breezes of youth blow
Over each sleeping head, and out of the plane trees Ilissus,
Murmuring, makes himself known and nightly the wave of the
        Sea-God,
Which, predicting new days, to new deeds lures them on and inspires
        them,
Sounds from afar and grants enlivening dreams to his loved ones.
And already their crops, the golden, spring up and burst into flower
In the trampled fields, and piously, patiently tended,
Olive trees are in leaf, and once again at Colonus
In their old pasture, at peace, Athenian horses are grazing.

   But to please the maternal earth and honour the god of the waters
Now the city revives, a glorious artifice, firmly
Founded as galaxies, wrought by genius that readily thus will
Make himself fetters of love, and thus in majestic constructions,
Raised for his restless self, maintains a durable dwelling.
Look, and the forest serves that creator; Pentele, like other

Mountains near by, provides rich ores and offers him marble,
But alive as he is, and glad and splendid it seems to
Leap from his hands, and his work seems easily done, like the sun's
        work.
Fountains rise from the ground, and over the hills in pure conduits
Quickly the spring is conveyed and rushes to fill the bright basin;
Round about them, bright, as heroes dressed up for a banquet
Gleam round the communal cup, a circle of houses; above it
Looms the Prytanean hall, and now the gymnasia are open.
Temples are built for the gods and, near to immortals, a thought as
Holy as it is bold, the Olympion rises to Aether
From the sacred grove; still many a heavenly hall rose,
Mother Athene, for you; and prouder your glorious hill rose
From its affliction, and long it flourished there, also for your sake,
God of the waters, yours too, and happily gathered your loved ones
Often yet would intone their paean to you on the foothills.

O die Kinder des Glüks, die frommen! wandeln sie fern nun
Bei den Vätern daheim, und der Schiksaalstage vergessen,
Drüben am Lethestrom, und bringt kein Sehnen sie wieder?
Sieht mein Auge sie nie? ach! findet über den tausend

Pfaden der grünenden Erd', ihr göttergleichen Gestalten!
Euch das Suchende nie, und vernahm ich darum die Sprache,
Darum die Sage von euch, daß immertrauernd die Seele
Vor der Zeit mir hinab zu euern Schatten entfliehe?
Aber näher zu euch, wo eure Haine noch wachsen,
Wo sein einsames Haupt in Wolken der heilige Berg hüllt,
Zum Parnassos will ich, und wenn im Dunkel der Eiche
Schimmernd, mir Irrenden dort Kastalias Quelle begegnet,
Will ich, mit Thränen gemischt, aus blüthenumdufteter Schaale
Dort, auf keimendes Grün, das Wasser gießen, damit doch,
O ihr Schlafenden all! ein Todtenopfer euch werde.
Dort im schweigenden Thal, an Tempes hangenden Felsen,

Will ich wohnen mit euch, dort oft, ihr herrlichen Nahmen!
Her euch rufen bei Nacht, und wenn ihr zürnend erscheinet,
Weil der Pflug die Gräber entweiht, mit der Stimme des Herzens

Will ich, mit frommem Gesang euch sühnen, heilige Schatten!
Bis zu leben mit euch, sich ganz die Seele gewöhnet.
Fragen wird der Geweihtere dann euch manches, ihr Todten!
Euch, ihr Lebenden auch, ihr hohen Kräfte des Himmels,
Wenn ihr über dem Schutt mit euren Jahren vorbeigeht,
Ihr in der sicheren Bahn! denn oft ergreiffet das Irrsaal
Unter den Sternen mir, wie schaurige Lüfte, den Busen,
Daß ich spähe nach Rath, und lang schon reden sie nimmer

Trost den Bedürftigen zu, die prophetischen Haine Dodonas,
Stumm ist der delphische Gott, und einsam liegen und öde
Längst die Pfade, wo einst, von Hoffnungen leise geleitet,
Fragend der Mann zur Stadt des redlichen Sehers heraufstieg.
Aber droben das Licht, es spricht noch heute zu Menschen,
Schöner Deutungen voll und des großen Donnerers Stimme
Ruft es: denket ihr mein? und die trauernde Wooge des Meergotts
Hallt es wieder: gedenkt ihr nimmer meiner, wie vormals?
Denn es ruhn die Himmlischen gern am fühlenden Herzen;

O the children of bliss, the godly, far off are they walking
With their ancestors now, at home, on the far side of Lethe,
Fate's own days quite forgotten? And never will yearning recall them?
Shall my eyes never see them? Nor yet, though he tries all the
   thousand
Paths of the greening earth, the seeker his life long discover
You, most godlike of men? And was it for this that I heard your
Language, your legend, that now for ever saddened my soul should
Flee me before it is time, drawn down to your shadowy regions?
Yet more close to you rather, where still your orchards are growing,
Where the holy mountain's lone head lies cloud-veiled as ever,
To Parnassus I'll go, and when there in the darkness of oak-trees,
Gleaming, Castalia's spring appears to me, aimlessly roving,
Then, mixed with tears, from the cup that blossoms make fragrant
Water I'll pour on a site all green again now and all budding,
One libation at least for you sleepers who will not awaken.
There in the valley now hushed, where Tempe's great rocks hang
   suspended,
I will live with you all and often invoke you, the glorious
Names of the dead, in the night, and if then you appear, but in anger
Since your graves are profaned by the plough, with the voice of the
   heart, with
Pious song I'll appease you all, holy shades, till my soul is
Wholly accustomed and fit to live with you, heroes and wise men.
Many a question, you dead, then the more hallowed will ask you,
You, the living, no less, exalted and heavenly powers,
When with your years you pass by above the Grecian rubble,
You of the certain course! For often, like shivery breezes
Wild confusion grips me till lost I wander in starlight,
Looking for guidance, advice, and long now they've ceased to speak
   words of
Comfort to men in such need, the prophetic groves of Dodona,
Mute is the Delphian god, and desolate, long now deserted
Lie the pathways where once, while hopes would gently escort him,
Up walked the questioning man to the town of the truth-loving seer.
But the light above speaks kindly to mortals as ever,
Full of promises, hints, and the great Thunderer's voice, it
Cries: do you think of me? and the sorrowing wave of the Sea God
Echoes it back: do you never think of me now, as you once did?
For the Heavenly like to repose on a human heart that can feel them;

Immer, wie sonst, geleiten sie noch, die begeisternden Kräfte,
Gerne den strebenden Mann und über Bergen der Heimath
Ruht und waltet und lebt allgegenwärtig der Aether,
Daß ein liebendes Volk in des Vaters Armen gesammelt,
Menschlich freudig, wie sonst, und Ein Geist allen gemein sei.
Aber weh! es wandelt in Nacht, es wohnt, wie im Orkus,
Ohne Göttliches unser Geschlecht. Ans eigene Treiben
Sind sie geschmiedet allein, und sich in der tosenden Werkstatt
Höret jeglicher nur und viel arbeiten die Wilden
Mit gewaltigem Arm, rastlos, doch immer und immer
Unfruchtbar, wie die Furien, bleibt die Mühe der Armen.
Bis, erwacht vom ängstigen Traum, die Seele den Menschen
Aufgeht, jugendlich froh, und der Liebe seegnender Othem
Wieder, wie vormals oft, bei Hellas blühenden Kindern,
Wehet in neuer Zeit und über freierer Stirne
Uns der Geist der Natur, der fernherwandelnde, wieder
Stilleweilend der Gott in goldnen Wolken erscheinet.
Ach! und säumest du noch? und jene, die göttlichgebornen,

Wohnen immer, o Tag! noch als in Tiefen der Erde
Einsam unten, indeß ein immerlebender Frühling
Unbesungen über dem Haupt den Schlafenden dämmert?
Aber länger nicht mehr! schon hör' ich ferne des Festtags
Chorgesang auf grünem Gebirg' und das Echo der Haine,
Wo der Jünglinge Brust sich hebt, wo die Seele des Volks sich

Stillvereint im freieren Lied, zur Ehre des Gottes,
Dem die Höhe gebührt, doch auch die Thale sind heilig;
Denn, wo fröhlich der Strom in wachsender Jugend hinauseilt,
Unter Blumen des Lands, und wo auf sonnigen Ebnen
Edles Korn und der Obstwald reift, da kränzen am Feste
Gerne die Frommen sich auch, und auf dem Hügel der Stadt glänzt,
Menschlicher Wohnung gleich, die himmlische Halle der Freude.
Denn voll göttlichen Sinns ist alles Leben geworden,
Und vollendend, wie sonst, erscheinst du wieder den Kindern
Überall, o Natur! und, wie vom Quellengebirg, rinnt

Seegen von da und dort in die keimende Seele dem Volke.
Dann, dann, o ihr Freuden Athens! ihr Thaten in Sparta!
Köstliche Frühlingszeit im Griechenlande! wenn unser

Still the enrapturing powers, as ever, are glad to escort a
Man who seeks and aspires, and still does ubiquitous Aether
Rest and govern and live above the old hills of their homeland,
So that a loving people conjoined in the arms of the Father
Shall be humanly glad, *one* spirit be common to all men.
Ah, but our kind walks in darkness, it dwells as in Orcus,
Severed from all that's divine. To his own industry only
Each man is forged, and can hear only himself in the workshop's
Deafening noise; and much the savages toil there, for ever
Moving their powerful arms, they labour, yet always and always
Vain, like the Furies, unfruitful the wretches' exertions remain there.
Till the nightmare ends, and the human spirit, awakened,
Burgeons, youthfully glad, and love like a gentle warm breath blows
Over this new age as often once it would blow over Hellas,
Blessing her children in flower, and over our brows less constricted
Nature's spirit that comes to men from far-distant places,
Calmly abiding, in clouds all golden the god reappears now.
What, and you hesitate still? And they, though their birth was divine,
        still
Live as they did before, O day, as though lonely, confined in
Gloomy depths of the earth, while a springtime eternally living
Glimmers away unsung above the heads of those sleepers?
Not a moment longer! Already I hear on far foothills
Choric song, the feast-day's, and hear the green groves all re-echo,
Where the young men more deeply breathe, where the soul of the
        people
Quietly gathers in freer singing in praise of that god whose
Realm is the mountain heights, but the valleys also are holy;
For where youthful and growing the river lightheartedly hurries
Out amid flowers of the land, and where on sun-flooded plains the
Noble corn and the orchards mature, there too on the feast-day
Pious folk like to wear bright garlands, and up in the town gleams,
Not unlike human homes, the heavenly hall of pure gladness.
For the gods have restored to all life their spirit, their meaning,
And perfecting, as once you did, you appear to your children
Everywhere, Nature, once more, and as from the brook-threaded
        mountains
Blessings from this place and that transfuse the new soul of the people.
Then, O then, you joys of Athens, you deeds done at Sparta,
You delicious springtime in Grecian lands! When our autumn

Herbst kömmt, wenn ihr gereift, ihr Geister alle der Vorwelt!
Wiederkehret und siehe! des Jahrs Vollendung ist nahe!
Dann erhalte das Fest auch euch, vergangene Tage!
Hin nach Hellas schaue das Volk, und weinend und dankend
Sänftige sich in Erinnerungen der stolze Triumphtag!

Aber blühet indeß, bis unsre Früchte beginnen,
Blüht, ihr Gärten Ioniens! nur, und die an Athens Schutt
Grünen, ihr Holden! verbergt dem schauenden Tage die Trauer!
Kränzt mit ewigem Laub, ihr Lorbeerwälder! die Hügel
Eurer Todten umher, bei Marathon dort, wo die Knaben
Siegend starben, ach! dort auf Chäroneas Gefilden,
Wo mit den Waffen ins Blut die lezten Athener enteilten,
Fliehend vor dem Tage der Schmach, dort, dort von den Bergen
Klagt ins Schlachtthal täglich herab, dort singet von Oetas
Gipfeln das Schiksaalslied, ihr wandelnden Wasser, herunter!
Aber du, unsterblich, wenn auch der Griechengesang schon
Dich nicht feiert, wie sonst, aus deinen Woogen, o Meergott!

Töne mir in die Seele noch oft, daß über den Wassern
Furchtlosrege der Geist, dem Schwimmer gleich, in der Starken
Frischem Glüke sich üb', und die Göttersprache, das Wechseln

Und das Werden versteh', und wenn die reißende Zeit mir
Zu gewaltig das Haupt ergreifft und die Noth und das Irrsaal
Unter Sterblichen mir mein sterblich Leben erschüttert,
Laß der Stille mich dann in deiner Tiefe gedenken.

Menons Klagen um Diotima

I

Täglich geh' ich heraus, und such' ein Anderes immer,
    Habe längst sie befragt alle die Pfade des Lands;
Droben die kühlenden Höhn, die Schatten alle besuch' ich,
    Und die Quellen; hinauf irret der Geist und hinab,
Ruh' erbittend; so flieht das getroffene Wild in die Wälder,
    Wo es um Mittag sonst sicher im Dunkel geruht;

Comes, when you all, grown mature, you genii known in the ancient
World return – and, look, the year's consummation approaches –
Then may the feast-day preserve you also, great era long ended,
May the people look towards Hellas and thanksgiving, weeping,
Make the proud day of their triumph gentle with solemn
      remembrance!

Meanwhile, however, flower, till our fruition commences,
Flower, Ionian gardens, no less, and you others, you dear ones
Green behind Athens' rubble, hide her, lest day see her sadness!
And with evergreen leaves, you laurel woods, garland the gravemounds
Of your dead there at Marathon, where in the act of winning
Boys fell dead, and oh, there too, on the plains of Chaeronea
Where the last Athenians rushed into blood with their weapons,
Fleeing the day of disgrace, and there, over there, from the mountains
Daily down to the battlefield sound your lament, from Oeta's
Peaks give voice to your hymn of destiny, wandering waters!
You, however, immortal although the great hymns of the Grecians
Now do not praise you, may you, O God of the Sea, from your
      breakers
Often yet with your music infuse my soul, so that on your
Waters fearlessly nimble my mind like a swimmer may practise
Joy which the strong know, fresh joy, and master the language of gods,
      of
All that changes and grows; and if Time, as it rushes on ruthless
Seizes my head too firmly, and need, and this walking bewildered,
Lost, among mortals at last should shatter my mortal existence,
Then in your deeps the tranquillity let me remember.

Menon's Lament for Diotima

    I

Daily I search, now here, now there my wandering takes me
    Countless times I have probed every highway and path;
Coolness I seek on those hilltops, all the shades I revisit,
    Then the well-springs again; up my mind roves and down
Begging for rest; so a wounded deer will flee to the forests
    Where he used to lie low, safe in the dark towards noon;

Aber nimmer erquikt sein grünes Lager das Herz ihm,
  Jammernd und schlummerlos treibt es der Stachel umher.
Nicht die Wärme des Lichts, und nicht die Kühle der Nacht hilft,

  Und in Woogen des Stroms taucht es die Wunden umsonst.
Und wie ihm vergebens die Erd' ihr fröhliches Heilkraut
  Reicht, und das gährende Blut keiner der Zephyre stillt,
So, ihr Lieben! auch mir, so will es scheinen, und niemand
  Kann von der Stirne mir nehmen den traurigen Traum?

2

Ja! es frommet auch nicht, ihr Todesgötter! wenn einmal
  Ihr ihn haltet, und fest habt den bezwungenen Mann,
Wenn ihr Bösen hinab in die schaurige Nacht ihn genommen,
  Dann zu suchen, zu flehn, oder zu zürnen mit euch,
Oder geduldig auch wohl im furchtsamen Banne zu wohnen,
  Und mit Lächeln von euch hören das nüchterne Lied.
Soll es seyn, so vergiß dein Heil, und schlummere klanglos!
  Aber doch quillt ein Laut hoffend im Busen dir auf,
Immer kannst du noch nicht, o meine Seele! noch kannst du's
  Nicht gewohnen, und träumst mitten im eisernen Schlaf!
Festzeit hab' ich nicht, doch möcht' ich die Loke bekränzen;
  Bin ich allein denn nicht? aber ein Freundliches muß
Fernher nahe mir seyn, und lächeln muß ich und staunen,
  Wie so seelig doch auch mitten im Leide mir ist.

3

Licht der Liebe! scheinest du denn auch Todten, du goldnes!
  Bilder aus hellerer Zeit leuchtet ihr mir in die Nacht?
Liebliche Gärten seid, ihr abendröthlichen Berge,
  Seid willkommen und ihr, schweigende Pfade des Hains,
Zeugen himmlischen Glüks, und ihr, hochschauende Sterne,
  Die mir damals so oft seegnende Blike gegönnt!
Euch, ihr Liebenden auch, ihr schönen Kinder des Maitags,
  Stille Rosen und euch, Lilien, nenn' ich noch oft!
Wohl gehn Frühlinge fort, ein Jahr verdränget das andre,
  Wechselnd und streitend, so tost droben vorüber die Zeit

Yet his green lair no longer now can refresh him or soothe him,
    Crying and sleepless he roams, cruelly pricked by the thorn,
Neither the warmth of the daylight nor the cool darkness of night
        helps,
    In the river's waves too vainly he washes his wounds.
And as vainly to him now Earth offers herbs that might heal them,
    Cheer him, and none of the winds quiets his feverish blood,
So, beloved ones, it seems, with me it is too, and can no one
    Lift this dead weight from my brow, break the all-saddening dream?

2

And indeed, gods of death, when once you have utterly caught him,
    Seized and fettered the man, so that he cringes, subdued,
When you evil ones down into horrible night have conveyed him
    Useless it is to implore, then to be angry with you,
Useless even to bear that grim coercion with patience,
    Smiling to hear you each day chant him the sobering song.
If you must, then forget your welfare and drowse away tuneless!
    Yet in your heart even now, hoping, a sound rises up,
Still, my soul, even now you cling to your habit of music,
    Will not give in yet, and dream deep in the lead of dull sleep!
Cause I have none to be festive, but long to put on a green garland;
    Am I not quite alone? Yet something kind now must be
Close to me from afar, so that I smile as I wonder
    How in the midst of my grief I can feel happy and blessed.

3

Golden light of love, for dead men, for shades, do you shine then?
    Radiant visions recalled, even this night, then, you pierce?
Pleasant gardens, and mountains tinged with crimson at sunset,
    Welcome I call you, and you, murmurless path of the grove,
Witness to heavenly joy, and stars more loftily gazing,
    Who so freely would grant looks that were blessings to me!
And you lovers, you too, the May-day's beautiful children,
    Quiet roses, and you, lilies, I often invoke!
Springs, it is true, go by, one year still supplanting the other,
    Changing and warring, so Time over us mortal men's heads

Über sterblichem Haupt, doch nicht vor seeligen Augen,
  Und den Liebenden ist anderes Leben geschenkt.
Denn sie alle die Tag' und Jahre der Sterne, sie waren
  Diotima! um uns innig und ewig vereint;

4

Aber wir, zufrieden gesellt, wie die liebenden Schwäne,
  Wenn sie ruhen am See, oder, auf Wellen gewiegt,
Niedersehn in die Wasser, wo silberne Wolken sich spiegeln,
  Und ätherisches Blau unter den Schiffenden wallt,
So auf Erden wandelten wir. Und drohte der Nord auch,

  Er, der Liebenden Feind, klagenbereitend, und fiel
Von den Ästen das Laub, und flog im Winde der Reegen,

  Ruhig lächelten wir, fühlten den eigenen Gott
Unter trautem Gespräch; in Einem Seelengesange,
  Ganz in Frieden mit uns kindlich und freudig allein.
Aber das Haus ist öde mir nun, und sie haben mein Auge
  Mir genommen, auch mich hab' ich verloren mit ihr.
Darum irr' ich umher, und wohl, wie die Schatten, so muß ich
  Leben, und sinnlos dünkt lange das Übrige mir.

5

Feiern möcht' ich; aber wofür? und singen mit Andern,
  Aber so einsam fehlt jegliches Göttliche mir.
Diß ist's, diß mein Gebrechen, ich weiß, es lähmet ein Fluch mir
  Darum die Sehnen, und wirft, wo ich beginne, mich hin,
Daß ich fühllos size den Tag, und stumm wie die Kinder,
  Nur vom Auge mir kalt öfters die Thräne noch schleicht,
Und die Pflanze des Felds, und der Vögel Singen mich trüb macht,
  Weil mit Freuden auch sie Boten des Himmlischen sind,
Aber mir in schaudernder Brust die beseelende Sonne,
  Kühl und fruchtlos mir dämmert, wie Stralen der Nacht,
Ach! und nichtig und leer, wie Gefängnißwände, der Himmel
  Eine beugende Last über dem Haupte mir hängt!

Rushes past up above, but not in the eyes of the blessed ones,
    Nor of lovers, to whom different life is vouchsafed.
For all these, all the days and years of the heavenly planets,
    Diotima, round us closely, for ever, conjoined;

4

Meanwhile we – like the mated swans in their summer contentment
    When by the lake they rest or on the waves, lightly rocked,
Down they look, at the water, and silvery clouds through that mirror
    Drift, and ethereal blue flows where the voyagers pass –
Moved and dwelled on this earth. And though the North Wind was
        threatening
    Hostile to lovers, he, gathering sorrows, and down
Came dead leaves from the boughs, and rain filled the spluttering
        storm-gusts
    Calmly we smiled, aware, sure of the tutelar god
Present in talk only ours, one song that our two souls were singing,
    Wholly at peace with ourselves, childishly, raptly alone.
Desolate now is my house, and not only her they have taken,
    No, but my own two eyes, myself I have lost, losing her.
That is why, astray, like wandering phantoms I live now,
    Must live, I fear, and the rest long has seemed senseless to me.

5

Celebrate – yes, but what? And gladly with others I'd sing now,
    Yet alone as I am nothing that's godlike rings true,
This, I know, is it, my failing, a curse maims my sinews
    Only because of this, making me flag from the start,
So that numb all day long I sit like a child that is moping
    Dumb, though at times a tear coldly creeps out of my eyes,
And the flowers of the field, the singing of birds make me sad now,
    Being heralds of heaven, bearers of heavenly joy,
But to me, in my heart's dank vault, now the soul giving sun dawns
    Cool, infertile, in vain, feeble as rays of the night,
Oh, and futile and empty, walls of a prison, the heavens
    Press, a smothering load heaped on my head from above!

6

Sonst mir anders bekannt! o Jugend, und bringen Gebete

Dich nicht wieder, dich nie? führet kein Pfad mich zurük?
Soll es werden auch mir, wie den Götterlosen, die vormals
    Glänzenden Auges doch auch saßen an seeligem Tisch',
Aber übersättiget bald, die schwärmenden Gäste,
    Nun verstummet, und nun, unter der Lüfte Gesang,
Unter blühender Erd' entschlafen sind, bis dereinst sie
    Eines Wunders Gewalt sie, die Versunkenen, zwingt,
Wiederzukehren, und neu auf grünendem Boden zu wandeln. –
    Heiliger Othem durchströmt göttlich die lichte Gestalt,
Wenn das Fest sich beseelt, und Fluthen der Liebe sich regen,
    Und vom Himmel getränkt, rauscht der lebendige Strom,
Wenn es drunten ertönt, und ihre Schäze die Nacht zollt,
    Und aus Bächen herauf glänzt das begrabene Gold. –

7

Aber o du, die schon am Scheidewege mir damals,
    Da ich versank vor dir, tröstend ein Schöneres wies,
Du, die Großes zu sehn, und froher die Götter zu singen,
    Schweigend, wie sie, mich einst stille begeisternd gelehrt;
Götterkind! erscheinest du mir, und grüßest, wie einst, mich,
    Redest wieder, wie einst, höhere Dinge mir zu?
Siehe! weinen vor dir, und klagen muß ich, wenn schon noch,
    Denkend edlerer Zeit, dessen die Seele sich schämt.
Denn so lange, so lang auf matten Pfaden der Erde
    Hab' ich, deiner gewohnt, dich in der Irre gesucht,
Freudiger Schuzgeist! aber umsonst, und Jahre zerrannen,
    Seit wir ahnend um uns glänzen die Abende sahn.

8

Dich nur, dich erhält dein Licht, o Heldinn! im Lichte,
    Und dein Dulden erhält liebend, o Gütige, dich;
Und nicht einmal bist du allein; Gespielen genug sind,
    Wo du blühest und ruhst unter den Rosen des Jahrs;
Und der Vater, er selbst, durch sanftumathmende Musen
    Sendet die zärtlichen Wiegengesänge dir zu.
Ja! noch ist sie es ganz! noch schwebt vom Haupte zur Sohle,
    Stillherwandelnd, wie sonst, mir die Athenerinn vor.

6

Once, how different it was! O youth, will no prayer bring you back,
then,
    Never again? And no path ever again lead me back?
Shall it be my fate, as once it was that of the godless,
    Bright-eyed to sit for a time feasting at heavenly boards
But to be cloyed with that food, all those fantastical guests now
    Fallen silent, and now, deaf to the music of winds,
Under the flowering earth asleep, till a miracle's power shall
    Force them one day to return, deep though they lie now, at rest,
Force them to walk anew the soil that is sprouting new verdure. –
    Holy breath, then, divine, through their bright bodies will flow
While the feast is inspired and love like great floodwaters gathers,
    Fed by the heavens themselves, on sweeps the river, alive,
When the deep places boom, Night pays her tribute of riches
    And from the beds of streams up glitters gold long submerged. –

7

You, though, who ever then, already then at the crossroads
    When I fell at your feet, comforting showed me the way,
Taught me to see what is great, to sing with a beauty more mellow,
    Joy more serene, the gods, silent as gods are yourself,
Child of the gods, will you appear to me, greet me once more now,
    Quietly raising me up, speak to me now of those things?
Look, in your presence I weep, lament, though remembering always
    Worthier times that are past, deep, in my soul I feel shame.
For so very long on weary paths of the earth now,
    Still accustomed to you, you I have sought in the wilds,
Tutelar spirit, but all in vain, and whole years have gone by since
    Late in the evenings we walked, bathed in that ominous glow.

8

You, only you, your own light, O heroine, keeps in the light still,
    And your patience still keeps you both loving and kind;
Nor indeed are you lonely; playmates enough are provided
    Where amid roses you bloom, rest with the flowers of the year;
And the Father himself by means of the balm-breathing Muses
    Sends you those cradle-songs warm as a southerly breeze.
Yes, she is quite the same! From her head to her heels the Athenian,
    Quiet and poised as before hovers in front of my eyes.

Und wie, freundlicher Geist! von heitersinnender Stirne
   Seegnend und sicher dein Stral unter die Sterblichen fällt;
So bezeugest du mir's, und sagst mir's, daß ich es andern
   Wiedersage, denn auch Andere glauben es nicht,
Daß unsterblicher doch, denn Sorg' und Zürnen, die Freude
   Und ein goldener Tag täglich am Ende noch ist.

9

So will ich, ihr Himmlischen! denn auch danken, und endlich
   Athmet aus leichter Brust wieder des Sängers Gebet.
Und wie, wenn ich mit ihr, auf sonniger Höhe mit ihr stand,
   Spricht belebend ein Gott innen vom Tempel mich an.
Leben will ich denn auch! schon grünt's! wie von heiliger Leier
   Ruft es von silbernen Bergen Apollons voran!
Komm! es war wie ein Traum! Die blutenden Fittige sind ja
   Schon genesen, verjüngt leben die Hoffnungen all.
Großes zu finden, ist viel, ist viel noch übrig, und wer so

   Liebte, gehet, er muß, gehet zu Göttern die Bahn.
Und geleitet ihr uns, ihr Weihestunden! ihr ernsten,
   Jugendlichen! o bleibt, heilige Ahnungen, ihr
Fromme Bitten! und ihr Begeisterungen und all ihr
   Guten Genien, die gerne bei Liebenden sind;
Bleibt so lange mit uns, bis wir auf gemeinsamem Boden
   Dort, wo die Seeligen all niederzukehren bereit,
Dort, wo die Adler sind, die Gestirne, die Boten des Vaters,
   Dort, wo die Musen, woher Helden und Liebende sind,
Dort uns, oder auch hier, auf thauender Insel begegnen,
   Wo die Unsrigen erst, blühend in Gärten gesellt,
Wo die Gesänge wahr, und länger die Frühlinge schön sind,
   Und von neuem ein Jahr unserer Seele beginnt.

And as blessing and sure your radiance falls upon mortals,
    Tender soul, from your brow rapt in deep thought, yet serene,
So you prove it to me, and tell me, that also to others
    Then I may pass it on, others who doubt as I doubt,
That more enduring than care and anger is holy rejoicing
    And that golden the day daily still shines in the end.

9

Thanks, once more, then, I'll give to you up in heaven; once more now
    Freely at last can my prayer rise from a heart unoppressed.
And, as before, when with her I stood on a sun-gilded hilltop,
    Quickening, to me now a god speaks from the temple within.
I will live, then! New verdure! As though from a lyre that is hallowed
    Onward! from silvery peaks, Apollo's mountains ring out.
Come, it was all like a dream, the wounds in your wings have already
    Healed, and restored to youth all your old hopes leap alive.
Knowledge of greatness is much, yet much still remains to be done,
        and
    One who loved as you loved only to gods can move on.
You conduct us, then, you solemn ones, Hours of Communion,
    Youthful ones, stay with us, holy Presentiments also,
Pious prayers, and you, Inspirations, and all of you kindly
    Spirits who like to attend lovers, to be where they are.
Stay with us two until on communal ground, reunited
    Where, when their coming is due, all the blessed souls will return,
Where the eagles are, the planets, the Father's own heralds,
    Where the Muses are still, heroes and lovers began,
There we shall meet again, or here, on a dew-covered island
    Where what is ours for once, blooms that a garden conjoins,
All our poems are true and springs remain beautiful longer
    And another, a new year of our souls can begin.

Der Wanderer

Einsam stand ich und sah in die Afrikanischen dürren
   Ebnen hinaus; vom Olymp reegnete Feuer herab,
Reißendes! milder kaum, wie damals, da das Gebirg hier

   Spaltend mit Stralen der Gott Höhen und Tiefen gebaut.

Aber auf denen springt kein frischaufgrünender Wald nicht
   In die tönende Luft üppig und herrlich empor.
Unbekränzt ist die Stirne des Bergs und beredtsame Bäche
   Kennet er kaum, es erreicht selten die Quelle das Thal.
Keiner Heerde vergeht am plätschernden Brunnen der Mittag,
   Freundlich aus Bäumen hervor blikte kein gastliches Dach.
Unter dem Strauche saß ein ernster Vogel gesanglos,
   Aber die Wanderer flohn eilend, die Störche, vorbei.
Da bat ich um Wasser dich nicht, Natur! in der Wüste,
   Wasser bewahrte mir treulich das fromme Kameel.
Um der Haine Gesang, ach! um die Gärten des Vaters
   Bat ich vom wandernden Vogel der Heimath gemahnt.
Aber du sprachst zu mir; auch hier sind Götter und walten,
   Groß ist ihr Maas, doch es mißt gern mit der Spanne der Mensch.

Und es trieb die Rede mich an, noch Andres zu suchen,
   Fern zum nördlichen Pol kam ich in Schiffen herauf.
Still in der Hülse von Schnee schlief da das gefesselte Leben,
   Und der eiserne Schlaf harrte seit Jahren des Tags.
Denn zu lang nicht schlang um die Erde den Arm der Olymp hier,
   Wie Pygmalions Arm um die Geliebte sich schlang.
Hier bewegt' er ihr nicht mit dem Sonnenblike den Busen,
   Und in Reegen und Thau sprach er nicht freundlich zu ihr;
Und mich wunderte deß und thörig sprach ich: o Mutter
   Erde, verlierst du denn immer, als Wittwe, die Zeit?

Nichts zu erzeugen ist ja und nichts zu pflegen in Liebe,
   Alternd im Kinde sich nicht wieder zu sehn, wie der Tod.
Aber vieleicht erwarmst du dereinst am Strale des Himmels,
   Aus dem dürftigen Schlaf schmeichelt sein Othem dich auf;

The Traveller

Lonely I stood and looked out into African desert, unbroken
    Plains; and, standing there, saw fire from Olympus rain down,
Ravening fire scarcely more gentle than when in the same mountain
        ranges,
    Blasting their bulk with his rays, God made the heights and the
        depths.
Never on these, though, a forest with newly green leafage
    Into the resonant air, luscious and glorious, will rise.
All ungarlanded is the brow of this mountain, and eloquent torrents
    Hardly are known to it, brooks rarely complete their descent.
Noon by no murmuring well-spring goes by for the somnolent cattle,
    Not one hospitable roof amiably beckoned from trees.
Under dry bushes there sat a serious bird, never singing.
    But those migrants, the storks, hurriedly passed on their way.
Nature, not you did I ask for water there in the desert,
    But on the good camel's back only for drink could rely.
For the song of the groves, ah, and the gardens, my father's,
    Yes, I did ask – by the birds, migrants from homeland, recalled.
Then, though, you said to me: here also gods are, and they govern,
    Great is their measure, but men take as their measure the span.

And those words impelled me to look for other things also,
    Far off to the northern pole sailing I made my way.
Packed in its wrapping of snow a fettered life seemed to sleep there
    And for years iron sleep there had been waiting for day.
For not too long around Earth did Olympus wrap a fond arm here
    As Pygmalion's arm round his beloved was wrapped.
Here with his sunny gaze he awakens no warmth in her bosom,
    Never with rain or with dew whispered those words that seduce;
And I marvelled at that, and I foolishly said to her: Mother
    Earth, will you always, then, waste, widowed, your time and your
        life?
When to give birth to nothing and nothing to lovingly care for,
    Never to see your own self imaged in children, is death.
Or in the heavenly beam after all still one day you'll be basking,
    Out of the dearth of your sleep raised by his breath after all;

Daß, wie ein Saamkorn, du die eherne Schaale zersprengest,

Los sich reißt und das Licht grüßt die entbundene Welt,
All' die gesammelte Kraft aufflammt in üppigem Frühling,
Rosen glühen und Wein sprudelt im kärglichen Nord.

Also sagt' ich und jezt kehr' ich an den Rhein, in die Heimath,
Zärtlich, wie vormals, weh'n Lüfte der Jugend mich an;
Und das strebende Herz besänftigen mir die vertrauten
Offnen Bäume, die einst mich in den Armen gewiegt,
Und das heilige Grün, der Zeuge des seeligen, tiefen
Lebens der Welt, es erfrischt, wandelt zum Jüngling mich um.
Alt bin ich geworden indeß, mich blaichte der Eispol,

Und im Feuer des Süds fielen die Loken mir aus.
Aber wenn einer auch am lezten der sterblichen Tage,
Fernher kommend und müd bis in die Seele noch jezt
Wiedersähe diß Land, noch Einmal müßte die Wang' ihm
Blüh'n, und erloschen fast glänzte sein Auge noch auf.
Seeliges Thal des Rheins! kein Hügel ist ohne den Weinstok,
Und mit der Traube Laub Mauer und Garten bekränzt,
Und des heiligen Tranks sind voll im Strome die Schiffe,
Städt' und Inseln sie sind trunken von Weinen und Obst.
Aber lächelnd und ernst ruht droben der Alte, der Taunus,
Und mit Eichen bekränzt neiget der Freie das Haupt.

Und jezt kommt vom Walde der Hirsch, aus Wolken das Tagslicht,

Hoch in heiterer Luft siehet der Falke sich um.
Aber unten im Thal, wo die Blume sich nähret von Quellen,

Strekt das Dörfchen bequem über die Wiese sich aus.
Still ists hier. Fern rauscht die immer geschäfftige Mühle,
Aber das Neigen des Tags künden die Gloken mir an.
Lieblich tönt die gehämmerte Sens' und die Stimme des Landmanns,
Der heimkehrend dem Stier gerne die Schritte gebeut,

And, like the living seed-grain, burst out of the husk that constricts
      you,
  So that the world, unbound, tears itself loose and greets light,
All the strength so long gathered flares up in a springtime luxuriance,
  Roses glow and rich wine gushes in northerly dearth.

So I addressed her, and now I return to the Rhine, to my homeland,
  Feel, as I used to do, childhood's mild breeze on my face;
And my heart, the far-roaming, is soothed again by familiar
  Welcoming trees that before cradled the child in their arms,
And the holy verdure betokening blissful and deeper
  Life in this world makes it new, changes the man to a youth.
Old in the meantime I've grown, and was blanched by the ice of the
      Arctic,
  In the fire of the South lost many locks of my hair.
Yet if a man on his very last day as a mortal,
  Coming from far away, weary right down to his soul,
Were to revisit this country, once more to his cheeks must the colour
  Rise, and his eyes almost dimmed brightly would gleam once again.
Blessed valley, the Rhine's! Not one hill but is covered with vineyards,
  And with leaves of the grape garden and wall are adorned,
And on the rivers the ships are full of the drink that is holy,
  Cities and islands are all drunken with wines and with fruit.
Smiling and serious above them the ancient one, Taunus, reposes
  And his head crowned with oaks proudly the free one inclines.

And from the wood comes the stag now, from clouds comes the
      daylight,
  Up in a sky that is clear now hangs the hawk and looks round.
But in the valley below where the flowers are nourished by
      well-springs,
  Look, the small village spreads out among meadows, relaxed.
Quiet it's here. From afar comes the noise of the mill-wheels revolving,
  But the day's decline church bells convey to my ear.
Pleasantly clangs the hammered scythe and the voice of the farmer
  Who, going home with his bull, likes to command and to curb,

Lieblich der Mutter Gesang, die im Grase sizt mit dem Söhnlein;
  Satt vom Sehen entschliefs; aber die Wolken sind roth,

Und am glänzenden See, wo der Hain das offene Hofthor
  Übergrünt und das Licht golden die Fenster umspielt,
Dort empfängt mich das Haus und des Gartens heimliches Dunkel,
  Wo mit den Pflanzen mich einst liebend der Vater erzog;
Wo ich frei, wie Geflügelte, spielt' auf luftigen Ästen,

  Oder ins treue Blau blikte vom Gipfel des Hains.
Treu auch bist du von je, treu auch dem Flüchtlinge blieben,
  Freundlich nimmst du, wie einst, Himmel der Heimath, mich auf.

Noch gedeihn die Pfirsiche mir, mich wundern die Blüthen,
  Fast, wie die Bäume, steht herrlich mit Rosen der Strauch.
Schwer ist worden indeß von Früchten dunkel mein Kirschbaum,
  Und der pflükenden Hand reichen die Zweige sich selbst.
Auch zum Walde zieht mich, wie sonst, in die freiere Laube
  Aus dem Garten der Pfad oder hinab an den Bach,
Wo ich lag, und den Muth erfreut' am Ruhme der Männer
  Ahnender Schiffer; und das konnten die Sagen von euch,
Daß in die Meer' ich fort, in die Wüsten mußt', ihr Gewalt'gen!
  Ach! indeß mich umsonst Vater und Mutter gesucht.
Aber wo sind sie? du schweigst? du zögerst? Hüter des Haußes!

  Hab' ich gezögert doch auch! habe die Schritte gezählt,
Da ich nahet', und bin, gleich Pilgern, stille gestanden.

  Aber gehe hinein, melde den Fremden, den Sohn,
Daß sich öffnen die Arm' und mir ihr Seegen begegne,

  Daß ich geweiht und gegönnt wieder die Schwelle mir sei!
Aber ich ahn' es schon, in heilige Fremde dahin sind
  Nun auch sie mir, und nie kehret ihr Lieben zurük.

Vater und Mutter? und wenn noch Freunde leben, sie haben

Andres gewonnen, sie sind nimmer die Meinigen mehr.

Pleasant the mother's song as she sits in the grass with her infant;
   Sated with seeing he sleeps; clouds, though, are tinged now with
      red,
And by the glistening lake where the orchard extends its full branches
   Over the open yard gate, window-panes glitter with gold,
There I'm received by the house and the garden's secretive half-light,
   Where together with plants fondly my father reared me;
Where as free as the winged ones I played in the boughs' airy
      greenness
   Or from the orchard's crest gazed into spaces all blue.
Loyal you were, and loyal remain to the fugitive even,
   Kindly as ever you were, heaven of home, take me back.

Still do the peaches grow ripe for me, still at the blossom I marvel,
   Almost as tall as the trees gloriously rose-bushes flower.
Heavy meanwhile with fruit and dark has my cherry-tree grown now,
   And to the gathering hand branches now proffer themselves.
Still to the woods by the path, as before, to the free-lying bower
   Out of the garden I'm drawn, down to the stream, where before
I would lie, with my mind cheered by the fame of those men, the
   Prescient mariners; and such was the power of your love
That to the oceans, the deserts, your valour compelled me to follow,
   Ah, while in vain they looked, father and mother, for me.
But where are they? You're silent? You hesitate, you, my home's
      keeper?
   Hesitate? Well, so did I, counting my steps to the door,
As I drew near and, like pilgrims, awe-stricken slowed them, and
      halted.
   Go inside, nonetheless, say: there's a stranger, your son,
So that they open their arms and receive me once more with their
      blessing,
   So that they sanctify me, grant me the threshold once more.
Yet already I guess it: to holy remoteness they also
   Now have passed on and to me never again will return.

Father and mother? And if there are friends living still, they as well
      have
   Found new pursuits, other gains, are not the friends who were mine.

Kommen werd' ich, wie sonst, und die alten, die Nahmen der Liebe
  Nennen, beschwören das Herz, ob es noch schlage, wie sonst,
Aber stille werden sie seyn. So bindet und scheidet
  Manches die Zeit. Ich dünk' ihnen gestorben, sie mir.
Und so bin ich allein. Du aber, über den Wolken,
  Vater des Vaterlands! mächtiger Aether! und du
Erd' und Licht! ihr einigen drei, die walten und lieben,
  Ewige Götter! mit euch brechen die Bande mir nie.
Ausgegangen von euch, mit euch auch bin ich gewandert,
  Euch, ihr Freudigen, euch bring' ich erfahrner zurük.
Darum reiche mir nun, bis oben an von des Rheines
  Warmen Bergen mit Wein reiche den Becher gefüllt!
Daß ich den Göttern zuerst und das Angedenken der Helden
  Trinke, der Schiffer, und dann eures, ihr Trautesten! auch
Eltern und Freund'! und der Mühn und aller Leiden vergesse
  Heut' und morgen und schnell unter den Heimischen sei.

Stutgard

AN SIEGFRIED SCHMIDT

I

Wieder ein Glük ist erlebt. Die gefährliche Dürre geneset,
  Und die Schärfe des Lichts senget die Blüthe nicht mehr.
Offen steht jezt wieder ein Saal, und gesund ist der Garten,
  Und von Reegen erfrischt rauschet das glänzende Thal,
Hoch von Gewächsen, es schwellen die Bäch' und alle gebundnen

  Fittige wagen sich wieder ins Reich des Gesangs.
Voll ist die Luft von Fröhlichen jezt und die Stadt und der Hain ist
  Rings von zufriedenen Kindern des Himmels erfüllt.
Gerne begegnen sie sich, und irren untereinander,
  Sorgenlos, und es scheint keines zu wenig, zu viel.
Denn so ordnet das Herz es an, und zu athmen die Anmuth,
  Sie, die geschikliche, schenkt ihnen ein göttlicher Geist.
Aber die Wanderer auch sind wohlgeleitet und haben
  Kränze genug und Gesang, haben den heiligen Stab

Though as before I come and address by love's names, by the old ones,
    All that I see, and adjure heart-beats that once would respond,
Utter silence will meet me. For so it is: much is bound by,
    Much is severed by time. I to them will seem dead, they to me;
And I'm left all alone. But with you, up there above clouds, my
    Fatherland's father, you, powerful Aether, and you
Earth and Light, unanimous three who love and who govern,
    Deathless gods, with you never my bonds I shall break.
Out of you originated, with you I have also travelled,
    You, the joyous ones, you, filled with more knowledge, bring back.
Therefore pass to me now the cup that is filled, overflowing
    With the wine from those grapes grown on warm hills of the Rhine,
That I may drink to the gods at first and then remember those others,
    Mariners, heroes, and then you, the still closer to me,
Parents and friends, and forget my whole load of afflictions and labours
    This and the next day, and soon be among those of my kind.

Stuttgart
TO SIEGFRIED SCHMIDT

I

Once again a joy has been lived. The dangerous dryness recovers
    And the sharp edge of light singes no leaf and no flower.
Open once more stands the hall, and the garden also is healthy
    And the rill-rushing vale glistens, refreshed by the rain,
Lush with new growth, and the brooks swell up and the
        long-constricted
    Wings now venture again into the purlieus of song.
Full is the air of merry ones now and the city and woodland
    All around are filled, teem with those children of air.
Happy they are to meet and ramble one with another,
    Carefree, and nothing to them now seems too little, too much.
For it's so the heart would have it, to breathe in such beauty,
    Grace that is destined, a god's spirit now grants as a gift.
But the travellers too are well-directed, not lacking
    Garlands enough or song, carry the sanctified stave

Vollgeschmükt mit Trauben und Laub bei sich und der Fichte
    Schatten; von Dorfe zu Dorf jauchzt es, von Tage zu Tag,
Und wie Wagen, bespannt mit freiem Wilde, so ziehn die
    Berge voran und so träget und eilet der Pfad.

2

Aber meinest du nun, es haben die Thore vergebens
    Aufgethan und den Weg freudig die Götter gemacht?
Und es schenken umsonst zu des Gastmahls Fülle die Guten
    Nebst dem Weine noch auch Beeren und Honig und Obst?
Schenken das purpurne Licht zu Festgesängen und kühl und
    Ruhig zu tieferem Freundesgespräche die Nacht?
Hält ein Ernsteres dich, so spars dem Winter und willst du
    Freien, habe Geduld, Freier beglüket der Mai.
Jezt ist Anderes Noth, jezt komm' und feire des Herbstes
    Alte Sitte, noch jezt blühet die Edle mit uns.
Eins nur gilt für den Tag, das Vaterland und des Opfers
    Festlicher Flamme wirft jeder sein Eigenes zu.
Darum kränzt der gemeinsame Gott umsäuselnd das Haar uns,
    Und den eigenen Sinn schmelzet, wie Perlen, der Wein.
Diß bedeutet der Tisch, der geehrte, wenn, wie die Bienen,
    Rund um den Eichbaum, wir sizen und singen um ihn,
Diß der Pokale Klang, und darum zwinget die wilden
    Seelen der streitenden Männer zusammen der Chor.

3

Aber damit uns nicht, gleich Allzuklugen, entfliehe
    Diese neigende Zeit, komm' ich entgegen sogleich,
Bis an die Grenze des Lands, wo mir den lieben Geburtsort
    Und die Insel des Stroms blaues Gewässer umfließt.
Heilig ist mir der Ort, an beiden Ufern, der Fels auch,
    Der mit Garten und Haus grün aus den Wellen sich hebt.
Dort begegnen wir uns; o gütiges Licht! wo zuerst mich
    Deiner gefühlteren Stralen mich einer betraf.

Dort begann und beginnt das liebe Leben von neuem;
    Aber des Vaters Grab seh' ich und weine dir schon?
Wein' und halt' und habe den Freund und höre das Wort, das
    Einst mir in himmlischer Kunst Leiden der Liebe geheilt.

Richly adorned with grapes and foliage and shade of the fir-tree;
    As their cheer spills from village to village, from day to day,
And like chariots drawn by wild beasts, so the mountains
    Surge ahead and so leads and so hurries the path.

2

Could it be, you think, that for nothing the gods have thrown open
    Gates that were closed and in vain opened a pathway for joy?
That for nothing the kindly ones add to the plentiful banquet
    Not only wine but more, berries and honey and fruit?
Give us the crimson light for festive music and, cool and
    Calm for discourse more deep, friendship's, the blessing of night?
If you have graver cares on your mind, save them up for the winter,
    If it's a wife you want, wait, lovers do better in May.
Now there is need for other things. Come and celebrate autumn's
    Ancient ritual, for still we and great Earth are in flower.
One thing only counts for this day, the fatherland; each of us offers
    Up to the festive flame that which is his to cast in.
Therefore the communal god is a wind in our hair, is a garland,
    And our selfhood, each one's, melts, as a pearl does, in wine.
This the table betokens, the honoured, whenever, as bees do,
    Round the oak-tree we sit, singing and clustering there,
This the ringing of cups, and for this are the fierce souls of fighters
    Brought into unison, fused by a common compulsion, the choir's.

3

Not, though, like those all too clever, letting it slip and elude me,
    Now that the season declines, promptly to meet it I come,
Up to the bordering regions, our country's, where bluish water
    Laps the birthplace I love, laps the small river-girt isle.
Holy the place is to me, and on both of the banks, as the rock is
    Which with garden and house rises all green from the waves.
There, kindly light, we can meet, for there too for the first time
    One of your rays, the more felt, touching me, marked what it
        touched.
There began and begins anew now a life truly living;
    Yet my father's grave – one little look, and I burst into tears?
Weep and go to and cling to the friend and hear the same word that
    Once amid heavenly art healed all the anguish of love.

Andres erwacht! ich muß die Landesheroën ihm nennen,
    Barbarossa! dich auch, gütiger Kristoph, und dich,
Konradin! wie du fielst, so fallen Starke, der Epheu
    Grünt am Fels und die Burg dekt das bacchantische Laub,
Doch Vergangenes ist, wie Künftiges heilig den Sängern,
    Und in Tagen des Herbsts sühnen die Schatten wir uns.

4

So der Gewaltgen gedenk und des herzerhebenden Schiksaals,
    Thatlos selber, und leicht, aber vom Aether doch auch
Angeschauet und fromm, wie die Alten, die göttlicherzognen
    Freudigen Dichter ziehn freudig das Land wir hinauf.
Groß ist das Werden umher. Dort von den äußersten Bergen

    Stammen der Jünglinge viel, steigen die Hügel herab.
Quellen rauschen von dort und hundert geschäfftige Bäche,
    Kommen bei Tag und Nacht nieder und bauen das Land.
Aber der Meister pflügt die Mitte des Landes, die Furchen
    Ziehet der Nekarstrom, ziehet den Seegen herab.
Und es kommen mit ihm Italiens Lüfte, die See schikt
    Ihre Wolken, sie schikt prächtige Sonnen mit ihm.
Darum wächset uns auch fast über das Haupt die gewaltge
    Fülle, denn hieher ward, hier in die Ebne das Gut
Reicher den Lieben gebracht, den Landesleuten, doch neidet
    Keiner an Bergen dort ihnen die Gärten, den Wein
Oder das üppige Gras und das Korn und die glühenden Bäume,
    Die am Wege gereiht über den Wanderern stehn.

5

Aber indeß wir schaun und die mächtige Freude durchwandeln,
    Fliehet der Weg und der Tag uns, wie den Trunkenen, hin.
Denn mit heiligem Laub umkränzt erhebet die Stadt schon
    Die gepriesene, dort leuchtend ihr priesterlich Haupt.
Herrlich steht sie und hält den Rebenstab und die Tanne
    Hoch in die seeligen purpurnen Wolken empor.
Sei uns hold! dem Gast und dem Sohn, o Fürstin der Heimath!
    Glükliches Stutgard, nimm freundlich den Fremdling mir auf!
Immer hast du Gesang mit Flöten und Saiten gebilligt,
    Wie ich glaub' und des Lieds kindlich Geschwäz und der Mühn

Other things waken. I name, I have to, my homeland's own heroes,
　　Barbarossa, and you, kind-hearted Christoph, and you,
Conradin, how you fell, strong men fall so, and the ivy
　　Green on the rock and the keep dark with bacchantical leaves,
But things past, like the things yet to come, are holy to singers,
　　And on autumnal days shades we seek out and appease.

4

So recalling those powerful ones and the fate that raises our hearts up,
　　Deedless ourselves, of small weight, but by Aether nevertheless
Not overlooked, devout as the ancients, those god-instructed
　　Joy-breathing poets, we joyously roam through the land.
Great is the growth all around. Up there, from the bordering
　　mountains,
　　Many a youth descends, born there, the gentle-sloped hills,
Well-springs bubble from there and a hundred brooklets, as busy,
　　Come both by day and by night into the lowlands, to till.
But the master it is who ploughs up the heartland and centre,
　　Draws the furrows himself, Neckar, draws blessings down.
With him there come the Italian breezes, the sea sends
　　Clouds for his way and sends sunshine, magnificent suns.
Hence it is that almost over our heads it may rise then,
　　Superabundant, for here, down to the lowlands the wealth
Even more richly was brought to the favoured, the region's people,
　　Yet not one of the mountain-folk ever begrudges them wine,
Gardens, luxuriant grass or their corn or their glowing
　　Fruit-trees that line the roads, shadow us wayfaring men.

5

While we look on, though, and move through profusion of gladness,
　　Both our road and our day pass like a drunken man's, flee.
For already the city, the famed, with garlands of hallowing leafage,
　　Luminous over there, raises her reverend head.
Glorious she stands with thyrsus held up and the fir-tree
　　High, as far as the clouds, crimsonly blessed by the light.
Now be gracious to us! To the guest and your son now returning,
　　Fortunate Stuttgart, with grace welcome the stranger for me.
Anthems with flute or with strings you have always approved of,
　　So I believe, and the song's childlike babble, and sweet

Süße Vergessenheit bei gegenwärtigem Geiste,
    Drum erfreuest du auch gerne den Sängern das Herz.
Aber ihr, ihr Größeren auch, ihr Frohen, die allzeit
    Leben und walten, erkannt, oder gewaltiger auch,
Wenn ihr wirket und schafft in heiliger Nacht und allein herrscht
    Und allmächtig empor ziehet ein ahnendes Volk,
Bis die Jünglinge sich der Väter droben erinnern,
    Mündig und hell vor euch steht der besonnene Mensch –

6

Engel des Vaterlands! o ihr, vor denen das Auge,
    Sei's auch stark und das Knie bricht dem vereinzelten Mann,
Daß er halten sich muß an die Freund' und bitten die Theuern,
    Daß sie tragen mit ihm all die beglükende Last,
Habt, o Gütige, Dank für den und alle die Andern,
    Die mein Leben, mein Gut unter den Sterblichen sind.
Aber die Nacht kommt! laß uns eilen, zu feiern das Herbstfest
    Heut noch! voll ist das Herz, aber das Leben ist kurz,

Und was uns der himmlische Tag zu sagen geboten,
    Das zu nennen, mein Schmidt! reichen wir beide nicht aus.

Trefliche bring' ich dir und das Freudenfeuer wird hoch auf
    Schlagen und heiliger soll sprechen das kühnere Wort.
Siehe! da ist es rein! und des Gottes freundliche Gaaben
    Die wir theilen, sie sind zwischen den Liebenden nur.
Anderes nicht – o kommt! o macht es wahr! denn allein ja
    Bin ich und niemand nimmt mir von der Stirne den Traum?
Kommt und reicht, ihr Lieben, die Hand! das möge genug seyn,
    Aber die größere Lust sparen dem Enkel wir auf.

Rest from labour, oblivion that's entered with minds that are wakeful,
    Always prepared to please singers and gladden their hearts.
Yet you still greater ones, you the serene who at all times
    Live and hold sway, whether known, named, or more mighty still
When in holy night you're at work and create and alone you
    Rule and almightily draw upward a people by signs,
Till the young remember their forefathers gathered above them,
    And before you, matured, stands a more thoughtful mankind –

        6
Angels of home, our country's, O you in whose presence the vision,
    Strong though it be, and the knees break of a man on his own,
So that to friends he must look for support and the dear ones
    That they may help him to bear all the great load of his joy,
Kind ones, accept my thanks for him and for all the others
    Who are my life and my wealth here amid mortals, on earth.
Night is coming, though. Let us hurry to celebrate autumn
    This very day. Though the heart, full, may forget it, our lives are
        short
And those things that a heavenly day has commanded we speak of,
    Them to make known, dear friend, is too much both for you and for
        me.
Excellent men I bring you, the fire of rejoicing high up shall
    Leap and more sacredly then speak the more venturesome word.
Look, there it's pure. And the generous presents the god gives,
    When we share them, cohere only when love makes the bond.
Nothing else can. Oh, come, then, and make it true. For alone I
    Am, after all; and can none lift the bad dream from my brow?
Come, dear friends, and hold out your hands. Let that token suffice us,
    While for the grandson we save greater and deeper delight.

Brod und Wein

AN HEINZE

I

Rings um ruhet die Stadt; still wird die erleuchtete Gasse,
    Und, mit Fakeln geschmükt, rauschen die Wagen hinweg.
Satt gehn heim von Freuden des Tags zu ruhen die Menschen,
    Und Gewinn und Verlust wäget ein sinniges Haupt
Wohlzufrieden zu Haus; leer steht von Trauben und Blumen,
    Und von Werken der Hand ruht der geschäfftige Markt.
Aber das Saitenspiel tönt fern aus Gärten; vieleicht, daß
    Dort ein Liebendes spielt oder ein einsamer Mann
Ferner Freunde gedenkt und der Jugendzeit; und die Brunnen
    Immerquillend und frisch rauschen an duftendem Beet.
Still in dämmriger Luft ertönen geläutete Gloken,
    Und der Stunden gedenk rufet ein Wächter die Zahl.
Jezt auch kommet ein Wehn und regt die Gipfel des Hains auf,
    Sieh! und das Schattenbild unserer Erde, der Mond
Kommet geheim nun auch; die Schwärmerische, die Nacht kommt,
    Voll mit Sternen und wohl wenig bekümmert um uns,
Glänzt die Erstaunende dort, die Fremdlingin unter den Menschen
    Über Gebirgeshöhn traurig und prächtig herauf.

2

Wunderbar ist die Gunst der Hocherhabnen und niemand
    Weiß von wannen und was einem geschiehet von ihr.
So bewegt sie die Welt und die hoffende Seele der Menschen,
    Selbst kein Weiser versteht, was sie bereitet, denn so
Will es der oberste Gott, der sehr dich liebet, und darum
    Ist noch lieber, wie sie, dir der besonnene Tag.
Aber zuweilen liebt auch klares Auge den Schatten
    Und versuchet zu Lust, eh' es die Noth ist, den Schlaf,
Oder es blikt auch gern ein treuer Mann in die Nacht hin,
    Ja, es ziemet sich ihr Kränze zu weihn und Gesang,
Weil den Irrenden sie geheiliget ist und den Todten,
    Selber aber besteht, ewig, in freiestem Geist.
Aber sie muß uns auch, daß in der zaudernden Weile,
    Daß im Finstern für uns einiges Haltbare sei,

Bread and Wine
TO HEINSE

1

Round us the town is at rest; the street, in pale lamplight, falls quiet
   And, their torches ablaze, coaches rush through and away.
People go home to rest, replete with the day and its pleasures,
   There to weigh up in their heads, pensive, the gain and the loss,
Finding the balance good; stripped bare now of grapes and of flowers,
   As of their handmade goods, quiet the market stalls lie.
But faint music of strings comes drifting from gardens; it could be
   Someone in love who plays there, could be a man all alone
Thinking of distant friends, the days of his youth; and the fountains,
   Ever welling and new, plash amid balm-breathing beds.
Church bells ring; every stroke hangs still in the quivering half-light
   And the watchman calls out, mindful, no less, of the hour.
Now a breeze rises too and ruffles the crests of the coppice,
   Look, and in secret our globe's shadowy image, the moon,
Slowly is rising too; and Night, the fantastical, comes now
   Full of stars and, I think, little concerned about us,
Night, the astonishing, there, the stranger to all that is human,
   Over the mountain-tops mournful and gleaming draws on.

2

Marvellous is her favour, Night's, the exalted, and no one
   Knows what it is or whence comes all she does and bestows.
So she works on the world and works on our souls ever hoping,
   Not even wise men can tell what is her purpose, for so
God, the Highest, has willed, who very much loves you, and therefore
   Dearer even than Night reasoning Day is to you.
Nonetheless there are times when clear eyes too love the shadows,
   Tasting sleep uncompelled, trying the pleasure it gives,
Or a loyal man too will gaze into Night and enjoy it,
   Yes, and rightly to her garlands we dedicate, hymns,
Since to all those astray, the mad and the dead, she is sacred,
   Yet herself remains firm, always, her spirit most free.
But to us in her turn, so that in the wavering moment,
   Deep in the dark there shall be something at least that endures,

Uns die Vergessenheit und das Heiligtrunkene gönnen,
    Gönnen das strömende Wort, das, wie die Liebenden, sei,
Schlummerlos und vollern Pokal und kühneres Leben,
    Heilig Gedächtniß auch, wachend zu bleiben bei Nacht.

3

Auch verbergen umsonst das Herz im Busen, umsonst nur
    Halten den Muth noch wir, Meister und Knaben, denn wer
Möcht' es hindern und wer möcht' uns die Freude verbieten?
    Göttliches Feuer auch treibet, bei Tag und bei Nacht,
Aufzubrechen. So komm! daß wir das Offene schauen,
    Daß ein Eigenes wir suchen, so weit es auch ist.
Fest bleibt Eins; es sei um Mittag oder es gehe
    Bis in die Mitternacht, immer bestehet ein Maas,
Allen gemein, doch jeglichem auch ist eignes beschieden,
    Dahin gehet und kommt jeder, wohin er es kann.
Drum! und spotten des Spotts mag gern frohlokkender Wahnsinn,
    Wenn er in heiliger Nacht plözlich die Sänger ergreift.
Drum an den Isthmos komm! dorthin, wo das offene Meer rauscht
    Am Parnaß und der Schnee delphische Felsen umglänzt,
Dort ins Land des Olymps, dort auf die Höhe Cithärons,
    Unter die Fichten dort, unter die Trauben, von wo
Thebe drunten und Ismenos rauscht im Lande des Kadmos,
    Dorther kommt und zurük deutet der kommende Gott.

4

Seeliges Griechenland! du Haus der Himmlischen alle,
    Also ist wahr, was einst wir in der Jugend gehört?
Festlicher Saal! der Boden ist Meer! und Tische die Berge,
    Wahrlich zu einzigem Brauche vor Alters gebaut!
Aber die Thronen, wo? die Tempel, und wo die Gefäße,
    Wo mit Nectar gefüllt, Göttern zu Lust der Gesang?
Wo, wo leuchten sie denn, die fernhintreffenden Sprüche?
    Delphi schlummert und wo tönet das große Geschik?
Wo ist das schnelle? wo brichts, allgegenwärtigen Glüks voll
    Donnernd aus heiterer Luft über die Augen herein?
Vater Aether! so riefs und flog von Zunge zu Zunge
    Tausendfach, es ertrug keiner das Leben allein;

Holy drunkenness she must grant and frenzied oblivion,
    Grant the on-rushing word, sleepless as lovers are too,
And a wine-cup more full, a life more intense and more daring,
    Holy remembrance too, keeping us wakeful at night.

      3

And in vain we conceal our hearts deep within us, in vain we,
    Master and novice alike, still keep our courage in check.
For who now would stop us, who would forbid us rejoicing?
    Day-long, night-long we're urged on by a fire that's divine.
Urged to be gone. Let us go, then! Off to see open spaces,
    Where we may seek what is ours, distant, remote though it be!
One thing is sure even now: at noon or just before midnight,
    Whether it's early or late, always a measure exists,
Common to all, though his own to each one is also allotted,
    Each of us makes for the place, reaches the place that he can.
Well, then, may jubilant madness laugh at those who deride it,
    When in hallowed Night poets are seized by its power;
Off to the Isthmus, then! To land where wide open the sea roars
    Near Parnassus and snow glistens on Delphian rocks;
Off to Olympian regions, up to the heights of Cithaeron,
    Up to the pine-trees there, up to the grapes, from which rush
Thebe down there and Ismenos, loud in the country of Cadmus:
    Thence has come and back there points the god who's to come.

      4

Happy land of the Greeks, you house of them all, of the Heavenly,
    So it is true what we heard then, in the days of our youth?
Festive hall, whose floor is ocean, whose tables are mountains,
    Truly, in time out of mind built for a purpose unique!
But the thrones, where are they? Where are the temples, the vessels,
    Where, to delight the gods, brim-full with nectar, the songs?
Where, then, where do they shine, the oracles winged for far targets?
    Delphi's asleep, and where now is great fate to be heard?
Where is the swift? And full of joy omnipresent, where does it
    Flash upon dazzled eyes, thundering fall from clear skies?
Father Aether! one cried, and tongue after tongue took it up then,
    Thousands, no man could bear life so intense on his own;

Ausgetheilet erfreut solch Gut und getauschet, mit Fremden,

    Wirds ein Jubel, es wächst schlafend des Wortes Gewalt
Vater! heiter! und hallt, so weit es gehet, das uralt
    Zeichen, von Eltern geerbt, treffend und schaffend hinab.
Denn so kehren die Himmlischen ein, tiefschütternd gelangt so
    Aus den Schatten herab unter die Menschen ihr Tag.

    5

Unempfunden kommen sie erst, es streben entgegen
    Ihnen die Kinder, zu hell kommet, zu blendend das Glük,
Und es scheut sie der Mensch, kaum weiß zu sagen ein Halbgott,
    Wer mit Nahmen sie sind, die mit den Gaaben ihm nahn.
Aber der Muth von ihnen ist groß, es füllen das Herz ihm
    Ihre Freuden und kaum weiß er zu brauchen das Gut,
Schafft, verschwendet und fast ward ihm Unheiliges heilig,
    Das er mit seegnender Hand thörig und gütig berührt.
Möglichst dulden die Himmlischen diß; dann aber in Wahrheit
    Kommen sie selbst und gewohnt werden die Menschen des Glüks
Und des Tags und zu schaun die Offenbaren, das Antliz
    Derer, welche, schon längst Eines und Alles genannt,
Tief die verschwiegene Brust mit freier Genüge gefüllet,
    Und zuerst und allein alles Verlangen beglükt;
So ist der Mensch; wenn da ist das Gut, und es sorget mit Gaaben
    Selber ein Gott für ihn, kennet und sieht er es nicht.
Tragen muß er, zuvor; nun aber nennt er sein Liebstes,
    Nun, nun müssen dafür Worte, wie Blumen, entstehn.

    6

Und nun denkt er zu ehren in Ernst die seeligen Götter,
    Wirklich und wahrhaft muß alles verkünden ihr Lob.
Nichts darf schauen das Licht, was nicht den Hohen gefället,
    Vor den Aether gebührt müßigversuchendes nicht.
Drum in der Gegenwart der Himmlischen würdig zu stehen,
    Richten in herrlichen Ordnungen Völker sich auf
Untereinander und baun die schönen Tempel und Städte
    Vest und edel, sie gehn über Gestaden empor –
Aber wo sind sie? wo blühn die Bekannten, die Kronen des Festes?

    Thebe welkt und Athen; rauschen die Waffen nicht mehr

Shared, such wealth gives delight and later, when bartered with
    strangers,
  Turns to rapture; the word gathers new strength when asleep:
Father! Clear light! and long resounding it travels, the ancient
  Sign handed down, and far, striking, creating, rings out.
So do the Heavenly enter, shaking the deepest foundations,
  Only so from the gloom down to mankind comes their Day.

5

Unperceived at first they come, and only the children
  Surge towards them, too bright, dazzling, this joy enters in,
So that men are afraid, a demigod hardly can tell yet
  Who they are, and name those who approach him with gifts.
Yet their courage is great, his heart soon is full of their gladness
  And he hardly knows what's to be done with such wealth,
Busily runs and wastes it, almost regarding as sacred
  Trash which his blessing hand foolishly, kindly has touched.
This, while they can, the Heavenly bear with; but then they appear in
  Truth, in person, and now men grow accustomed to joy,
And to Day, and the sight of godhead revealed, and their faces –
  One and All long ago, once and for all, they were named –
Who with free self-content had deeply suffused silent bosoms,
  From the first and alone satisfied every desire.
Such is man; when the wealth is there, and no less than a god in
  Person tends him with gifts, blind he remains, unaware.
First he must suffer; but now he names his most treasured possession,
  Now for it words like flowers leaping alive he must find.

6

Now in earnest he means to honour the gods who have blessed him,
  Now in truth and in deed all must re-echo their praise.
Nothing must see the light but what to those high ones is pleasing,
  Idle and bungled work never for Aether was fit.
So, to be worthy and stand unashamed in the heavenly presence,
  Nations rise up and soon, gloriously ordered, compete
One with the other in building beautiful temples and cities,
  Noble and firm they tower high above river and sea –
Only, where are they? Where thrive those famed ones, the festival's
    garlands?
  Athens is withered, and Thebes; now do no weapons ring out

In Olympia, nicht die goldnen Wagen des Kampfspiels,
    Und bekränzen sich denn nimmer die Schiffe Korinths?
Warum schweigen auch sie, die alten heilgen Theater?
    Warum freuet sich denn nicht der geweihete Tanz?
Warum zeichnet, wie sonst, die Stirne des Mannes ein Gott nicht,
    Drükt den Stempel, wie sonst, nicht dem Getroffenen auf?
Oder er kam auch selbst und nahm des Menschen Gestalt an
    Und vollendet' und schloß tröstend das himmlische Fest.

7

Aber Freund! wir kommen zu spät. Zwar leben die Götter,
    Aber über dem Haupt droben in anderer Welt.
Endlos wirken sie da und scheinens wenig zu achten,
    Ob wir leben, so sehr schonen die Himmlischen uns.
Denn nicht immer vermag ein schwaches Gefäß sie zu fassen,
    Nur zu Zeiten erträgt göttliche Fülle der Mensch.
Traum von ihnen ist drauf das Leben. Aber das Irrsaal
    Hilft, wie Schlummer und stark machet die Noth und die Nacht,
Biß daß Helden genug in der ehernen Wiege gewachsen,
    Herzen an Kraft, wie sonst, ähnlich den Himmlischen sind.
Donnernd kommen sie drauf. Indessen dünket mir öfters
    Besser zu schlafen, wie so ohne Genossen zu seyn,
So zu harren und was zu thun indeß und zu sagen,
    Weiß ich nicht und wozu Dichter in dürftiger Zeit?
Aber sie sind, sagst du, wie des Weingotts heilige Priester,
    Welche von Lande zu Land zogen in heiliger Nacht.

8

Nemlich, als vor einiger Zeit, uns dünket sie lange,
    Aufwärts stiegen sie all, welche das Leben beglükt,
Als der Vater gewandt sein Angesicht von den Menschen,
    Und das Trauern mit Recht über der Erde begann,
Als erschienen zu lezt ein stiller Genius, himmlisch
    Tröstend, welcher des Tags Ende verkündet' und schwand,
Ließ zum Zeichen, daß einst er da gewesen und wieder

    Käme, der himmlische Chor einige Gaaben zurük,
Derer menschlich, wie sonst, wir uns zu freuen vermöchten,
    Denn zur Freude, mit Geist, wurde das Größre zu groß

In Olympia, nor now those chariots, all golden, in games there,
   And no longer are wreaths hung on Corinthian ships?
Why are they silent too, the theatres, ancient and hallowed?
   Why not now does the dance celebrate, consecrate joy?
Why no more does a god imprint on the brow of a mortal
   Struck, as by lightning, the mark, brand him, as once he would do?
Else he would come himself, assuming a shape that was human,
   And, consoling the guests, crowned and concluded the feast.

        7
But, my friend, we have come too late. Though the gods are living,
   Over our heads they live, up in a different world.
Endlessly there they act and, such is their kind wish to spare us,
   Little they seem to care whether we live or do not.
For not always a frail, a delicate vessel can hold them,
   Only at times can our kind bear the full impact of gods.
Ever after our life is dream about them. But frenzy,
   Wandering, helps, like sleep; Night and distress make us strong
Till in that cradle of steel heroes enough have been fostered,
   Hearts in strength can match heavenly strength as before.
Thundering then they come. But meanwhile too often I think it's
   Better to sleep than to be friendless as we are, alone,
Always waiting, and what to do or to say in the meantime
   I don't know, and who wants poets at all in lean years?
But they are, you say, like those holy ones, priests of the wine-god
   Who in holy Night roamed from one place to the next.

        8
For, when some time ago now – to us it seems ages –
   Up rose all those by whom life had been brightened, made glad,
When the Father had turned his face from the sight of us mortals
   And all over the earth, rightly, they started to mourn,
Lastly a Genius had come, dispensing heavenly comfort,
   He who proclaimed the Day's end, then himself went away,
Then, as a token that once they had been down here and once more
      would
   Come, the heavenly choir left a few presents behind,
Gifts in which now as ever humanly men might take pleasure,
   Since for spiritual joy great things had now grown too great

Unter den Menschen und noch, noch fehlen die Starken zu höchsten
Freuden, aber es lebt stille noch einiger Dank.
Brod ist der Erde Frucht, doch ists vom Lichte geseegnet,
Und vom donnernden Gott kommet die Freude des Weins.
Darum denken wir auch dabei der Himmlischen, die sonst
Da gewesen und die kehren in richtiger Zeit,
Darum singen sie auch mit Ernst die Sänger den Weingott
Und nicht eitel erdacht tönet dem Alten das Lob.

9

Ja! sie sagen mit Recht, er söhne den Tag mit der Nacht aus,
Führe des Himmels Gestirn ewig hinunter, hinauf,
Allzeit froh, wie das Laub der immergrünenden Fichte,
Das er liebt, und der Kranz, den er von Epheu gewählt,
Weil er bleibet und selbst die Spur der entflohenen Götter
Götterlosen hinab unter das Finstere bringt.
Was der Alten Gesang von Kindern Gottes geweissagt,
Siehe! wir sind es, wir; Frucht von Hesperien ists!
Wunderbar und genau ists als an Menschen erfüllet,
Glaube, wer es geprüft! aber so vieles geschieht,
Keines wirket, denn wir sind herzlos, Schatten, bis unser
Vater Aether erkannt jeden und allen gehört.
Aber indessen kommt als Fakelschwinger des Höchsten
Sohn, der Syrier, unter die Schatten herab.
Seelige Weise sehns; ein Lächeln aus der gefangnen
Seele leuchtet, dem Licht thauet ihr Auge noch auf.
Sanfter träumet und schläft in Armen der Erde der Titan,
Selbst der neidische, selbst Cerberus trinket und schläft.

Heimkunft

AN DIE VERWANDTEN

1

Drinn in den Alpen ists noch helle Nacht und die Wolke,
Freudiges dichtend, sie dekt drinnen das gähnende Thal.
Dahin, dorthin toset und stürzt die scherzende Bergluft,
Schroff durch Tannen herab glänzet und schwindet ein Stral.

Here, among men, and even now there's a lack of those strong for
    Joy's extremity, but silent some thanks do live on.
Bread is a fruit of Earth, yet touched by the blessing of sunlight,
    From the thundering god issues the gladness of wine.
Therefore in tasting them we think of the Heavenly who once were
    Here and shall come again, come when their advent is due;
Therefore also the poets in serious hymns to the wine-god,
    Never idly devised, sound that most ancient one's praise.

9

Yes, and rightly they say he reconciles Day with our Night-time,
    Leads the stars of the sky upward and down without end,
Always glad, like the living boughs of the evergreen pine tree
    Which he loves, and the wreath wound out of ivy for choice
Since it lasts and conveys the trace of the gods now departed
    Down to the godless below, into the midst of their gloom.
What of the children of God was foretold in the songs of the ancients,
    Look, we are it, ourselves; fruit of Hesperia it is!
Strictly it has come true, fulfilled as in men by a marvel,
    Let those who have seen it believe! Much, however, occurs,
Nothing succeeds, because we are heartless, mere shadows until our
    Father Aether, made known, recognized, fathers us all.
Meanwhile, though, to us shadows comes the Son of the Highest,
    Comes the Syrian and down into our gloom bears his torch.
Blissful, the wise men see it; in souls that were captive there gleams a
    Smile, and their eyes shall yet thaw in response to the light.
Dreams more gentle and sleep in the arms of Earth lull the Titan,
    Even that envious one, Cerberus, drinks and lies down.

Homecoming
TO HIS RELATIVES

I

There in the Alps a gleaming night still delays and, composing
    Portents of gladness, the cloud covers a valley agape.
This way, that way roars and rushes the breeze of the mountains,
    Teasing, sheer through the firs falls a bright beam, and is lost.

Langsam eilt und kämpft das freudigschauernde Chaos,
  Jung an Gestalt, doch stark, feiert es liebenden Streit
Unter den Felsen, es gährt und wankt in den ewigen Schranken,
  Denn bacchantischer zieht drinnen der Morgen herauf.
Denn es wächst unendlicher dort das Jahr und die heilgen
  Stunden, die Tage, sie sind kühner geordnet, gemischt.
Dennoch merket die Zeit der Gewittervogel und zwischen
  Bergen, hoch in der Luft weilt er und rufet den Tag.
Jezt auch wachet und schaut in der Tiefe drinnen das Dörflein
  Furchtlos, Hohem vertraut, unter den Gipfeln hinauf.
Wachstum ahnend, denn schon, wie Blize, fallen die alten
  Wasserquellen, der Grund unter den Stürzenden dampft,
Echo tönet umher, und die unermeßliche Werkstatt
  Reget bei Tag und Nacht, Gaaben versendend, den Arm.

2

Ruhig glänzen indeß die silbernen Höhen darüber,
  Voll mit Rosen ist schon droben der leuchtende Schnee.
Und noch höher hinauf wohnt über dem Lichte der reine
  Seelige Gott vom Spiel heiliger Stralen erfreut.

Stille wohnt er allein und hell erscheinet sein Antliz,
  Der ätherische scheint Leben zu geben geneigt,
Freude zu schaffen, mit uns, wie oft, wenn, kundig des Maases,
  Kundig der Athmenden auch zögernd und schonend der Gott
Wohlgediegenes Glük den Städten und Häußern und milde
  Reegen, zu öffnen das Land, brütende Wolken, und euch,
Trauteste Lüfte dann, euch, sanfte Frühlinge, sendet,

  Und mit langsamer Hand Traurige wieder erfreut,
Wenn er die Zeiten erneut, der Schöpferische, die stillen
  Herzen der alternden Menschen erfrischt und ergreifft,
Und hinab in die Tiefe wirkt, und öffnet und aufhellt,
  Wie ers liebet, und jezt wieder ein Leben beginnt,
Anmuth blühet, wie einst, und gegenwärtiger Geist kömmt,
  Und ein freudiger Muth wieder die Fittige schwellt.

Slowly it hurries and wars, this Chaos trembling with pleasure,
    Young in appearance, but strong, celebrates here amid rocks
Loving discord, and seethes, shakes in its bounds that are timeless,
    For more bacchantically now morning approaches within.
For more endlessly there the year expands, and the holy
    Hours and the days in there more boldly are ordered and mixed.
Yet the bird of thunder marks and observes the time, and
    High in the air, between peaks, hangs and calls out a new day.
Now, deep inside, the small village also awakens and fearless
    Looks at the summits around, long now familiar with height;
Growth it foreknows, for already ancient torrents like lightning
    Crash, and the ground below steams with the spray of their fall.
Echo sounds all around and, measureless, tireless the workshop,
    Sending out gifts, is astir, active by day and by night.

2

Quiet, meanwhile, above, the silvery peaks lie aglitter,
    Full of roses up there, flushed with dawn's rays, lies the snow.
Even higher, beyond the light, does the pure, never clouded
    God have his dwelling, whom beams, holy, make glad with their
        play.
Silent, alone he dwells, and bright his countenance shines now,
    He, the aethereal one, seems kindly, disposed to give life,
Generate joys, with us men, as often when, knowing the measure,
    Knowing those who draw breath, hesitant, sparing the God
Sends well-allotted fortune both to the cities and houses,
    Showers to open the land, gentle, and you, brooding clouds,
You, then, most dearly loved breezes, followed by temperate
        springtime,
    And with a slow hand once more gladdens us mortals grown sad,
When he renews the seasons, he, the creative, and quickens,
    Moves once again those hearts weary and numb with old age,
Works on the lowest depths to open them up and to brighten
    All, as he loves to do; so now does life bud anew,
Beauty abounds, as before, and spirit is present, returned now,
    And a joyful zest urges furled wings to unfold.

3

Vieles sprach ich zu ihm, denn, was auch Dichtende sinnen
  Oder singen, es gilt meistens den Engeln und ihm;
Vieles bat ich, zu lieb dem Vaterlande, damit nicht
  Ungebeten uns einst plözlich befiele der Geist;
Vieles für euch auch, die im Vaterlande besorgt sind,

  Denen der heilige Dank lächelnd die Flüchtlinge bringt,
Landesleute! für euch, indessen wiegte der See mich,
  Und der Ruderer saß ruhig und lobte die Fahrt.
Weit in des Sees Ebene wars Ein freudiges Wallen
  Unter den Seegeln und jezt blühet und hellet die Stadt
Dort in der Frühe sich auf, wohl her von schattigen Alpen
  Kommt geleitet und ruht nun in dem Hafen das Schiff.
Warm ist das Ufer hier und freundlich offene Thale,
  Schön von Pfaden erhellt grünen und schimmern mich an.
Gärten stehen gesellt und die glänzende Knospe beginnt schon,
  Und des Vogels Gesang ladet den Wanderer ein.
Alles scheinet vertraut, der vorübereilende Gruß auch
  Scheint von Freunden, es scheint jegliche Miene verwandt.

4

Freilich wohl! das Geburtsland ists, der Boden der Heimath,
  Was du suchest, es ist nahe, begegnet dir schon.
Und umsonst nicht steht, wie ein Sohn, am wellenumrauschten
  Thor' und siehet und sucht liebende Nahmen für dich,
Mit Gesang ein wandernder Mann, glükseeliges Lindau!
  Eine der gastlichen Pforten des Landes ist diß,
Reizend hinauszugehn in die vielversprechende Ferne,
  Dort, wo die Wunder sind, dort, wo das göttliche Wild
Hoch in die Ebnen herab der Rhein die verwegene Bahn bricht,
  Und aus Felsen hervor ziehet das jauchzende Thal,
Dort hinein, durchs helle Gebirg, nach Komo zu wandern,

  Oder hinab, wie der Tag wandelt, den offenen See;
Aber reizender mir bist du, geweihete Pforte!
  Heimzugehn; wo bekannt blühende Wege mir sind,

3

Much I said to him; for whatever the poets may ponder,
    Sing, it mostly concerns either the angels or him.
Much I besought, on my country's behalf, lest unbidden one day the
    Spirit should suddenly come, take us by storm unprepared;
Much, too, for your sake to whom, though troubled now in our
        country,
    Holy gratitude brings fugitives back with a smile,
Fellow Germans, for your sake! Meanwhile the lake gently rocked me,
    Calmly the boatman sat, praising the weather, the breeze.
Out on the level lake one impulse of joy had enlivened
    All the sails, and at last, there in a new day's first hour
Brightening, the town unfurls, and safely conveyed from the shadows
    Cast by the Alps, now the boat glides to its mooring and rests.
Warm the shore is here, and valleys open in welcome,
    Pleasantly lit by paths, greenly allure me and gleam.
Gardens, forgathered, lie here and already the dew-laden bud breaks
    And a bird's early song welcomes the traveller home.
All seems familiar; even the word or the nod caught in passing
    Seems like a friend's, every face looks like a relative's face.

4

And no wonder! Your native country and soil you are walking,
    What you seek, it is near, now comes to meet you halfway.
Nor by mere chance like a son a wandering man now stands gazing
    Here by the wavelet-loud gate, looking for names to convey
Love to you in his poem, Lindau, the favoured and happy!
    Not the least of our land's many hospitable doors,
Urging men to go out allured by the promise of distance,
    Go where the wonders are, go where that godlike wild beast,
High up the Rhine blasts his reckless way to the plains of the lowlands,
    Where out of rocks at last bursts the lush valley's delight,
Wander in there, through the sunlit mountain range, making for
        Como,
    Or, as the day drifts on, drift on the wide open lake;
Yet, you door that are hallowed, me much more strongly you urge to
    Make for home where I know blossoming pathways and lanes,

Dort zu besuchen das Land und die schönen Thale des Nekars,
    Und die Wälder, das Grün heiliger Bäume, wo gern
Sich die Eiche gesellt mit stillen Birken und Buchen,
    Und in Bergen ein Ort freundlich gefangen mich nimmt.

5

Dort empfangen sie mich. O Stimme der Stadt, der Mutter!
    O du triffest, du regst Langegelerntes mir auf!
Dennoch sind sie es noch! noch blühet die Sonn' und die Freud' euch,
    O ihr Liebsten! und fast heller im Auge, wie sonst.
Ja! das Alte noch ists! Es gedeihet und reifet, doch keines
    Was da lebet und liebt, lässet die Treue zurük.
Aber das Beste, der Fund, der unter des heiligen Friedens
    Bogen lieget, er ist Jungen und Alten gespart.
Thörig red ich. Es ist die Freude. Doch morgen und künftig
    Wenn wir gehen und schaun draußen das lebende Feld
Unter den Blüthen des Baums, in den Feiertagen des Frühlings
    Red' und hoff' ich mit euch vieles, ihr Lieben! davon.
Vieles hab' ich gehört vom großen Vater und habe

    Lange geschwiegen von ihm, welcher die wandernde Zeit
Droben in Höhen erfrischt, und waltet über Gebirgen
    Der gewähret uns bald himmlische Gaaben und ruft
Hellern Gesang und schikt viel gute Geister. O säumt nicht,
    Kommt, Erhaltenden ihr! Engel des Jahres! und ihr,

6

Engel des Haußes, kommt! in die Adern alle des Lebens,
    Alle freuend zugleich, theile das Himmlische sich!
Adle! verjünge! damit nichts Menschlichgutes, damit nicht
    Eine Stunde des Tags ohne die Frohen und auch
Solche Freude, wie jezt, wenn Liebende wieder sich finden,
    Wie es gehört für sie, schiklich geheiliget sei.
Wenn wir seegnen das Mahl, wen darf ich nennen und wenn wir
    Ruhn vom Leben des Tags, saget, wie bring' ich den Dank?
Nenn' ich den Hohen dabei? Unschikliches liebet ein Gott nicht,

    Ihn zu fassen, ist fast unsere Freude zu klein.
Schweigen müssen wir oft; es fehlen heilige Nahmen,
    Herzen schlagen und doch bleibet die Rede zurük?

There to visit the fields and the Neckar's beautiful valleys,
    And the woods, green leaves holy to me, where the oak
Does not disdain to consort with quiet birches and beeches,
    Where amid mountains one place holds me, a captive content.

5

There they too receive me. Voice of my town, of my mother!
    How to your sound respond things that I learned long ago!
Yet they are still themselves! More radiantly, almost, than ever,
    Dearest ones, in your eyes joy and the sun are alight.
Yes, it's all what it was. It thrives and grows ripe, but no creature
    Living and loving there ever abandons its faith.
But the best thing of all, the find that's been saved up beneath the
    Holy rainbow of peace, waits for the young and the old.
Like a fool I speak. In my joy. But tomorrow and later
    When we go outside, look at the living green field
Under the trees in blossom, on holidays due in the springtime,
    Much of those things with you, dear ones, I'll speak and I'll hope.
Much in the meantime I've heard of him, the great Father, and long
      now
    I have kept silent about him who on summits renews
Wandering Time up above and governs the high mountain ranges,
    Him who soon now will grant heavenly gifts and calls forth
Song more effulgent, and sends us many good spirits. No longer
    Wait now, preservers, the year's angels, O come now, and you,

6

Angels, too, of our house, re-enter the veins of all life now,
    Gladdening all at once, let what is heavenly be shared!
Make us noble and new! Till nothing that's humanly good, no
    Hour of the day without them, them the most joyful, or such
Joy as now too is known when lovers return to each other,
    Passes, as fitting for them, hallowed as angels demand.
When we bless the meal, whose name may I speak, and when late we
    Rest from the life of each day, tell me, to whom give my thanks?
Him, the most High, should I name then? A god does not love what's
      unseemly,
    Him to embrace and to hold our joy is too small.
Silence often behoves us: deficient in names that are holy,
    Hearts may beat high, while the lips hesitate, wary of speech?

Aber ein Saitenspiel leiht jeder Stunde die Töne,
  Und erfreuet vieleicht Himmlische, welche sich nahn.
Das bereitet und so ist auch beinahe die Sorge
  Schon befriediget, die unter das Freudige kam.
Sorgen, wie diese, muß, gern oder nicht, in der Seele
  Tragen ein Sänger und oft, aber die anderen nicht.

Yet a lyre to each hour lends the right mode, the right music,
   And, it may be, delights heavenly ones who draw near.
This make ready, and almost nothing remains of the care that
   Darkened our festive day, troubled the promise of joy.
Whether he like it or not, and often, a singer must harbour
   Cares like these in his soul; not, though, the wrong sore of cares.

THE HYMNS
(1799–1803)

Lebensalter

Ihr Städte des Euphrats!
Ihr Gassen von Palmyra!
Ihr Säulenwälder in der Eb'ne der Wüste,
Was seid ihr?
Euch hat die Kronen,
Dieweil ihr über die Gränze
Der Othmenden seid gegangen,
Von Himmlischen der Rauchdampf und
Hinweg das Feuer genommen;
Jezt aber siz' ich unter Wolken, darin
Ein jedes eine Ruh' hat eigen, unter
Wohleingerichteten Eichen, auf
Der Heide des Rehs, und fremd
Erscheinen und gestorben mir
Der Seeligen Geister.

Hälfte des Lebens

Mit gelben Birnen hänget
Und voll mit wilden Rosen
Das Land in den See,
Ihr holden Schwäne,
Und trunken von Küssen
Tunkt ihr das Haupt
Ins heilignüchterne Wasser.

Weh mir, wo nehm' ich, wenn
Es Winter ist, die Blumen, und wo
Den Sonnenschein,
Und Schatten der Erde?
Die Mauern stehn
Sprachlos und kalt, im Winde
Klirren die Fahnen.

The Ages of Life

You cities of Euphrates,
You streets at Palmyra,
You forests of pillars in the desert plain,
What are you?
Your crests, as you passed beyond
The bounds of those who breathe,
By smoke of heavenly powers and
By fire were taken away;
But now I sit beneath clouds, in which
Peculiar quiet comes to each one, beneath
A pleasing order of oak-trees, on
The heath where the roe-deer feed, and strange
To me, remote and dead seem
The souls of the blessèd.

Half of Life

With yellow pears hangs down
And full of wild roses
The land into the lake,
You loving swans,
And drunk with kisses
You dip your heads
Into water, the holy-and-sober.

But oh, where shall I find
When winter comes, the flowers, and where
The sunshine
And shade of the earth?
The walls loom
Speechless and cold, in the wind
Weathercocks clatter.

Der Winkel von Hahrdt

Hinunter sinket der Wald,
Und Knospen ähnlich, hängen
Einwärts die Blätter, denen
Blüht unten auf ein Grund,
Nicht gar unmündig.
Da nemlich ist Ulrich
Gegangen; oft sinnt, über den Fußtritt,
Ein groß Schiksaal
Bereit, an übrigem Orte.

Wie wenn am Feiertage . . .

Wie wenn am Feiertage, das Feld zu sehn
Ein Landmann geht, des Morgens, wenn
Aus heißer Nacht die kühlenden Blize fielen
Die ganze Zeit und fern noch tönet der Donner,
In sein Gestade wieder tritt der Strom,
Und frisch der Boden grünt
Und von des Himmels erfreuendem Reegen
Der Weinstok trauft und glänzend
In stiller Sonne stehn die Bäume des Haines:

So stehn sie unter günstiger Witterung
Sie die kein Meister allein, die wunderbar
Allgegenwärtig erzieht in leichtem Umfangen
Die mächtige, die göttlichschöne Natur.
Drum wenn zu schlafen sie scheint zu Zeiten des Jahrs
Am Himmel oder unter den Pflanzen oder den Völkern
So trauert der Dichter Angesicht auch,
Sie scheinen allein zu seyn, doch ahnen sie immer.
Denn ahnend ruhet sie selbst auch.

Jezt aber tagts! Ich harrt und sah es kommen,
Und was ich sah, das Heilige sei mein Wort.
Denn sie, sie selbst, die älter denn die Zeiten

The Nook at Hardt

Down slopes the forest
And, bud-like, inward
Hang the leaves, for which
Down below a ground blossoms forth,
Quite able to speak for itself.
For there Ulrich
Once walked; and often, over the footprint,
A great destiny ponders,
Made ready, on the residual site.

As on a holiday . . .

As on a holiday, to see the field
A countryman goes out, at morning, when
Out of hot night the cooling flashes had fallen
For hours on end, and thunder still rumbles afar,
The river enters its banks once more,
New verdure sprouts from the soil,
And with the gladdening rain of heaven
The grapevine drips, and gleaming
In tranquil sunlight stand the trees of the grove:

So now in favourable weather they stand
Whom no mere master teaches, but in
A light embrace, miraculously omnipresent,
God-like in power and beauty, Nature brings up.
So when she seems to be sleeping at times of the year
Up in the sky or among plants or the peoples,
The poets' faces likewise are sad,
They seem to be alone, but are always divining,
For divining too she herself is at rest.

But now day breaks! I waited and saw it come,
And what I saw, the hallowed, my word shall convey,
For she, she herself, who is older than the ages

Und über die Götter des Abends und Orients ist,
Die Natur ist jezt mit Waffenklang erwacht,
Und hoch vom Aether bis zum Abgrund nieder
Nach vestem Geseze, wie einst, aus heiligem Chaos gezeugt,
Fühlt neu die Begeisterung sich,
Die Allerschaffende wieder.

Und wie im Aug' ein Feuer dem Manne glänzt,
Wenn hohes er entwarf; so ist
Von neuem an den Zeichen, den Thaten der Welt jezt
Ein Feuer angezündet in Seelen der Dichter.
Und was zuvor geschah, doch kaum gefühlt,
Ist offenbar erst jezt,
Und die uns lächelnd den Aker gebauet,
In Knechtsgestalt, sie sind erkannt,
Die Allebendigen, die Kräfte der Götter.

Erfrägst du sie? im Liede wehet ihr Geist
Wenn es der Sonne des Tags und warmer Erd
Entwächst, und Wettern, die in der Luft, und andern
Die vorbereiteter in Tiefen der Zeit,
Und deutungsvoller, und vernehmlicher uns
Hinwandeln zwischen Himmel und Erd und unter den Völkern.
Des gemeinsamen Geistes Gedanken sind,
Still endend in der Seele des Dichters.

Daß schnellbetroffen sie, Unendlichem
Bekannt seit langer Zeit, von Erinnerung
Erbebt, und ihr, von heilgem Stral entzündet,
Die Frucht in Liebe geboren, der Götter und Menschen Werk
Der Gesang, damit er beiden zeuge, glükt.
So fiel, wie Dichter sagen, da sie sichtbar
Den Gott zu sehen begehrte, sein Bliz auf Semeles Haus
Und die göttlichgetroffne gebahr,
Die Frucht des Gewitters, den heiligen Bacchus.

Und daher trinken himmlisches Feuer jezt
Die Erdensöhne ohne Gefahr.
Doch uns gebührt es, unter Gottes Gewittern,
Ihr Dichter! mit entblößtem Haupte zu stehen

And higher than the gods of Orient and Occident,
Nature has now awoken amid the clang of arms,
And from high Aether down to the low abyss,
According to fixed law, begotten, as in the past, on holy Chaos,
Delight, the all-creative,
Delights in self-renewal.

And as a fire gleams in the eye of that man
Who has conceived a lofty design,
Once more by the tokens, the deeds of the world now
A fire has been lit in the souls of the poets.
And that which happened before, but hardly was felt,
Only now is manifest,
And they who smiling worked our fields for us,
Assuming the shape of labourers, now are known,
The all-alive, all-animating powers of the gods.

Do you ask where they are? In song their spirit wafts
When from the sun of day and from warm soil
It grows, and storms that are in the air, and others
That, more prepared in the depths of time,
More full of meaning and more audible to us,
Drift on between Heaven and Earth and amid the peoples.
The thoughts of the communal spirit they are,
And quietly come to rest in the poet's soul,

So that quickly struck and long familiar
To infinite powers, it shakes
With recollection and kindled by
The holy ray, that fruit conceived in love, the work of gods and men,
To bear witness to both, the song succeeds.
So once, the poets tell, when she desired to see
The god in person, visible, did his lightning fall
On Semele's house, and the divinely struck gave birth to
The thunder-storm's fruit, to holy Bacchus.

And hence it is that without danger now
The sons of Earth drink heavenly fire.
Yet, fellow poets, us it behoves to stand
Bareheaded beneath God's thunder-storms,

Des Vaters Stral, ihn selbst, mit eigner Hand
Zu fassen und dem Volk ins Lied
Gehüllt die himmlische Gaabe zu reichen.
Denn sind nur reinen Herzens,
Wie Kinder, wir, sind schuldlos unsere Hände,

   Des Vaters Stral, der reine versengt es nicht
Und tieferschüttert, die Leiden des Stärkeren
Mitleidend, bleibt in den hochherstürzenden Stürmen

Des Gottes, wenn er nahet, das Herz doch fest.
Doch weh mir! wenn von

Weh mir!

   Und sag ich gleich,

Ich sei genaht, die Himmlischen zu schauen,
Sie selbst, sie werfen mich tief unter die Lebenden
Den falschen Priester, ins Dunkel, daß ich
Das warnende Lied den Gelehrigen singe.
Dort

Am Quell der Donau

   Denn, wie wenn hoch von der herrlichgestimmten, der Orgel
Im heiligen Saal,
Reinquillend aus den unerschöpflichen Röhren,
Das Vorspiel, wekend, des Morgens beginnt
Und weitumher, von Halle zu Halle,
Der erfrischende nun, der melodische Strom rinnt,
Bis in den kalten Schatten das Haus
Von Begeisterungen erfüllt,
Nun aber erwacht ist, nun, aufsteigend ihr,
Der Sonne des Fests, antwortet

To grasp the Father's ray, no less, with our own two hands
And, wrapping in song the heavenly gift,
To offer it to the people.
For if only we are pure in heart,
Like children, and our hands are guiltless,

 The Father's ray, the pure, will not sear our hearts
And, deeply convulsed, and sharing his sufferings
Who is stronger than we are, yet in the far-flung down-rushing storms
      of
The God, when he draws near, will the heart stand fast.
But, oh, my shame! when of

My shame!

   And let me say at once

That I approached to see the Heavenly,
And they themselves cast me down, deep down
Below the living, into the dark cast down
The false priest that I am, to sing,
For those who have ears to hear, the warning song.
There

At the Source of the Danube

 For as when high from the gloriously voiced, the organ
Within a holy hall
Untainted welling from inexhaustible pipes,
The prelude, awakening men, rings out in the morning
And far and wide, from mansion to mansion,
Now pours the refreshing, the melodious current,
Down to the chilly shadows even filling
The house with inspirations,
But now awake and rising to it, to
The sun of celebration, responds the

Der Chor der Gemeinde; so kam
Das Wort aus Osten zu uns,
Und an Parnassos Felsen und am Kithäron hör' ich
O Asia, das Echo von dir und es bricht sich
Am Kapitol und jählings herab von den Alpen

Kommt eine Fremdlingin sie
Zu uns, die Erwekerin,
Die menschenbildende Stimme.

Da faßt' ein Staunen die Seele
Der Getroffenen all und Nacht
War über den Augen der Besten.
Denn vieles vermag
Und die Fluth und den Fels und Feuersgewalt auch
Bezwinget mit Kunst der Mensch
Und achtet, der Hochgesinnte, das Schwerdt
Nicht, aber es steht
Vor Göttlichem der Starke niedergeschlagen,

Und gleichet dem Wild fast; das,
Von süßer Jugend getrieben,
Schweift rastlos über die Berg'
Und fühlet die eigene Kraft
In der Mittagshizze. Wenn aber
Herabgeführt, in spielenden Lüften,
Das heilige Licht, und mit dem kühleren Stral
Der freudige Geist kommt zu
Der seeligen Erde, dann erliegt es, ungewohnt
Des Schönsten und schlummert wachenden Schlaf,
Noch ehe Gestirn naht. So auch wir. Denn manchen erlosch
Das Augenlicht schon vor den göttlichgesendeten Gaben,

Den freundlichen, die aus Ionien uns,
Auch aus Arabia kamen, und froh ward
Der theuern Lehr' und auch der holden Gesänge
Die Seele jener Entschlafenen nie,
Doch einige wachten. Und sie wandelten oft
Zufrieden unter euch, ihr Bürger schöner Städte,
Beim Kampfspiel, wo sonst unsichtbar der Heros

Community's choir – so the word
Came down to us from the East,
And by the rocks of Parnassus and by Cithaeron,
O Asia, I hear the echo of you, and it breaks
Upon the Capitol and sudden down from the Alps

    A stranger it comes
To us, that quickening word,
The voice that moulds and makes human.

    Amazement then took hold of
The souls of all who were struck, and night
Obscured the eyes of the best men.
For much can our kind
Accomplish, and flood and rock and even the might of fire
With art can subdue,
Nor, noble in mind, recoils from
The sword-blade, but faced with powers divine
The strong will stand abashed,

    And almost are like the beast of the wilds; which
Impelled by sweet youth
Roams restless over the hills
And feels its own strength in
The noonday heat. But when,
Led down, in frolicking breezes,
The holy light, and with its cool beam
The joyful spirit descend
To blessèd Earth, it succumbs, unfamiliar
With utmost beauty, and drowses in waking sleep,
Though stars are not rising yet. So it is with us. For many's
The man whose vision went out in face of those god-sent gifts,

    The kindly, that from Ionia came
To us, from Arabia too, and never
The souls of these now gone to their rest were glad
Of precious doctrine nor yet of the lovely songs,
Yet some kept awake. And often, you citizens
Of beautiful towns, they walked among you contented,
At Games, where once in secret the hero

Geheim bei Dichtern saß, die Ringer schaut und lächelnd
Pries, der gepriesene, die müßigernsten Kinder.
Ein unaufhörlich Lieben wars und ists.
Und wohlgeschieden, aber darum denken
Wir aneinander doch, ihr Fröhlichen am Isthmos,
Und am Cephyß und am Taygetos,
Auch eurer denken wir, ihr Thale des Kaukasos,
So alt ihr seid, ihr Paradiese dort
Und deiner Patriarchen und deiner Propheten,

O Asia, deiner Starken, o Mutter!
Die furchtlos vor den Zeichen der Welt,
Und den Himmel auf Schultern und alles Schiksaal,
Taglang auf Bergen gewurzelt,
Zuerst es verstanden,
Allein zu reden
Zu Gott. Die ruhn nun. Aber wenn ihr
Und diß ist zu sagen,
Ihr Alten all, nicht sagtet, woher?
Wir nennen dich, heiliggenöthiget, nennen,
Natur! dich wir, und neu, wie dem Bad entsteigt
Dir alles Göttlichgeborne.

Zwar gehn wir fast, wie die Waisen;
Wohl ists, wie sonst, nur jene Pflege nicht wieder;
Doch Jünglinge, der Kindheit gedenk,
Im Haußhe sind auch diese nicht fremde.
Sie leben dreifach, eben wie auch
Die ersten Söhne des Himmels.
Und nicht umsonst ward uns
In die Seele die Treue gegeben.
Nicht uns, auch Eures bewahrt sie,
Und bei den Heiligtümern, den Waffen des Worts
Die scheidend ihr den Ungeschikteren uns
Ihr Schiksaalssöhne, zurükgelassen

Invisible sat with poets, watched the wrestlers and smiling
Praised – he, the recipient of praise – those idly serious children.
An endless loving it was, and is.
And rightly severed; yet nonetheless we think
Of one another still, you happy ones at the Isthmus,
And by Cephissus and by Taygetus,
And you we think of, vales of the Caucasus,
However ancient, you paradises there,
And of your patriarchs and of your prophets,

    O Asia, of all your mighty ones, Mother,
Who fearless in face of the signs of the world,
The heavens heaped upon shoulders and all manner of fate,
For days were rooted on mountains
And were the first who knew
How to speak alone
To God. These now are at rest. But if,
And this must be said, you ancients
Would never tell us whence it is that
We name you, under a holy compulsion we
Now name you Nature, and new, as from a bath
From you emerges all that's divinely born.

    True, like orphans almost we walk;
Though much is what it was, that tutelage now is lacking;
But youths who are mindful of childhood,
These are not strangers now in the house.
Threefold they live, as did
The very first-born of Heaven.
And not for nothing in
Our souls was loyalty fixed.
Not us alone, but that which is yours it preserves
And in those holy relics, the weapons of the word
Which, parting, you sons of Fate,
You left behind for us the less fated,
The less endowed with rightness,

Ihr guten Geister, da seid ihr auch,
Oftmals, wenn einen dann die heilige Wolk umschwebt,
Da staunen wir und wissens nicht zu deuten.
Ihr aber würzt mit Nectar uns den Othem
Und dann frohloken wir oft oder es befällt uns
Ein Sinnen, wenn ihr aber einen zu sehr liebt
Er ruht nicht, bis er euer einer geworden.
Darum, ihr Gütigen! umgebet mich leicht,
Damit ich bleiben möge, denn noch ist manches zu singen,
Jezt aber endiget, seeligweinend,
Wie eine Sage der Liebe,
Mir der Gesang, und so auch ist er
Mir, mit Erröthen, Erblassen,
Von Anfang her gegangen. Doch Alles geht so.

Die Wanderung

Glükseelig Suevien, meine Mutter,
Auch du, der glänzenderen, der Schwester
Lombarda drüben gleich,
Von hundert Bächen durchflossen!
Und Bäume genug, weißblühend und röthlich,
Und dunklere, wild, tiefgrünenden Laubs voll
Und Alpengebirg der Schweiz auch überschattet
Benachbartes dich; denn nah dem Heerde des Haußes
Wohnst du, und hörst, wie drinnen
Aus silbernen Opferschaalen
Der Quell rauscht, ausgeschüttet
Von reinen Händen, wenn berührt

Von warmen Stralen
Krystallenes Eis und umgestürzt
Vom leichtanregenden Lichte
Der schneeige Gipfel übergießt die Erde
Mit reinestem Wassser. Darum ist
Dir angeboren die Treue. Schwer verläßt,

You kindly spirits, in them you are present too,
And often, when the holy cloud is hovering round a man,
We are amazed and do not know the meaning.
But you with nectar spice our breath, and then
We may exult or else a pondering befalls us,
But when too greatly you love a man
He finds no rest till he is one of you.
Therefore, benign ones, surround me lightly,
And let me stay a while, for much remains to be sung;
But now, like a legend of love,
Blissfully weeping, my song
Comes to its end, and so too,
Amid blushing and blanching, it's gone
With me from the start. But that is how all things go.

The Journey

Most happy Swabia, my mother,
Whom like the more shining, your sister
Lombarda over there
A hundred rivulets thread!
And trees enough, white-flowering and reddish
And darker ones, wild, full of deeply greening foliage,
And alpine ranges of Switzerland cast their shade
On you, the neighbouring, too; for close to the hearth of
The house you dwell, and hear how within
From silver votive vessels
The well-spring purls, poured out
By hands that are pure, when touched

By warming beams
The crystalline ice and, tumbled
By gently quickening light
The snowy summit drenches the earth
With purest water. Therefore
Innate in you is loyalty. For whatever dwells

Was nahe dem Ursprung wohnet, den Ort.
Und deine Kinder, die Städte,
Am weithindämmernden See,
An Nekars Weiden, am Rheine,
Sie alle meinen, es wäre
Sonst nirgend besser zu wohnen.

Ich aber will dem Kaukasos zu!
Denn sagen hört' ich
Noch heut in den Lüften:
Frei sei'n, wie Schwalben, die Dichter.
Auch hat mir ohnediß
In jüngeren Tagen Eines vertraut,
Es seien vor alter Zeit
Die Eltern einst, das deutsche Geschlecht,
Still fortgezogen von Wellen der Donau
Am Sommertage, da diese
Sich Schatten suchten, zusammen
Mit Kindern der Sonn'
Am schwarzen Meere gekommen;
Und nicht umsonst sei diß
Das gastfreundliche genennet.

Denn, als sie erst sich angesehen,
Da nahten die Anderen erst; dann sazten auch
Die Unseren sich neugierig unter den Ölbaum.
Doch als sich ihre Gewande berührt,
Und keiner vernehmen konnte
Die eigene Rede des andern, wäre wohl
Entstanden ein Zwist, wenn nicht aus Zweigen herunter
Gekommen wäre die Kühlung,
Die Lächeln über das Angesicht
Der Streitenden öfters breitet, und eine Weile
Sahn still sie auf, dann reichten sie sich
Die Hände liebend einander. Und bald

Vertauschten sie Waffen und all
Die lieben Güter des Haußes,
Vertauschten das Wort auch und es wünschten

Close to its origin is loath to leave the place.
And so your children, the towns by
The distantly glimmering lake,
By Neckar's willows and by the Rhine,
All these affirm that
No dwelling-place could be better.

But I am bound for the Caucasus!
For only today
I heard it said in the breezes
That free as swallows the poets are.
Besides, when I was younger
Someone confided to me
That time out of mind our parents,
The German people, had quietly
Departed from the waves of the Danube
One summer day, and when those
Were looking for shade, had met
With children of the Sun
Not far from the Black Sea's beaches;
And not for nothing that sea
Was called the hospitable.

For when they first exchanged glances
It was the others who first approached; only then did
Our people too, inquisitive, seat themselves under the olive tree.
But when their garments had touched
And none could comprehend
The other's peculiar speech, a quarrel
Might well have begun, if coolness had not fallen
Upon them from the boughs,
Eliciting a smile, as it often does,
From faces that frowned with anger; and for a while
They raised their eyes in silence, then
They lovingly held out their hands. And soon

They bartered weapons and all
The precious goods of the house,
And bartered the word, and not in vain

Die freundlichen Väter umsonst nichts
Beim Hochzeitjubel den Kindern.
Denn aus den heiligvermählten
Wuchs schöner, denn Alles,
Was vor und nach
Von Menschen sich nannt', ein Geschlecht auf. Wo,
Wo aber wohnt ihr, liebe Verwandten,
Daß wir das Bündniß wiederbegehn
Und der theuern Ahnen gedenken?

   Dort an den Ufern, unter den Bäumen
Ionias, in Ebenen des Kaisters,
Wo Kraniche, des Aethers froh,
Umschlossen sind von fernhindämmernden Bergen;
Dort wart auch ihr, ihr Schönsten! oder pfleget
Der Inseln, die mit Wein bekränzt,
Voll tönten von Gesang; noch andere wohnten
Am Tayget, am vielgepriesnen Himettos,
Die blühten zulezt; doch von
Parnassos Quell bis zu des Tmolos
Goldglänzenden Bächen erklang
Ein ewiges Lied; so rauschten
Damals die Wälder und all
Die Saitenspiele zusamt
Von himmlischer Milde gerühret.

   O Land des Homer!
Am purpurnen Kirschbaum oder wenn
Von dir gesandt im Weinberg mir
Die jungen Pfirsiche grünen,
Und die Schwalbe fernher kommt und vieles erzählend
An meinen Wänden ihr Haus baut, in
Den Tagen des Mais, auch unter den Sternen
Gedenk' ich, o Ionia, dein! doch Menschen
Ist Gegenwärtiges lieb. Drum bin ich
Gekommen, euch, ihr Inseln, zu sehn, und euch,
Ihr Mündungen der Ströme, o ihr Hallen der Thetis,
Ihr Wälder, euch, und euch, ihr Wolken des Ida!

Did kindly fathers bless there with any wish
Their children's jubilant nuptials.
For from the sacredly married
There sprang a people more beautiful
Than all who before or since
Have called themselves human. But where,
O where do you dwell, dear kin,
So that we may renew the pact
And remember those worthy forebears?

    There on the shores, beneath the trees of
Ionia, on plains of the Cayster
Where, gladdened by Aether, cranes
Are surrounded by mountains distantly glimmering,
There you were also, loveliest ones, or haunted
The islands garlanded with vines
And filled with resonant song; or others dwelled
Beside Taygetus, by widely praised Hymettus,
These were the last to thrive; but from
Parnassus' well-spring down to the brooks,
Gold-glittering, of Tmolus rang
An everlasting melody; so then did all
The holy woods and all
The lyres in unison resound
When heavenly gentleness touched them.

    O land of Homer!
Beside the crimson cherry-tree, or when,
Your emissaries, in the vineyard for me
The young green peaches cling
And the swallow comes from afar and, telling many a tale,
Builds on my walls her house,
In May-time days, and also under the stars,
Ionia, I think of you! And that is why
I've come to see you, you islands, and you,
The river estuaries, halls of Thetis,
You woods, and you, the clouds over Ida!

Doch nicht zu bleiben gedenk ich.
Unfreundlich ist und schwer zu gewinnen
Die Verschlossene, der ich entkommen, die Mutter.
Von ihren Söhnen einer, der Rhein,
Mit Gewalt wollt' er ans Herz ihr stürzen und schwand
Der Zurükgestoßene, niemand weiß, wohin, in die Ferne.
Doch so nicht wünscht' ich gegangen zu seyn,
Von ihr und nur, euch einzuladen,
Bin ich zu euch, ihr Gratien Griechenlands,
Ihr Himmelstöchter, gegangen,
Daß, wenn die Reise zu weit nicht ist,
Zu uns ihr kommet, ihr Holden!

Wenn milder athmen die Lüfte,
Und liebende Pfeile der Morgen
Uns Allzugedultigen schikt,
Und leichte Gewölke blühn
Uns über den schüchternen Augen,
Dann werden wir sagen, wie kommt
Ihr, Charitinnen, zu Wilden?
Die Dienerinnen des Himmels
Sind aber wunderbar,
Wie alles Göttlichgeborne.
Zum Traume wirds ihm, will es Einer
Beschleichen und straft den, der
Ihm gleichen will mit Gewalt;
Oft überraschet es einen,
Der eben kaum es gedacht hat.

Germanien

Nicht sie, die Seeligen, die erschienen sind,
Die Götterbilder in dem alten Lande,
Sie darf ich ja nicht rufen mehr, wenn aber
Ihr heimatlichen Wasser! jezt mit euch
Des Herzens Liebe klagt, was will es anders,
Das Heiligtrauernde? Denn voll Erwartung liegt
Das Land und als in heißen Tagen

Yet not to stay I am minded.
Ungracious and intractable is
The taciturn whom I fled from, my mother.
One of her sons, the Rhine,
By force once tried to rush to her heart and vanished,
Repulsed, no one knows where, in the distance;
Not so, however, would I depart
From her and only to invite you here,
You Graces of Hellas, you daughters
Of Heaven, I went to you,
So that, if the journey is not too far,
You may come to us, beloved ones.

When milder the breezes blow
And morning sends loving arrows
To us the all too patient,
And downy clouds like blossom
Drift over our diffident eyes,
Then we shall say, how did
You Charities come to barbarians?
But like all that's divinely born,
The servant girls of Heaven
Are strange, miraculous.
If someone tries to grasp it by stealth, he holds
A dream in his hand, and him who uses force
To make himself its peer, it punishes.
Yet often it takes by surprise
A man whose mind it has hardly entered.

Germania

Not them, the blessed, who once appeared,
Those images of gods in the ancient land,
Them, it is true, I may not now invoke, but if,
You waters of my homeland, now with you
The love of my heart laments, what else does it want, in
Its hallowed sadness? For full of expectation lies
The country, and as though it had been lowered

Herabgesenkt, umschattet heut
Ihr Sehnenden! uns ahnungsvoll ein Himmel.
Voll ist er von Verheißungen und scheint
Mir drohend auch, doch will ich bei ihm bleiben,
Und rükwärts soll die Seele mir nicht fliehn
Zu euch, Vergangene! die zu lieb mir sind.
Denn euer schönes Angesicht zu sehn,
Als wärs, wie sonst, ich fürcht' es, tödlich ists,
Und kaum erlaubt, Gestorbene zu weken.

Entflohene Götter! auch ihr, ihr gegenwärtigen, damals
Wahrhaftiger, ihr hattet eure Zeiten!
Nichts läugnen will ich hier und nichts erbitten.
Denn wenn es aus ist, und der Tag erloschen
Wohl trifts den Priester erst, doch liebend folgt
Der Tempel und das Bild ihm auch und seine Sitte
Zum dunkeln Land und keines mag noch scheinen.
Nur als von Grabesflammen, ziehet dann
Ein goldner Rauch, die Sage drob hinüber,
Und dämmert jezt uns Zweifelnden um das Haupt,
Und keiner weiß, wie ihm geschieht. Er fühlt
Die Schatten derer, so gewesen sind,
Die Alten, so die Erde neubesuchen.
Denn die da kommen sollen, drängen uns,
Und länger säumt von Göttermenschen
Die heilige Schaar nicht mehr im blauen Himmel.

Schon grünet ja, im Vorspiel rauherer Zeit
Für sie erzogen das Feld, bereitet ist die Gaabe
Zum Opfermahl und Thal und Ströme sind
Weitoffen um prophetische Berge,
Daß schauen mag bis in den Orient
Der Mann und ihn von dort der Wandlungen viele bewegen.
Vom Aether aber fällt
Das treue Bild und Göttersprüche reegnen
Unzählbare von ihm, und es tönt im innersten Haine.
Und der Adler, der vom Indus kömmt,
Und über des Parnassos
Beschneite Gipfel fliegt, hoch über den Opferhügeln
Italias, und frohe Beute sucht

In sultry dogdays, on us a heaven today,
You yearning rivers, casts prophetic shade.
With promises it is fraught, and to me
Seems threatening too, yet I will stay with it,
And backward now my soul shall not escape
To you, the vanished, whom I love too much.
To look upon your beautiful brows, as though
They were unchanged, I am afraid, for deadly
And scarcely permitted it is to awaken the dead.

Gods who are fled! And you also, present still,
But once more real, you had your time, your ages!
No, nothing here I'll deny and ask no favours.
For when it's over, and Day's light gone out,
The priest is the first to be struck, but lovingly
The temple and the image and the cult
Follow him down into darkness, and none of them now may shine.
Only as from a funeral pyre henceforth
A golden smoke, the legend of it, drifts
And glimmers on around our doubting heads
And no one knows what's happening to him. He feels
The shadowy shapes of those who once were here,
The ancients, newly visiting the earth.
For those who are to come now jostle us,
Nor longer will that holy host of beings
Divinely human linger in azure Heaven.

Already, in the prelude of a rougher age
Raised up for them, the field grows green, prepared
Are offerings for the votive feast and valley
And rivers lie wide open round prophetic mountains,
So that into the very Orient
A man may look and thence be moved by many transformations.
But down from Aether falls
The faithful image, and words of gods rain down
Innumerable from it, and the innermost grove resounds.
And the eagle that comes from the Indus
And flies over the snow-covered peaks of
Parnassus, high above the votive hills
Of Italy, and seeks glad booty for

Dem Vater, nicht wie sonst, geübter im Fluge
Der Alte, jauchzend überschwingt er
Zulezt die Alpen und sieht die vielgearteten Länder.

   Die Priesterin, die stillste Tochter Gottes,
Sie, die zu gern in tiefer Einfalt schweigt,
Sie suchet er, die offnen Auges schaute,
Als wüßte sie es nicht, jüngst, da ein Sturm
Todtdrohend über ihrem Haupt ertönte;
Es ahnete das Kind ein Besseres,
Und endlich ward ein Staunen weit im Himmel
Weil Eines groß an Glauben, wie sie selbst,
Die seegnende, die Macht der Höhe sei;
Drum sandten sie den Boten, der, sie schnell erkennend,
Denkt lächelnd so: Dich, unzerbrechliche, muß
Ein ander Wort erprüfen und ruft es laut,
Der Jugendliche, nach Germania schauend:
»Du bist es, auserwählt,
Allliebend und ein schweres Glük
»Bist du zu tragen stark geworden,

   Seit damals, da im Walde verstekt und blühendem Mohn
Voll süßen Schlummers, trunkene, meiner du
Nicht achtetest, lang, ehe noch auch geringere fühlten
Der Jungfrau Stolz und staunten weß du wärst und woher,
Doch du es selbst nicht wußtest. Ich miskannte dich nicht,
Und heimlich, da du träumtest, ließ ich
Am Mittag scheidend dir ein Freundeszeichen,
Die Blume des Mundes zurük und du redetest einsam.
Doch Fülle der goldenen Worte sandtest du auch
Glükseelige! mit den Strömen und sie quillen unerschöpflich
In die Gegenden all. Denn fast, wie der heiligen,
Die Mutter ist von allem,
Die Verborgene sonst genannt von Menschen,
So ist von Lieben und Leiden
Und voll von Ahnungen dir
Und voll von Frieden der Busen.

The Father, not as he used to, more practised in flight,
That ancient one, exultant, over the Alps
Wings on at last and sees the diverse countries.

  The priestess, her, the quietest daughter of God,
Too fond of keeping silent in deep ingenuousness,
Her now he seeks, who open-eyed looked up
As though she did not know it, lately when a storm,
Threatening death, rang out above her head;
A better destiny the child divined,
And in the end amazement spread in heaven
Because one being was as great in faith
As they themselves, the blessing powers on high;
Therefore they sent the messenger, who, quick to recognize her,
Smilingly thus reflects: you the unbreakable
A different word must try, and then proclaims,
The youthful, looking towards Germania:
'Yes, it is you, elected
All-loving and to bear
A burdensome good fortune have grown strong,

  'Since, hidden in the woods and flowering poppies
Filled with sweet drowsiness, you, drunken, did not heed
Me for a long time, before lesser ones even felt
The virgin's pride, and marvelled whose you are and where from,
But you yourself did not know. Yet I did not misjudge you
And secretly, while you dreamed, at noon,
Departing I left a token of friendship,
The flower of the mouth behind, and lonely you spoke.
Yet you, the greatly blessed, with the rivers too
Dispatched a wealth of golden words, and they well unceasing
Into all regions now. For almost as is the holy,
The Mother of all things, upholder of the abyss,
Whom men at other times call the Concealed,
Now full of loves and sorrows
And full of presentiments
And full of peace is your bosom.

O trinke Morgenlüfte,
Biß daß du offen bist,
Und nenne, was vor Augen dir ist,
Nicht länger darf Geheimniß mehr
Das Ungesprochene bleiben,
Nachdem es lange verhüllt ist;
Denn Sterblichen geziemet die Schaam,
Und so zu reden die meiste Zeit,
Ist weise auch von Göttern.
Wo aber überflüssiger, denn lautere Quellen
Das Gold und ernst geworden ist der Zorn an dem Himmel,
Muß zwischen Tag und Nacht
Einsmals ein Wahres erscheinen.
Dreifach umschreibe du es,
Doch ungesprochen auch, wie es da ist,
Unschuldige, muß es bleiben.

O nenne Tochter du der heiligen Erd'
Einmal die Mutter. Es rauschen die Wasser am Fels
Und Wetter im Wald und bei dem Nahmen derselben
Tönt auf aus alter Zeit Vergangengöttliches wieder.
Wie anders ists! und rechthin glänzt und spricht
Zukünftiges auch erfreulich aus den Fernen.
Doch in der Mitte der Zeit
Lebt ruhig mit geweihter
Jungfräulicher Erde der Aether
Und gerne, zur Erinnerung, sind
Die unbedürftigen sie
Gastfreundlich bei den unbedürftgen
Bei deinen Feiertaggn
Germania, wo du Priesterin bist
Und wehrlos Rath giebst rings
Den Königen und den Völkern.

'O drink the morning breezes
Until you are opened up
And name what you see before you;
No longer now the unspoken
May remain a mystery
Though long it has been veiled;
For shame behoves us mortals
And most of the time to speak thus
Of gods indeed is wise.
But where more superabundant than purest well-springs
The gold has become and the anger in Heaven earnest,
For once between Day and Night must
A truth be made manifest.
Now threefold circumscribe it,
Yet unuttered also, just as you found it,
Innocent virgin, let it remain.

'Once only, daughter of holy Earth,
Pronounce your Mother's name. The waters roar on the rock
And thunderstorms in the wood, and at their name
Divine things past ring out from time immemorial.
How all is changed! And to the right there gleam
And speak things yet to come, joy-giving, from the distance.
Yet at the centre of Time
In peace with hallowed,
With virginal Earth lives Aether
And gladly, for remembrance, they
The never-needy dwell
Hospitably amid the never-needy,
Amid your holidays,
Germania, where you are priestess and
Defenceless proffer all round
Advice to the kings and the peoples.'

Der Rhein
AN ISAAK VON SINCLAIR

Im dunkeln Epheu saß ich, an der Pforte
Des Waldes, eben, da der goldene Mittag,
Den Quell besuchend, herunterkam
Von Treppen des Alpengebirgs,
Das mir die göttlichgebaute,
Die Burg der Himmlischen heißt
Nach alter Meinung, wo aber
Geheim noch manches entschieden
Zu Menschen gelanget; von da
Vernahm ich ohne Vermuthen
Ein Schiksaal, denn noch kaum
War mir im warmen Schatten
Sich manches beredend, die Seele
Italia zu geschweift
Und fernhin an die Küsten Moreas.

Jezt aber, drinn im Gebirg,
Tief unter den silbernen Gipfeln
Und unter fröhlichem Grün,
Wo die Wälder schauernd zu ihm,
Und der Felsen Häupter übereinander
Hinabschaun, taglang, dort
Im kältesten Abgrund hört'
Ich um Erlösung jammern
Den Jüngling, es hörten ihn, wie er tobt',
Und die Mutter Erd' anklagt',
Und den Donnerer, der ihn gezeuget,
Erbarmend die Eltern, doch
Die Sterblichen flohn von dem Ort,
Denn furchtbar war, da lichtlos er
In den Fesseln sich wälzte,
Das Rasen des Halbgotts.

The Rhine

TO ISAAK VON SINCLAIR

  Amid dark ivy I was sitting, at
The forest's gate, just as a golden noon,
To visit the well-spring there, came down
From steps of the Alpine ranges
Which, following ancient lore,
I call the divinely built,
The fortress of the Heavenly,
But where, determined in secret
Much even now reaches men; from there
Without surmise I heard
A destiny, for, debating
Now this, now that in the warm shade,
My soul had hardly begun
To make for Italy
And far away for the shores of Morea.

  But now, within the mountains,
Deep down below the silvery summits
And in the midst of gay verdure,
Where shuddering the forests
And the heads of rocks overlapping
Look down at him, all day
There in the coldest chasm
I heard the youth implore
Release; and full of pity his parents heard
Him rage there and accuse
His Mother Earth and the Thunderer
Who fathered him, but mortals
Fled from the place, for dreadful,
As without light he writhed
Within his fetters, was
The demigod's raving.

Die Stimme wars des edelsten der Ströme,
Des freigeborenen Rheins,
Und anderes hoffte der, als droben von den Brüdern,
Dem Tessin und dem Rhodanus,
Er schied und wandern wollt', und ungeduldig ihn
Nach Asia trieb die königliche Seele.
Doch unverständig ist
Das Wünschen vor dem Schiksaal.
Die Blindesten aber
Sind Göttersöhne. Denn es kennet der Mensch
Sein Haus und dem Thier ward, wo
Es bauen solle, doch jenen ist
Der Fehl, daß sie nicht wissen wohin?
In die unerfahrne Seele gegeben.

Ein Räthsel ist Reinentsprungenes. Auch
Der Gesang kaum darf es enthüllen. Denn
Wie du anfiengst, wirst du bleiben,
So viel auch wirket die Noth,
Und die Zucht, das meiste nemlich
Vermag die Geburt,
Und der Lichtstral, der
Dem Neugebornen begegnet.
Wo aber ist einer,
Um frei zu bleiben
Sein Leben lang, und des Herzens Wunsch
Allein zu erfüllen, so
Aus günstigen Höhn, wie der Rhein,
Und so aus heiligem Schoose
Glüklich geboren, wie jener?

Drum ist ein Jauchzen sein Wort.
Nicht liebt er, wie andere Kinder,
In Wikelbanden zu weinen;
Denn wo die Ufer zuerst
An die Seit ihm schleichen, die krummen,
Und durstig umwindend ihn,
Den Unbedachten, zu ziehn
Und wohl zu behüten begehren

The voice it was of the noblest of rivers,
Of freeborn Rhine,
And different were his hopes when up there from his brothers
Ticino and Rhodanus
He parted and longed to roam, and impatiently
His regal soul drove him on towards Asia.
Yet in the face of fate
Imprudent it is to wish.
The sons of gods, though,
Are blindest of all. For human beings know
Their house, and the animals
Where they must build, but in
Their inexperienced souls the defect
Of not knowing where was implanted.

A mystery are those of pure origin.
Even song may hardly unveil it.
For as you began, so you will remain,
And much as need can effect,
And breeding, still greater power
Adheres to your birth
And the ray of light
That meets the newborn infant.
But where is anyone
So happily born as the Rhine
From such propitious heights
And from so holy a womb,
To remain free
His whole life long and alone fulfil
His heart's desire, like him?

And that is why his word is a jubilant roar,
Nor is he fond, like other children,
Of weeping in swaddling bands;
For where the banks at first
Slink to his side, the crooked,
And greedily entwining him,
Desire to educate
And carefully tend the feckless

Im eigenen Zahne, lachend
Zerreißt er die Schlangen und stürzt
Mit der Beut und wenn in der Eil'
Ein Größerer ihn nicht zähmt,
Ihn wachsen läßt, wie der Bliz, muß er
Die Erde spalten, und wie Bezauberte fliehn
Die Wälder ihm nach und zusammensinkend die Berge.

Ein Gott will aber sparen den Söhnen
Das eilende Leben und lächelt,
Wenn unenthaltsam, aber gehemmt
Von heiligen Alpen, ihm
In der Tiefe, wie jener, zürnen die Ströme.
In solcher Esse wird dann
Auch alles Lautre geschmiedet,
Und schön ists, wie er drauf,
Nachdem er die Berge verlassen,
Stillwandelnd sich im deutschen Lande
Begnüget und das Sehnen stillt
Im guten Geschäffte, wenn er das Land baut
Der Vater Rhein und liebe Kinder nährt
In Städten, die er gegründet.

Doch nimmer, nimmer vergißt ers.
Denn eher muß die Wohnung vergehn,
Und die Sazung und zum Unbild werden
Der Tag der Menschen, ehe vergessen
Ein solcher dürfte den Ursprung
Und die reine Stimme der Jugend.
Wer war es, der zuerst
Die Liebesbande verderbt
Und Strike von ihnen gemacht hat?
Dann haben des eigenen Rechts
Und gewiß des himmlischen Feuers
Gespottet die Trozigen, dann erst
Die sterblichen Pfade verachtend
Verwegnes erwählt
Und den Göttern gleich zu werden getrachtet.

Within their teeth, he laughs,
Tears up the serpents and rushes
Off with his prey, and if in haste
A greater one does not tame him,
But lets him grow, like lightning he
Must rend the earth and like things enchanted
The forests join his flight and, collapsing, the mountains.

A god, however, wishes to spare his sons
A life so fleeting and smiles
When, thus intemperate but restrained
By holy Alps, the rivers
Like this one rage at him in the depth.
In such a forge, then, all
That's pure is given shape
And it is good to see
How then, after leaving the mountains,
Content with German lands he calmly
Moves on and stills his longing
In useful industry, when he tills the land,
Now Father Rhine, and supports dear children
In cities which he has founded.

Yet never, never does he forget.
For sooner the dwelling shall be destroyed,
And all the laws, and the day of men
Become iniquitous, than such as he
Forget his origin
And the pure voice of his youth.
Who was the first to coarsen,
Corrupt the bonds of love
And turn them into ropes?
Then, sure of their own rights
And of the heavenly fire
Defiant rebels mocked, not till then
Despising mortal ways,
Chose foolhardy arrogance
And strove to become the equals of gods.

Es haben aber an eigner
Unsterblichkeit die Götter genug, und bedürfen
Die Himmlischen eines Dings,
So sinds Heroën und Menschen
Und Sterbliche sonst. Denn weil
Die Seeligsten nichts fühlen von selbst,
Muß wohl, wenn solches zu sagen
Erlaubt ist, in der Götter Nahmen
Theilnehmend fühlen ein Andrer,
Den brauchen sie; jedoch ihr Gericht
Ist, daß sein eigenes Haus
Zerbreche der und das Liebste
Wie den Feind schelt' und sich Vater und Kind
Begrabe unter den Trümmern,
Wenn einer, wie sie, seyn will und nicht
Ungleiches dulden, der Schwärmer.

Drum wohl ihm, welcher fand
Ein wohlbeschiedenes Schiksaal,
Wo noch der Wanderungen
Und süß der Leiden Erinnerung
Aufrauscht am sichern Gestade,
Daß da und dorthin gern
Er sehn mag bis an die Grenzen
Die bei der Geburt ihm Gott
Zum Aufenthalte gezeichnet.
Dann ruht er, seeligbescheiden,
Denn alles, was er gewollt,
Das Himmlische, von selber umfängt
Es unbezwungen, lächelnd
Jezt, da er ruhet, den Kühnen.

Halbgötter denk' ich jezt
Und kennen muß ich die Theuern,
Weil oft ihr Leben so
Die sehnende Brust mir beweget.
Wem aber, wie, Rousseau, dir,
Unüberwindlich die Seele
Die starkausdauernde ward,
Und sicherer Sinn

But their own immortality
Suffices the gods, and if
The Heavenly have need of one thing,
It is of heroes and human beings
And other mortals. For since
The most Blessed in themselves feel nothing
Another, if to say such a thing is
Permitted, must, I suppose,
Vicariously feel in the name of the gods,
And him they need; but their rule is that
He shall demolish his
Own house and curse like an enemy
Those dearest to him and under the rubble
Shall bury his father and child,
When one aspires to be like them, refusing
To bear with inequality, the fantast.

So happy he who has found
A well-allotted fate
Where still of his wanderings
And sweetly of his afflictions
The memory murmurs on banks that are sure,
So that this way, that way with pleasure
He looks as far as the bounds
Which God at birth assigned
To him for his term and site.
Then, blissfully humble, he rests,
For all that he has wanted,
Though heavenly, of itself surrounds
Him uncompelled, and smiles
Upon the bold one now that he's quiet.

Of demigods now I think
And I must know these dear ones
Because so often their lives
Move me and fill me with longing.
But he whose soul, like yours,
Rousseau, ever strong and patient,
Became invincible,
Endowed with steadfast purpose

Und süße Gaabe zu hören,
Zu reden so, daß er aus heiliger Fülle
Wie der Weingott, thörig göttlich
Und gesezlos sie die Sprache der Reinesten giebt
Verständlich den Guten, aber mit Recht
Die Achtungslosen mit Blindheit schlägt
Die entweihenden Knechte, wie nenn ich den Fremden?

    Die Söhne der Erde sind, wie die Mutter,
Allliebend, so empfangen sie auch
Mühlos, die Glüklichen, Alles.
Drum überraschet es auch
Und schrökt den sterblichen Mann,
Wenn er den Himmel, den
Er mit den liebenden Armen
Sich auf die Schultern gehäufft,
Und die Last der Freude bedenket;
Dann scheint ihm oft das Beste,
Fast ganz vergessen da,
Wo der Stral nicht brennt,
Im Schatten des Walds
Am Bielersee in frischer Grüne zu seyn,
Und sorglosarm an Tönen,
Anfängern gleich, bei Nachtigallen zu lernen.

    Und herrlich ists, aus heiligem Schlafe dann
Erstehen und aus Waldes Kühle
Erwachend, Abends nun
Dem milderen Licht entgegenzugehn,
Wenn, der die Berge gebaut
Und den Pfad der Ströme gezeichnet,
Nachdem er lächelnd auch
Der Menschen geschäfftiges Leben
Das othemarme, wie Seegel
Mit seinen Lüften gelenkt hat,
Auch ruht und zu der Schülerin jezt,
Der Bildner, Gutes mehr
Denn Böses findend,
Zur heutigen Erde der Tag sich neiget. –

And a sweet gift of hearing,
Of speaking, so that from holy profusion
Like the wine-god foolishly, divinely
And lawlessly he gives it away,
The language of the purest, comprehensible to the good,
But rightly strikes with blindness the irreverent,
The profaning rabble, what shall I call that stranger?

   The sons of Earth, like their mother are
All-loving, so without effort too
All things those blessèd ones receive.
And therefore it surprises
And startles the mortal man
When he considers the heaven
Which with loving arms he himself
Has heaped upon his shoulders,
And feels the burden of joy;
Then often to him it seems best
Almost wholly forgotten to be
Where the beam does not sear,
In the forest's shade
By Lake Bienne amid foliage newly green,
And blithely poor in tones,
Like beginners, to learn from nightingales.

   And glorious then it is to arise once more
From holy sleep and awakening
From coolness of the woods, at evening
Walk now toward the softer light
When he who built the mountains
And drafted the paths of the rivers,
Having also smiling directed
The busy lives of men,
So short of breath, like sails,
And filled them with his breezes,
Reposes also, and down to his pupil
The master craftsmen, finding
More good than evil,
Day now inclines to the present Earth.

Dann feiern das Brautfest Menschen und Götter,
Es feiern die Lebenden all,
Und ausgeglichen
Ist eine Weile das Schiksaal.
Und die Flüchtlinge suchen die Heerberg,
Und süßen Schlummer die Tapfern,
Die Liebenden aber
Sind, was sie waren, sie sind
Zu Haußhe, wo die Blume sich freuet
Unschädlicher Gluth und die finsteren Bäume
Der Geist umsäuselt, aber die Unversöhnten
Sind umgewandelt und eilen
Die Hände sich ehe zu reichen,
Bevor das freundliche Licht
Hinuntergeht und die Nacht kommt.

Doch einigen eilt
Diß schnell vorüber, andere
Behalten es länger.
Die ewigen Götter sind
Voll Lebens allzeit; bis in den Tod
Kann aber ein Mensch auch
Im Gedächtniß doch das Beste behalten,
Und dann erlebt er das Höchste.
Nur hat ein jeder sein Maas.
Denn schwer ist zu tragen
Das Unglük, aber schwerer das Glük.
Ein Weiser aber vermocht es
Vom Mittag bis in die Mitternacht,
Und bis der Morgen erglänzte,
Beim Gastmahl helle zu bleiben.

Dir mag auf heißem Pfade unter Tannen oder
Im Dunkel des Eichwalds gehüllt
In Stahl, mein Sinklair! Gott erscheinen oder
In Wolken, du kennst ihn, da du kennest, jugendlich,
Des Guten Kraft, und nimmer ist dir
Verborgen das Lächeln des Herrschers
Bei Tage, wenn
Es fieberhaft und angekettet das

Then gods and mortals celebrate their nuptials,
All the living celebrate,
And Fate for a while
Is levelled out, suspended.
And fugitives look for asylum,
For sweet slumber the brave,
But lovers are
What always they were, at home
Wherever flowers are glad
Of harmless fervour and the spirit wafts
Around the darkling trees, but those unreconciled
Are changed and hurry now
To hold out their hands to the other
Before the benevolent light
Goes down, and night comes.

For some, however,
This quickly passes, others
Retain it longer.
The eternal gods are full
Of life at all times; but until death
A mortal too can retain
And bear in mind what is best
And then is supremely favoured.
Yet each of us has his measure.
For hard to bear
Is misfortune, but good fortune harder.
A wise man, though, was able
From noon to midnight, and on
Till morning lit up the sky
To keep wide awake at the banquet.

To you in the heat of a path under fir-trees or
Within the oak forest's half-light, wrapped
In steel, my Sinclair, God may appear, or
In clouds, you'll know him, since, youthfully, you know
The good God's power, and never from you
The smile of the Ruler is hidden
By day, when all
That lives seems febrile

Lebendige scheinet oder auch
Bei Nacht, wenn alles gemischt
Ist ordnungslos und wiederkehrt
Uralte Verwirrung.

Friedensfeier

*Ich bitte dieses Blatt nur gutmüthig zu lesen. So wird es sicher nicht
unfaßlich, noch weniger anstößig seyn. Sollten aber dennoch einige eine solche
Sprache zu wenig konventionell finden, so muß ich ihnen gestehen: ich kann
nicht anders. An einem schönen Tage läßt sich ja fast jede Sangart hören,
und die Natur, wovon es her ist, nimmts auch wieder.*

*Der Verfasser gedenkt dem Publikum eine ganze Sammlung von dergleichen
Blättern vorzulegen, und dieses soll irgend eine Probe seyn davon.*

Der himmlischen, still wiederklingenden,
Der ruhigwandelnden Töne voll,
Und gelüftet ist der altgebaute,
Seeliggewohnte Saal; um grüne Teppiche duftet
Die Freudenwolk' und weithinglänzend stehn,
Gereiftester Früchte voll und goldbekränzter Kelche,
Wohlangeordnet, eine prächtige Reihe,
Zur Seite da und dort aufsteigend über dem
Geebneten Boden die Tische.
Denn ferne kommend haben
Hieher, zur Abendstunde,
Sich liebende Gäste beschieden.

Und dämmernden Auges denk' ich schon,
Vom ernsten Tagwerk lächelnd,
Ihn selbst zu sehn, den Fürsten des Fests.
Doch wenn du schon dein Ausland gern verläugnest,
Und als vom langen Heldenzuge müd,
Dein Auge senkst, vergessen, leichtbeschattet,
Und Freundesgestalt annimmst, du Allbekannter, doch
Beugt fast die Knie das Hohe. Nichts vor dir,

And fettered, or also
By night, when all is mingled
Chaotically and back again comes
Primaeval confusion.

Celebration of Peace

All I ask is that the reader be kindly disposed towards these pages. In that case he will certainly not find them incomprehensible, far less objectionable. But if, nonetheless, some should think such a language too unconventional, I must confess to them: I cannot help it. On a fine day – they should consider – almost every mode of song makes itself heard; and Nature, whence it originates, also receives it again.

The author intends to offer the public an entire collection of such pieces, and this one should be regarded as a kind of sample.

With heavenly, quietly echoing,
With calmly modulating music filled,
And aired is the anciently built,
The sweetly familiar hall; upon green carpets wafts
The fragrant cloud of joy and, casting their brightness far,
Full of most mellow fruit and chalices wreathed with gold,
Arranged in seemly order, a splendid row,
Erected here and there on either side above
The levelled floor, stand the tables.
For, come from distant places,
Here, at the evening hour,
Loving guests have forgathered.

And already with eyes dusk-dim,
With solemn day-labour smiling,
I think that I see him in person, the prince of the feast-day.
But though you like to disavow your foreign land,
And weary, it seems, with long heroic war,
Cast down your eyes, oblivious, lightly shaded,
Assuming the shape of a friend, you known to all men, yet
Almost it bends our knees, such loftiness. Nothing in

Nur Eines weiß ich, Sterbliches bist du nicht.
Ein Weiser mag mir manches erhellen; wo aber
Ein Gott noch auch erscheint,
Da ist doch andere Klarheit.

Von heute aber nicht, nicht unverkündet ist er;
Und einer, der nicht Fluth noch Flamme gescheuet,
Erstaunet, da es stille worden, umsonst nicht, jezt,
Da Herrschaft nirgend ist zu sehn bei Geistern und Menschen.
Das ist, sie hören das Werk,
Längst vorbereitend, von Morgen nach Abend, jezt erst,
Denn unermeßlich braußt, in der Tiefe verhallend,
Des Donnerers Echo, das tausendjährige Wetter,
Zu schlafen, übertönt von Friedenslauten, hinunter.
Ihr aber, theuergewordne, o ihr Tage der Unschuld,
Ihr bringt auch heute das Fest, ihr Lieben! und es blüht
Rings abendlich der Geist in dieser Stille;
Und rathen muß ich, und wäre silbergrau
Die Loke, o ihr Freunde!
Für Kränze zu sorgen und Mahl, jezt ewigen Jünglingen ähnlich.

Und manchen möcht' ich laden, aber o du,
Der freundlichernst den Menschen zugethan,
Dort unter syrischer Palme,
Wo nahe lag die Stadt, am Brunnen gerne war;
Das Kornfeld rauschte rings, still athmete die Kühlung
Vom Schatten des geweiheten Gebirges,
Und die lieben Freunde, das treue Gewölk,
Umschatteten dich auch, damit der heiligkühne
Durch Wildniß mild dein Stral zu Menschen kam, o Jüngling!
Ach! aber dunkler umschattete, mitten im Wort, dich
Furchtbarentscheidend ein tödtlich Verhängniß. So ist schnell

Vergänglich alles Himmlische; aber umsonst nicht;

Denn schonend rührt des Maases allzeit kundig
Nur einen Augenblik die Wohnungen der Menschen
Ein Gott an, unversehn, und keiner weiß es, wenn?
Auch darf alsdann das Freche drüber gehn,

Your presence I know; but one thing: mortal you are not.
A wise man could elucidate much for me; but where
A God as well appears,
A different clarity shines.

Yet not sprung up today, nor unproclaimed he comes
And one who did not balk at either flood or flame
Not without reason astonishes us, now that all is quiet,
Dominion nowhere to be seen among spirits or mortals.
That is, only now do they hear
The work that long has prepared them, from Orient to Occident,
For now immeasurably, fading away in the deeps,
The Thunderer's echo, the millennial storm
Rolls down to sleep, intermingled with peaceful music.
But you, grown dear to us, O days of innocence,
It's you, beloved, that bring this feast-day too, and round us
The spirit flowers, vespertine in this quiet;
And, friends, I must advise you, though
Our hair had turned silver-grey,
To see to garlands and banquet, now like men immortally young.

And many there are I would invite, but you,
O you that benignly, gravely disposed to men
Down there beneath the Syrian palm-tree, where
The town lay near, by the well were glad to be;
Round you the cornfield rustled, quietly coolness breathed
From shadows of the hallowed mountainsides,
And your dear friends, the faithful clouds
Cast shade upon you too, so that the holy, the bold,
The beam through wilderness gently should fall on men, O youth.
But oh, more darkly, even as you spoke,
And dreadfully determining a deadly doom overshadowed you there.
So all
That's heavenly fleets on; but not for nothing;

For sparingly, at all times knowing the measure,
A God for a moment only will touch the dwellings
Of men, by none foreseen, and no one knows when.
And over it then all insolence may pass,

Und kommen muß zum heilgen Ort das Wilde
Von Enden fern, übt rauhbetastend den Wahn,
Und trift daran ein Schiksaal, aber Dank,
Nie folgt der gleich hernach dem gottgegebnen Geschenke;
Tiefprüfend ist es zu fassen.
Auch wär' uns, sparte der Gebende nicht
Schon längst vom Seegen des Heerds
Uns Gipfel und Boden entzündet.

    Des Göttlichen aber empfiengen wir
Doch viel. Es ward die Flamm' uns
In die Hände gegeben, und Ufer und Meersfluth.
Viel mehr, denn menschlicher Weise
Sind jene mit uns, die fremden Kräfte, vertrauet.
Und es lehret Gestirn dich, das
Vor Augen dir ist, doch nimmer kannst du ihm gleichen.
Vom Alllebendigen aber, von dem
Viel Freuden sind und Gesänge,
Ist einer ein Sohn, ein Ruhigmächtiger ist er,
Und nun erkennen wir ihn,
Nun, da wir kennen den Vater
Und Feiertage zu halten
Der hohe, der Geist
Der Welt sich zu Menschen geneigt hat.

    Denn längst war der zum Herrn der Zeit zu groß
Und weit aus reichte sein Feld, wann hats ihn aber erschöpfet?

Einmal mag aber ein Gott auch Tagewerk erwählen,
Gleich Sterblichen und theilen alles Schiksaal.
Schiksaalgesez ist diß, daß Alle sich erfahren,
Daß, wenn die Stille kehrt, auch eine Sprache sei.
Wo aber wirkt der Geist, sind wir auch mit, und streiten,
Was wohl das Beste sei. So dünkt mir jezt das Beste,
Wenn nun vollendet sein Bild und fertig ist der Meister,
Und selbst verklärt davon aus seiner Werkstatt tritt,
Der stille Gott der Zeit und nur der Liebe Gesez,
Das schönausgleichende gilt von hier an bis zum Himmel.

And to the holy place must come the savage
From ends remote, and roughly fingering works out his
Delusion, so fulfilling a fate, but thanks
Will never follow at once upon the godsent gift;
Probed deeply, this can be grasped,
And were not the giver sparing
The wealth of our hearth long ago would
Have fired both the roof and the floor.

    Yet much that's divine nonetheless we
Received. The flame was entrusted
To us, and shore and ocean flood.
Much more than humanly only
Are these, the alien powers, familiar with us.
And you are taught by the stars
In front of your eyes, but never you can be like them.
Yet to the All-Living from whom
Many joys and songs have sprung
There's one who is a son, and quietly powerful is he,
And now we recognize him,
Now that we know the Father
And to keep holidays
The exalted, the Spirit of
The World has inclined towards men.

    For long now he had been too great to rule
As Lord of Time, and wide his field extended, but when did it exhaust
       him?
For once, however, even a God may choose
Mere daily tasks, like mortals, and share all manner of fate.
This is a law of fate, that each shall know all others,
That when the silence returns there shall be a language too.
Yet where the Spirit is active, we too will stir and debate
What course might be the best. So now it seems best to me
If now the Master completes his image and, finished,
Himself transfigured by it, steps out of his workshop,
The quiet God of Time, and only the law of love,
That gently resolves all difference, prevails from here up to Heaven.

Viel hat von Morgen an,
Seit ein Gespräch wir sind und hören voneinander,
Erfahren der Mensch; bald sind wir aber Gesang.
Und das Zeitbild, das der große Geist entfaltet,
Ein Zeichen liegts vor uns, daß zwischen ihm und andern
Ein Bündniß zwischen ihm und andern Mächten ist.
Nicht er allein, die Unerzeugten, Ew'gen
Sind kennbar alle daran, gleichwie auch an den Pflanzen
Die Mutter Erde sich und Licht und Luft sich kennet.
Zulezt ist aber doch, ihr heiligen Mächte, für euch
Das Liebeszeichen, das Zeugniß
Daß ihrs noch seiet, der Festtag.

Der Allversammelnde, wo Himmlische nicht
Im Wunder offenbar, noch ungesehn im Wetter,
Wo aber bei Gesang gastfreundlich untereinander
In Chören gegenwärtig, eine heilige Zahl
Die Seeligen in jeglicher Weise
Beisammen sind, und ihr Geliebtestes auch,
An dem sie hängen, nicht fehlt; denn darum rief ich
Zum Gastmahl, das bereitet ist,
Dich, Unvergeßlicher, dich, zum Abend der Zeit,
O Jüngling, dich zum Fürsten des Festes; und eher legt
Sich schlafen unser Geschlecht nicht,
Bis ihr Verheißenen all,
All ihr Unsterblichen, uns
Von eurem Himmel zu sagen,
Da seid in unserem Haußе.

Leichtathmende Lüfte
Verkünden euch schon,
Euch kündet das rauchende Thal
Und der Boden, der vom Wetter noch dröhnet,
Doch Hoffnung röthet die Wangen,
Und vor der Thüre des Haußes
Sizt Mutter und Kind,
Und schauet den Frieden
Und wenige scheinen zu sterben

Much, from the morning onwards,
Since we have been a discourse and have heard from one another,
Has human kind learnt; but soon we shall be song.
That temporal image too, which the great Spirit reveals,
As a token lies before us that between him and others,
Himself and other powers, there is a pact of peace.
Not he alone, the Unconceived, Eternal
Can all be known by this, as likewise by the plants
Our Mother Earth and light and air are known.
Yet ultimately, you holy powers, our token
Of love for you, and the proof
That still you are holy to us, is the feast-day.

The all-assembling, where heavenly beings are
Not manifest in miracles, nor unseen in thunderstorms,
But where in hymns hospitably conjoined
And present in choirs, a holy number,
The blessèd in every way
Meet and forgather, and their best-beloved,
To whom they are attached, is not missing; for that is why
You to the banquet now prepared I called,
The unforgettable, you, at the Evening of Time,
O youth, called you to the prince of the feast-day; nor shall
Our nation ever lie down to sleep until
All you that were prophesied,
Every one of you Immortals,
To tell us about your Heaven
Are here with us in our house.

Winds lightly breathing
Already announce you,
The vapour that drifts from the valley
And the ground still resounding with thunder,
But hope now flushes our cheeks,
In front of the door of their house
Sit mother and child,
And look upon peace,
And few now seem to be dying;

Es hält ein Ahnen die Seele,
Vom goldnen Lichte gesendet,
Hält ein Versprechen die Ältesten auf.

   Wohl sind die Würze des Lebens,
Von oben bereitet und auch
Hinausgeführet, die Mühen.
Denn Alles gefällt jezt,
Einfältiges aber
Am meisten, denn die langgesuchte,
Die goldne Frucht,
Uraltem Stamm
In schütternden Stürmen entfallen,
Dann aber, als liebstes Gut, vom heiligen Schiksaal selbst,
Mit zärtlichen Waffen umschüzt,
Die Gestalt der Himmlischen ist es.

   Wie die Löwin, hast du geklagt,
O Mutter, da du sie,
Natur, die Kinder verloren.
Denn es stahl sie, Allzuliebende, dir
Dein Feind, da du ihn fast
Wie die eigenen Söhne genommen,
Und Satyren die Götter gesellt hast.
So hast du manches gebaut,
Und manches begraben,
Denn es haßt dich, was
Du, vor der Zeit
Allkräftige, zum Lichte gezogen.
   Nun kennest, nun lässest du diß;
Denn gerne fühllos ruht,
Bis daß es reift, furchtsamgeschäfftiges drunten.

The souls of the oldest even
Held back by a hint, a promise
Conveyed by the golden light.

   Indeed it is travails, designed from
Above and there carried out,
That are the spice of life.
For now all things are pleasing
But most of all the
Ingenuous, because the long sought,
The golden fruit,
In shattering gales fallen down from
An age-old bough
But then, as the dearest possession, by Fate herself
Protected with tender weapons,
The shape of the Heavenly it is.

   Like the lioness you lamented,
O Mother, when you lost
Your children, Nature,
For they were stolen from you, the all too loving, by
Your enemy, when almost
Like your own sons you had nursed him
And with satyrs made gods consort.
So there is much you built
And much you buried,
For you are hated by
That which too soon
All-powerful, you raised to the light.
   Now you know the fault, and desist,
For, till grown ripe, unfeeling
What's timidly busy likes to rest down below.

Der Einzige
ERSTE FASSUNG

Was ist es, das
An die alten seeligen Küsten
Mich fesselt, daß ich mehr noch
Sie liebe, als mein Vaterland?
Denn wie in himmlische
Gefangenschaft verkaufft
Dort bin ich, wo Apollo gieng
In Königsgestalt,
Und zu unschuldigen Jünglingen sich
Herablies Zevs und Söhn' in heiliger Art
Und Töchter zeugte
Der Hohe unter den Menschen?

Der hohen Gedanken
Sind nemlich viel
Entsprungen des Vaters Haupt
Und große Seelen
Von ihm zu Menschen gekommen.
Gehöret hab' ich
Von Elis und Olympia, bin
Gestanden oben auf dem Parnaß,
Und über Bergen des Isthmus,
Und drüben auch
Bei Smyrna und hinab
Bei Ephesos bin ich gegangen;

Viel hab' ich schönes gesehn,
Und gesungen Gottes Bild,
Hab' ich, das lebet unter
Den Menschen, aber dennoch
Ihr alten Götter und all
Ihr tapfern Söhne der Götter
Noch Einen such ich, den
Ich liebe unter euch,

The Only One
FIRST VERSION

What is it that
To the ancient, the happy shores
Binds me, so that I love them
Still more than my own homeland?
For as though into heavenly
Captivity sold,
I am where Apollo walked
In the guise of a king,
And Zeus condescended
To innocent youths, and sons in a holy fashion
Begot, and daughters,
The exalted, amid mankind.

For many a thought
Sublime and great
Has sprung from the Father's head
And lofty souls
Come down from him to mortals.
Of Elis and
Olympia I have heard, and stood
High up on the top of Parnassus
And up above hills of the Isthmus
And over there
By Smyrna too, and down
By Ephesus I have walked;

Have looked upon much that is lovely
And sung the image of God
As here among human kind
It lives, and yet, and yet,
You ancient gods and all
You valiant sons of the gods,
One other I look for whom
Within your ranks I love,

Wo ihr den lezten eures Geschlechts
Des Haußes Kleinod mir
Dem fremden Gaste verberget.

Mein Meister und Herr!
O du, mein Lehrer!
Was bist du ferne
Geblieben? und da
Ich fragte unter den Alten,
Die Helden und
Die Götter, warum bliebest
Du aus? Und jezt ist voll
Von Trauern meine Seele
Als eifertet, ihr Himmlischen, selbst
Daß, dien' ich einem, mir
Das andere fehlet.

Ich weiß es aber, eigene Schuld
Ists! Denn zu sehr,
O Christus! häng' ich an dir,
Wiewohl Herakles Bruder
Und kühn bekenn' ich, du
Bist Bruder auch des Eviers, der
An den Wagen spannte
Die Tyger und hinab
Bis an den Indus
Gebietend freudigen Dienst
Den Weinberg stiftet und
Den Grimm bezähmte der Völker.

Es hindert aber eine Schaam
Mich dir zu vergleichen
Die weltlichen Männer. Und freilich weiß
Ich, der dich zeugte, dein Vater,
Derselbe der,

Where hidden from the alien guest, from me,
You keep the last of your kind,
The treasured gem of the house.

    My Master and Lord!
O you, my teacher!
Why did you keep
Away? And when
I asked among the ancients,
The heroes and
The gods, then why were you
Not there? And now my soul
Is full of sadness as though
You Heavenly yourselves excitedly cried
That if I serve one I
Must lack the other.

    And yet I know, it is my
Own fault! For too greatly,
O Christ, I'm attached to you,
Although Heracles' brother.
And boldly I confess,
You are the brother also of Evius
Who to his chariot harnessed
The tigers and right down
As far as the Indus
Commanding joyful service,
First planted the vineyard and tamed
The fierceness and rage of the peoples.

    And yet a shame forbids me
To associate with you
The worldly men. And indeed I know
That he who begot you, your Father,
The same who

Denn nimmer herrscht er allein.

Es hänget aber an Einem
Die Liebe. Diesesmal
Ist nemlich vom eigenen Herzen
Zu sehr gegangen der Gesang,
Gut machen will ich den Fehl
Wenn ich noch andere singe.
Nie treff ich, wie ich wünsche,
Das Maas. Ein Gott weiß aber
Wenn kommet, was ich wünsche das Beste.
Denn wie der Master
Gewandelt auf Erden
Ein gefangener Aar.

Und viele, die
Ihn sahen, fürchteten sich,
Dieweil sein Äußerstes that
Der Vater und sein Bestes unter
Den Menschen wirkete wirklich,
Und sehr betrübt war auch
Der Sohn so lange, bis er
Gen Himmel fuhr in den Lüften,
Dem gleich ist gefangen die Seele der Helden.
Die Dichter müssen auch
Die geistigen weltlich seyn.

For never he reigns alone.

   To One alone, however,
Love clings. For this time too much
From my own heart the song
Has come; if other songs follow
I'll make amends for the fault.
Much though I wish to, never
I strike the right measure. But
A god knows when it comes, what I wish for, the best.
For as the Master
Once moved on earth,
A captive eagle,

      And many who
Looked on him were afraid,
While the Father did
His utmost, effectively bringing
The best to bear upon men,
And sorely troubled in mind
The Son was also until
To Heaven he rose in the winds,
So too, the souls of the heroes are captive.
The poets, and those no less who
Are spiritual, must be worldly.

Der Einzige
ZWEITE FASSUNG

Was ist es, das
An die alten seeligen Küsten
Mich fesselt, daß ich mehr noch
Sie liebe, als mein Vaterland?
Denn wie in himmlischer
Gefangenschaft gebükt, in flammender Luft
Dort bin ich, wo, wie Steine sagen Apollo gieng
In Königsgestalt,
Und zu unschuldigen Jünglingen sich
Herablies Zevs und Söhn in heiliger Art
Und Töchter zeugte
Der Hohe unter den Menschen?

Der hohen Gedanken
Sind nemlich viel
Entsprungen des Vaters Haupt
Und große Seelen
Von ihm zu Menschen gekommen.
Gehöret hab' ich
Von Elis und Olympia, bin
Gestanden oben auf dem Parnaß,
Und über Bergen des Isthmus,
Und drüben auch
Bei Smyrna und hinab
Bei Ephesos bin ich gegangen;

Viel hab' ich schönes gesehn,
Und gesungen Gottes Bild
Hab' ich, das lebet unter
Den Menschen, denn sehr dem Raum gleich ist
Das Himmlische reichlich in
Der Jugend zählbar, aber dennoch
O du der Sterne Leben und all
Ihr tapfern Söhne des Lebens
Noch Einen such ich, den
Ich liebe unter euch,

The Only One
SECOND VERSION

What is it that
To the ancient, the happy shores
Binds me, so that I love them
Still more than my own homeland?
For as though in heavenly
Captivity cowering, in flaming air
I am where the stones tell Apollo walked
In the guise of a king
And Zeus condescended
To innocent youths, and sons in a holy fashion
Begot, and daughters,
The exalted, amid mankind.

For many a thought
Sublime and great
Has sprung from the Father's head
And lofty souls
Come down from him to mortals.
Of Elis and
Olympia I have heard, and stood
High up on the top of Parnassus
And up above hills of the Isthmus
And over there
By Smyrna too, and down
By Ephesus I have walked;

Have looked upon much that is lovely
And sung the image of God
As here among human kind
It lives, for very much like space
In youth the Heavenly in plenty
Is numerable, and yet, and yet
O you the life of the stars and all
You valiant sons of life,
One other I look for whom
Within your ranks I love,

Wo ihr den lezten eures Geschlechts
Des Haußes Kleinod mir
Dem fremden Gaste verberget.

Mein Meister und Herr!
O du, mein Lehrer!
Was bist du ferne
Geblieben? und da
Ich fragte unter den Alten,
Die Helden und
Die Götter, warum bliebest
Du aus? Und jezt ist voll
Von Trauern meine Seele
Als eifertet, ihr Himmlischen, selbst
Daß, dien' ich einem, mir
Das andere fehlet.

Ich weiß es aber, eigene Schuld ists! Denn zu sehr
O Christus! häng' ich an dir, wiewohl Herakles Bruder
Und kühn bekenn' ich, du bist Bruder auch des Eviers, der
Die Todeslust der Völker aufhält und zerreißet den Fallstrik,
Fein sehen die Menschen, daß sie
Nicht gehn den Weg des Todes und hüten das Maas, daß einer
Etwas für sich ist, den Augenblik
Das Geschik der großen Zeit auch
Ihr Feuer fürchtend, treffen sie, und wo
Des Wegs ein anderes geht, da sehen sie
Auch, wo ein Geschik sei, machen aber
Das sicher, Menschen gleichend oder Gesezen.

Es entbrennet aber sein Zorn; daß nemlich
Das Zeichen die Erde berührt, allmälich
Aus Augen gekommen, als an einer Leiter.
Dißmal. Eigenwillig sonst, unmäßig
Gränzlos, daß der Menschen Hand
Anficht das Lebende, mehr auch, als sich schiket
Für einen Halbgott, heiliggeseztes übergeht
Der Entwurf. Seit nemlich böser Geist sich
Bemächtiget des glüklichen Altertums, unendlich,

Where hidden from the alien guest, from me
You keep the last of your kind,
The treasured gem of the house.

   My Master and Lord!
O you, my teacher,
Why did you keep
Away? And when
I asked among the ancients
The heroes and
The gods, why were you
Not there? And now my soul
Is full of sadness as though
You Heavenly yourselves excitedly cried
That if I serve one I
Must lack the other.

   And yet I know, it is my own fault. For too greatly
O Christ, I'm attached to you, although Heracles' brother,
And boldly I confess, you are the brother also of Evius, who
Restrains the deathwish of the peoples and breaks up the snare,
Well men can see now, so that
They do not go the way of death and keep the measure, so that
A man shall be something in himself and fear
The moment, the destiny of great eras and
Their fires no less, they strike, and where
Another goes that way, they also see
Where there's a destiny, but make
It safe, resembling human beings or laws.

   His fury flares up, however; that is, so that
The sign shall touch the earth, gradually
Released from eyes, as though by a ladder.
This time. Wilful at other times, immoderately
Boundless, so that the hands of men
Impugn whatever is living, more than is fitting for
A demigod, the design transgresses beyond
What's divinely ordained. For since evil spirit
Has taken possession of happy antiquity, unendingly

Langher währt Eines, gesangsfeind, klanglos, das
In Maasen vergeht, des Sinnes gewaltsames.

                                    Ungebundenes aber
Hasset Gott. Fürbittend aber

   Hält ihn der Tag von dieser Zeit, stillschaffend,
Des Weges gehend, die Blüthe der Jahre.
Und Kriegsgetön, und Geschichte der Helden unterhält,
                                    hartnäkig Geschik,
Die Sonne Christi, Gärten der Büßenden, und
Der Pilgrime Wandern und der Völker ihn, und des Wächters
Gesang und die Schrift
Des Barden oder Afrikaners. Ruhmloser auch
Geschik hält ihn, die an den Tag
Jezt erst recht kommen, das sind väterliche Fürsten. Denn
                                    viel ist der Stand
Gottgleicher, denn sonst. Denn Männern mehr
Gehöret das Licht. Nicht Jünglingen.
Das Vaterland auch. Nemlich frisch

   Noch unerschöpfet und voll mit Loken.
Der Vater der Erde freuet nemlich sich deß
Auch, daß Kinder sind, so bleibet eine Gewißheit
Des Guten. So auch freuet
Das ihn, daß eines bleibet.
Auch einige sind, gerettet, als
Auf schönen Inseln. Gelehrt sind die.
Versuchungen sind nemlich
Gränzlos an die gegangen.
Zahllose gefallen. Also gieng es, als
Der Erde Vater bereitet ständiges
In Stürmen der Zeit. Ist aber geendet.

Long now one power has prevailed, hostile to song, without resonance,
That within measures transgresses the violence of the mind.

                                        But God hates

The unbound. Yet interceding

   The day of this age holds him back, creating in silence,
Proceeding on its way, the blossom of the years.
And uproar of war and history of heroes holds him,

                                        stiff-necked destiny,

The sun of Christ, gardens of the penitent, and
The wandering of pilgrims and of the peoples, and the song
Of the watchman and the writings
Of the bard or the African. And the destiny
Of those unfamous holds him, who only now
Are really having their day, paternal princes, that is. For

                                        now that rank

Is much more godlike than before. For more to men
Now light belongs, not to youths.
Our homeland also. For fresh

   Still unexhausted and full of curls.
For the Father of Earth is glad of this too,
That there are children, so that a certainty
Of goodness remains. So too
He is glad that one remains.
And some there are, saved, as though
On beautiful islands. Learnèd are these,
For they have been subject to
Temptations without end.
Countless fallen. So it went when
The Father of Earth prepared what is constant
In storms of the age. But that is ended.

Patmos

DEM LANDGRAFTEN VON HOMBURG

Nah ist
Und schwer zu fassen der Gott.
Wo aber Gefahr ist, wächst
Das Rettende auch.
Im Finstern wohnen
Die Adler und furchtlos gehn
Die Söhne der Alpen über den Abgrund weg
Auf leichtgebaueten Brüken.
Drum, da gehäuft sind rings
Die Gipfel der Zeit, und die Liebsten
Nah wohnen, ermattend auf
Getrenntesten Bergen,
So gieb unschuldig Wasser,
O Fittige gieb uns, treuesten Sinns
Hinüberzugehn und wiederzukehren.

So sprach ich, da entführte
Mich schneller, denn ich vermuthet
Und weit, wohin ich nimmer
Zu kommen gedacht, ein Genius mich
Vom eigenen Hauß'. Es dämmerten
Im Zwielicht, da ich gieng
Der schattige Wald
Und die sehnsüchtigen Bäche
Der Heimath; nimmer kannt' ich die Länder;
Doch bald, in frischem Glanze,
Geheimnißvoll
Im goldenen Rauche, blühte
Schnellaufgewachsen,
Mit Schritten der Sonne,
Mit tausend Gipfeln duftend,

Mir Asia auf, und geblendet sucht'
Ich eines, das ich kennete, denn ungewohnt
War ich der breiten Gassen, wo herab
Vom Tmolus fährt

Patmos
FOR THE LANDGRAVE OF HOMBURG

Near is
And difficult to grasp, the God.
But where danger threatens
That which saves from it also grows.
In gloomy places dwell
The eagles, and fearless over
The chasm walk the sons of the Alps
On bridges lightly built.
Therefore, since round about
Are heaped the summits of Time
And the most loved live near, growing faint
On mountains most separate,
Give us innocent water,
O pinions give us, with minds most faithful
To cross over and to return.

So I spoke, when more swiftly
Than ever I had expected,
And far as I never thought
I should come, a Genius carried me
From my own house. There glimmered
In twilight, as I went,
The shadowy wood
And the yearning streams of
My homeland; no longer I knew those regions;
But soon, in a radiance fresh,
Mysteriously,
In the golden haze,
Quickly grown up,
With strides of the sun,
And fragrant with a thousand peaks,

Now Asia burst into flower for me, and dazzled
I looked for one thing there I might know, being unaccustomed
To those wide streets where down
From Tmolus drives

Der goldgeschmükte Pactol
Und Taurus stehet und Messogis,
Und voll von Blumen der Garten,
Ein stilles Feuer; aber im Lichte
Blüht hoch der silberne Schnee;
Und Zeug unsterblichen Lebens
An unzugangbaren Wänden
Uralt der Epheu wächst und getragen sind
Von lebenden Säulen, Cedern und Lorbeern
Die feierlichen,
Die göttlichgebauten Palläste.

Es rauschen aber um Asias Thore
Hinziehend da und dort
In ungewisser Meeresebene
Der schattenlosen Straßen genug,
Doch kennt die Inseln der Schiffer.
Und da ich hörte
Der nahegelegenen eine
Sei Patmos,
Verlangte mich sehr,
Dort einzukehren und dort
Der dunkeln Grotte zu nahn.
Denn nicht, wie Cypros,
Die quellenreiche, oder
Der anderen eine
Wohnt herrlich Patmos,

Gastfreundlich aber ist
Im ärmeren Hauße
Sie dennoch
Und wenn vom Schiffbruch oder klagend
Um die Heimath oder
Den abgeschiedenen Freund
Ihr nahet einer
Der Fremden, hört sie es gern, und ihre Kinder
Die Stimmen des heißen Hains,
Und wo der Sand fällt, und sich spaltet
Des Feldes Fläche, die Laute
Sie hören ihn und liebend tönt

The golden-bedded Pactolus,
And Taurus stands, and Messogis,
And full of flowers the garden,
A quiet fire; but in the light, high up
There blossoms the silver snow;
And, witness to life immortal,
On inaccessible walls
Pristine the ivy grows, and supported
On living pillars, cedars and laurels,
There stand the festive,
The palaces built by gods.

But around Asia's gates there murmur,
Extending this way and that
In the uncertain plain of the sea,
Shadowless roads enough;
Yet the boatman knows the islands.
And when I heard
That of the near islands one
Was Patmos,
I greatly desired
There to be lodged, and there
To approach the dark grotto.
For not like Cyprus,
The rich in well-springs,
Nor any of the others
Magnificently does Patmos dwell,

Hospitable nonetheless
In her poorer house
She is,
And when, after shipwreck or lamenting for
His homeland or else for
The friend departed from him,
A stranger draws near
To her, she is glad to hear it, and her children,
The voices of the hot noonday copse,
And where the sand falls, and the field's
Flat surface cracks, the sounds –
These hear him, and lovingly all is loud

Es wieder von den Klagen des Manns. So pflegte
Sie einst des gottgeliebten,
Des Sehers, der in seeliger Jugend war

   Gegangen mit
Dem Sohne des Höchsten, unzertrennlich, denn
Es liebte der Gewittertragende die Einfalt
Des Jüngers und es sahe der achtsame Mann
Das Angesicht des Gottes genau,
Da, beim Geheimnisse des Weinstoks, sie
Zusammensaßen, zu der Stunde des Gastmals,
Und in der großen Seele, ruhigahnend den Tod
Aussprach der Herr und die lezte Liebe, denn nie genug
Hatt' er von Güte zu sagen
Der Worte, damals, und zu erheitern, da
Ers sahe, das Zürnen der Welt.
Denn alles ist gut. Drauf starb er. Vieles wäre
Zu sagen davon. Und es sahn ihn, wie er siegend blikte
Den Freudigsten die Freunde noch zulezt,

   Doch trauerten sie, da nun
Es Abend worden, erstaunt,
Denn Großentschiedenes hatten in der Seele
Die Männer, aber sie liebten unter der Sonne
Das Leben und lassen wollten sie nicht
Vom Angesichte des Herrn
Und der Heimath. Eingetrieben war,
Wie Feuer im Eisen, das, und ihnen gieng
Zur Seite der Schatte des Lieben.
Drum sandt' er ihnen
Den Geist, und freilich bebte
Das Haus und die Wetter Gottes rollten
Ferndonnernd über
Die ahnenden Häupter, da, schwersinnend
Versammelt waren die Todeshelden.

   Izt, da er scheidend
Noch einmal ihnen erschien.
Denn izt erlosch der Sonne Tag
Der Königliche und zerbrach

With the man's re-echoed lament. So once
She tended the God-beloved,
The seer who in blessèd youth

   Had walked with
The son of the Highest, inseparable, for
The bearer of thunder loved the disciple's
Ingenuousness, and the attentive man
Saw the face of the God exactly
When over the mystery of the vine
They sat together at the hour of the communal meal
And in his great soul, calmly foreknowing,
The Lord pronounced death and the ultimate love, for never
He could find words enough
To say about kindness, then, and to soothe, when
He saw it, the wrath of the world.
For all things are good. After that he died. Much could
Be said of it. And the friends at the very last
Saw him, the gladdest, looking up triumphant,

   Yet they were sad, now that
The evening had come, amazed,
For the souls of these men contained
Things greatly predetermined, but under the sun they loved
This life and were loath to part from
The visible face of the Lord
And their homeland. Driven in,
Like fire into iron, was this, and beside them
The loved one's shadow walked.
Therefore he sent them
The Spirit, and mightily trembled
The house, and God's thunder-storms rolled
Distantly rumbling above
Their heads foreknowledge bowed, when deep in thought
Assembled were the heroes of death,

   Now that, departing,
Once more he appeared to them.
For now the kingly one extinguished
The day of the sun and broke

Den geradestralenden,
Den Zepter, göttlichleidend, von selbst,
Denn wiederkommen sollt es
Zu rechter Zeit. Nicht wär es gut
Gewesen, später, und schroffabbrechend, untreu,
Der Menschen Werk, und Freude war es
Von nun an,
Zu wohnen in liebender Nacht, und bewahren
In einfältigen Augen, unverwandt
Abgründe der Weisheit. Und es grünen
Tief an den Bergen auch lebendige Bilder.

Doch furchtbar ist, wie da und dort
Unendlich hin zerstreut das Lebende Gott.
Denn schon das Angesicht
Der theuern Freunde zu lassen
Und fernhin über die Berge zu gehn
Allein, wo zweifach
Erkannt, einstimmig
War himmlischer Geist; und nicht geweissagt war es, sondern
Die Loken ergriff es, gegenwärtig,
Wenn ihnen plözlich
Ferneilend zurük blikte
Der Gott und schwörend,
Damit er halte, wie an Seilen golden
Gebunden hinfort
Das Böse nennend, sie die Hände sich reichten –

Wenn aber stirbt alsdenn
An dem am meisten
Die Schönheit hieng, daß an der Gestalt
Ein Wunder war und die Himmlischen gedeutet
Auf ihn, und wenn, ein Räthsel ewig füreinander
Sie sich nicht fassen können
Einander, die zusammenlebten
Im Gedächtniß, und nicht den Sand nur oder
Die Weiden es hinwegnimmt und die Tempel
Ergreifft, wenn die Ehre
Des Halbgotts und der Seinen
Verweht und selber sein Angesicht

The straightly beaming, the sceptre,
Divinely suffering, yet of his own free will,
For it was to come back when
The time was due. To have done so later
Would not have been good, and the work of men
Abruptly broken off, disloyally, and from now on
A joy it was
To dwell in loving Night and in fixed,
Ingenuous eyes to preserve
Abysses of wisdom. And low down at
The foot of mountains, too, will living images thrive,

      Yet dreadful it is how here and there
Unendingly God disperses whatever lives.
For only to part from the sight
Of their dear friends
And far across the mountains to go
Alone, when doubly
Perceived, heavenly spirit before had been
Unanimous; and not predicted was this,
But seized them by the hair, on the instant,
When suddenly the God
Far off in haste looked back
At them, and vowing,
So that he would stay, from now on goldenly
Bound fast as to ropes,
Calling the evil by name, they linked hands –

      But when thereupon he dies
To whom beauty most adhered, so that
A miracle was wrought in his person and
The Heavenly had pointed at him,
And when, an enigma to one another
For ever, they cannot understand
One another who lived together
Conjoined by remembrance, and not only
The sand or the willows it takes away,
And seizes the temples, when even
The demigod's honour and that of his friends
Is blown away by the wind, and the Highest

Der Höchste wendet
Darob, daß nirgend ein
Unsterbliches mehr am Himmel zu sehn ist oder
Auf grüner Erde, was ist diß?

    Es ist der Wurf des Säemanns, wenn er faßt
Mit der Schaufel den Waizen,
Und wirft, dem Klaren zu, ihn schwingend über die Tenne.

Ihm fällt die Schaale vor den Füßen, aber
Ans Ende kommet das Korn,
Und nicht ein Übel ists, wenn einiges
Verloren gehet und von der Rede
Verhallet der lebendige Laut,
Denn göttliches Werk auch gleichet dem unsern,
Nicht alles will der Höchste zumal.
Zwar Eisen träget der Schacht,
Und glühende Harze der Aetna,
So hätt' ich Reichtum,
Ein Bild zu bilden, und ähnlich
Zu schaun, wie er gewesen, den Christ,

    Wenn aber einer spornte sich selbst,
Und traurig redend, unterweges, da ich wehrlos wäre
Mich überfiele, daß ich staunt' und von dem Gotte
Das Bild nachahmen möcht' ein Knecht –
Im Zorne sichtbar sah' ich einmal
Des Himmels Herrn, nicht, daß ich seyn sollt etwas, sondern
Zu lernen. Gütig sind sie, ihr Verhaßtestes aber ist,
So lange sie herrschen, das Falsche, und es gilt
Dann Menschliches unter Menschen nicht mehr.
Denn sie nicht walten, es waltet aber
Unsterblicher Schiksaal und es wandelt ihr Werk
Von selbst, und eilend geht es zu Ende.
Wenn nemlich höher gehet himmlischer
Triumphgang, wird genennet, der Sonne gleich
Von Starken der frohlokende Sohn des Höchsten,

Himself averts his face
Because nowhere now
An immortal is to be seen in the skies or
On our green earth, what is this?

   It is the sower's cast when he scoops up
The wheat in his shovel
And throws it, towards clear space, swinging it over the
        threshing-floor.
The husk falls at his feet, but
The grain reaches its end,
And there's no harm if some of it
Is lost, and of the speech
The living sound dies away,
For the work of gods, too, is like our own,
Not all things at once does the Highest intend.
The pit bears iron, though,
And glowing resins Etna,
And so I should have wealth
With which to form an image and see
The Christ as he truly was,

   But if someone spurred himself on
And, talking sadly, on the road, when I was
Defenceless, attacked me, so that amazed I tried
To copy the God's own image, I, a servant –
In anger visible once I saw
The Lord of Heaven, not that I should be something, but
To learn. Benign they are, but what they most abhor,
While their reign lasts, is falsehood, and then
What's human no longer counts among human kind.
For they do not govern, the fate
It is of immortals that governs, and their work
Proceeds by its own force and hurrying seeks its end.
For when heavenly triumph goes higher
The jubilant son of the Highest
Is called like the sun by the strong.

Ein Loosungszeichen, und hier ist der Stab
Des Gesanges, niederwinkend,
Denn nichts ist gemein. Die Todten weket
Er auf, die noch gefangen nicht
Vom Rohen sind. Es warten aber
Der scheuen Augen viele
Zu schauen das Licht. Nicht wollen
Am scharfen Strale sie blühn,
Wiewohl den Muth der goldene Zaum hält.
Wenn aber, als
Von schwellenden Augenbraunen
Der Welt vergessen
Stillleuchtende Kraft aus heiliger Schrift fällt, mögen
Der Gnade sich freuend, sie
Am stillen Blike sich üben.

Und wenn die Himmlischen jezt
So, wie ich glaube, mich lieben
Wie viel mehr Dich,
Denn Eines weiß ich,
Daß nemlich der Wille
Des ewigen Vaters viel
Dir gilt. Still ist sein Zeichen
Am donnernden Himmel. Und Einer stehet darunter
Sein Leben lang. Denn noch lebt Christus.
Es sind aber die Helden, seine Söhne
Gekommen all und heilige Schriften
Von ihm und den Bliz erklären
Die Thaten der Erde bis izt,
Ein Wettlauf unaufhaltsam. Er ist aber dabei. Denn seine Werke sind
Ihm alle bewußt von jeher.

Zu lang, zu lang schon ist
Die Ehre der Himmlischen unsichtbar.
Denn fast die Finger müssen sie
Uns führen und schmählich
Entreißt das Herz uns eine Gewalt.
Denn Opfer will der Himmlischen jedes,
Wenn aber eines versäumt ward,
Nie hat es Gutes gebracht.

A secret token, and here is the wand
Of song, signalling downward,
For nothing is common. The dead
He reawakens whom coarseness has not
Made captive yet. But many timid eyes
Are waiting to see the light.
They are reluctant to flower
Beneath the searing beam, though it is
The golden bridle that curbs their courage.
But when, as if
By swelling eyebrows made
Oblivious of the world
A quietly shining strength falls from holy scripture,
Rejoicing in grace, they
May practise upon the quiet gaze.

And if the Heavenly now
Love me as I believe,
How much more you
They surely love,
For one thing I know:
The eternal Father's will
Means much to you. Now silent is
His sign on thundering heaven. And there is one who stands
Beneath it his whole life long. For Christ lives yet.
But all the heroes, his sons,
Have come, and holy scriptures
About him, and lightning is explained by
The deeds of the world until now,
A race that cannot be stopped. But he is present in it. For known
To him are all his works from the beginning.

Too long, too long now
The honour of the Heavenly has been invisible.
For almost they must guide
Our fingers, and shamefully
A power is wresting our hearts from us.
For every one of the Heavenly wants sacrifices, and
When one of these was omitted
No good ever came of it.

Wir haben gedienet der Mutter Erd'
Und haben jüngst dem Sonnenlichte gedient,
Unwissend, der Vater aber liebt,
Der über allen waltet,
Am meisten, daß gepfleget werde
Der veste Buchstab, und bestehendes gut
Gedeutet. Dem folgt deutscher Gesang.

Patmos
BRUCHSTÜCKE DER SPÄTEREN FASSUNG

Voll Güt' ist; keiner aber fasset
Allein Gott.
Wo aber Gefahr ist, wächst
Das Rettende auch.
Im Finstern wohnen
Die Adler, und furchtlos gehn
Die Söhne der Alpen über den Abgrund weg
Auf leichtgebaueten Brüken.
Drum, da gehäuft sind rings, um Klarheit,
Die Gipfel der Zeit,
Und die Liebsten nahe wohnen, ermattend auf
Getrenntesten Bergen,
So gieb unschuldig Wasser,
O Fittige gieb uns, treuesten Sinns
Hinüberzugehn und wiederzukehren.

So sprach ich, da entführte
Mich künstlicher, denn ich vermuthet
Und weit, wohin ich nimmer
Zu kommen gedacht, ein Genius mich
Vom eigenen Hauß'. Es kleideten sich
Im Zwielicht, Menschen ähnlich, da ich gieng
Der schattige Wald
Und die sehnsüchtigen Bäche
Der Heimath; nimmer kannt' ich die Länder.
Viel aber mitgelitten haben wir, viel Maale. So

We have served Mother Earth
And lately have served the sunlight,
Unwittingly, but what the Father
Who reigns over all loves most
Is that the solid letter
Be given scrupulous care, and the existing
Be well interpreted. This German song observes.

Patmos
FRAGMENTS OF THE LATER VERSION

Most kind is; but no one by himself
Can grasp God.
But where danger threatens
That which saves from it also grows.
In gloomy places dwell
The eagles, and fearless over
The chasm walk the sons of the Alps
On bridges lightly built.
Therefore, since round about are heaped, around clearness,
The summits of Time,
And the most loved live near, growing faint
On mountains most separate,
Give us innocent water,
O pinions give us, with minds most faithful
To cross over and to return.

So I spoke when more ingeniously
Than ever I had expected
And far as I never thought
I should come, a Genius carried me
From my own house. There clothed themselves,
Like men, in the twilight, as I went,
The shadowy wood
And the yearning streams of
My homeland; no longer I knew those regions.
Yet much we have suffered with them, many times.

In frischem Glanze, geheimnißvoll,
In goldenem Rauche blühte
Schnellaufgewachsen,
Mit Schritten der Sonne,
Von tausend Tischen duftend, jezt,

Mir Asia auf und geblendet ganz
Sucht' eins ich, das ich kennete, denn ungewohnt
War ich der breiten Gassen, wo herab
Vom Tmolus fährt
Der goldgeschmükte Pactol
Und Taurus stehet und Messogis,
Und schläfrig fast von Blumen der Garten,

O Insel des Lichts!
Denn wenn erloschen ist der Ruhm die Augenlust und gehalten nicht
   mehr
Von Menschen, schattenlos, die Pfade zweifeln und die Bäume,

Und Reiche, das Jugendland der Augen sind vergangen
Athletischer,
Im Ruin,   und Unschuld angeborne
Zerrissen ist. Von Gott aus nemlich kommt gediegen
Und gehet das Gewissen, Offenbarung, die Hand des Herrn
Reich winkt aus richtendem Himmel, dann und eine Zeit ist
Untheilbar Gesez, und Amt, und die Hände
Zu erheben, das, und das Niederfallen
Böser Gedanken, los, zu ordnen. Grausam nemlich hasset
Allwissende Stirnen Gott. Rein aber bestand
Auf ungebundnem Boden Johannes. Wenn einer
Für irrdisches prophetisches Wort erklärt

So, in a radiance fresh, mysteriously,
In the golden haze
Quickly grown up,
With strides of the sun,
And fragrant with a thousand tables,

   Now, Asia burst into flower for me, and wholly dazzled
I looked for one thing there I might know, being unaccustomed
To those wide streets where down
From Tmolus drives
The golden-bedded Pactolus,
And Taurus stands, and Messogis,
And drowsy almost with flowers the garden,

   O island of light!
For when extinguished is fame, the delight in seeing, and no longer
      maintained
By human kind, shadowless, the paths succumb to doubt, and the
      trees,
And kingdoms, the youthful land of eyes, are perished,
More athletic
In ruin,   and inborn innocence
Is torn to shreds. For from God unalloyed
Does conscience come and go, revelation, the hand of the Lord
Richly beckons from judging Heaven, then and for a time there
Is indivisible law, and office, and hands to
Be raised, both this and to control
The falling of evil thoughts, loose. For cruelly
God hates omniscient brows. But pure
On a site unbound did John remain. When someone
Declares that a prophetic word is earthly

Vom Jordan und von Nazareth
Und fern vom See, an Capernaum,
Und Galiläa die Lüfte, und von Cana.
Eine Weile bleib ich, sprach er. Also mit Tropfen
Stillt er das Seufzen des Lichts, das durstigem Wild
War ähnlich in den Tagen, als um Syrien
Jammert der getödteten Kindlein heimatliche
Anmuth im Sterben, und das Haupt
Des Täuffers gepflükt, war unverwelklicher Schrift gleich
Sichtbar auf weilender Schüssel. Wie Feuer
Sind Stimmen Gottes. Schwer ists aber
Im Großen zu behalten das Große.
Nicht eine Waide. Daß einer
Bleibet im Anfang. Jezt aber
Geht dieses wieder, wie sonst.

Johannes. Christus. Diesen möcht'
Ich singen, gleich dem Herkules, oder
Der Insel, welche vestgehalten und gerettet, erfrischend
Die benachbarte mit kühlen Meereswassern aus der Wüste
Der Fluth, der weiten, Peleus. Das geht aber
Nicht. Anders ists ein Schiksaal. Wundervoller.
Reicher, zu singen. Unabsehlich
Seit jenem die Fabel. Und jezt
Möcht' ich die Fahrt der Edelleute nach
Jerusalem, und das Leiden irrend in Canossa,
Und den Heinrich singen. Daß aber
Der Muth nicht selber mich aussezze. Begreiffen müssen
Diß wir zuvor. Wie Morgenluft sind nemlich die Nahmen
Seit Christus. Werden Träume. Fallen, wie Irrtum
Auf das Herz und tödtend, wenn nicht einer

From Jordan and from Nazareth
And far from the lake, at Capernaum,
And Galilee the breezes, and from Canaan.
A little while I shall stay, he said. So with drops
He quenched the sighing of the light that was
Like thirsty wild beasts in those days, when for Syria
Lamented the native grace in dying of
Small children killed, and the Baptist's head,
Just picked, was visible like an unwithering script
On the abiding platter. Like fire
Are voices of God. Yet it is hard
In great events to preserve what is great.
Not a pasture. So that one shall
Abide in the beginning. But now
This goes on again, as before.

John. Christ. This latter now I wish
To sing, like Hercules or the island which
Was held and saved, refreshing
The neighbouring one with cool sea waters drawn
From ocean's desert, the vast, Peleus. But that's
Impossible. Differently it is a fate. More marvellous.
More rich to sing. Immeasurable
The fable ever since. And now
I wish to sing the journey of the nobles to
Jerusalem, and anguish wandering at Canossa,
And Heinrich himself. If only
My very courage does not expose me. This first we
Must understand. For like morning air are the names
Since Christ. Become dreams. Fall on the heart
Like error, and killing, if one does not

Erwäget, was sie sind und begreift.
Es sah aber der achtsame Mann
Das Angesicht des Gottes,
Damals, da, beim Geheimnisse des Weinstoks sie
Zusammensaßen, zu der Stunde des Gastmals,
Und in der großen Seele, wohlauswählend, den Tod
Aussprach der Herr, und die lezte Liebe, denn nie genug
Hatt er, von Güte, zu sagen
Der Worte, damals, und zu bejahn bejahendes. Aber sein Licht war

Tod. Denn karg ist das Zürnen der Welt.
Das aber erkannt' er. Alles ist gut. Drauf starb er.
Es sahen aber, gebükt, deß ungeachtet, vor Gott die Gestalt
Des Verläugnenden, wie wenn
Ein Jahrhundert sich biegt, nachdenklich, in der Freude der Wahrheit
Noch zulezt die Freunde.

Doch trauerten sie, da nun
Es Abend worden. Nemlich rein
Zu seyn, ist Geschik, ein Leben, das ein Herz hat,
Vor solchem Angesicht', und dauert über die Hälfte.
Zu meiden aber ist viel. Zu viel aber
Der Liebe, wo Anbetung ist,
Ist gefahrreich, triffet am meisten. Jene wollten aber
Vom Angesichte des Herrn
Nicht lassen und der Heimath. Eingeboren
Wie Feuer war in dem Eisen das, und ihnen
Zur Seite gieng, wie eine Seuche, der Schatte des Lieben.
Drum sandt er ihnen
Den Geist, und freilich bebte
Das Haus und die Wetter Gottes rollten
Ferndonnernd, Männer schaffend, wie wenn Drachenzähne,
                              prächtigen Schiksaals,

Consider what they are and understand.
But the attentive man saw
The face of God,
At that time, when over the mystery of the vine
They sat together, at the hour of the communal meal,
And in his great soul, carefully choosing, the Lord
Pronounced death, and the ultimate love, for never
He could find words enough
To say about kindness, then, and to affirm the affirmative. But his light
     was
Death. For niggardly is the wrath of the world.
Yet this he recognized. All is good. Thereupon he died.
But nevertheless, bowed down, the friends at the very last
Before God saw the denier's presence, as when
A century bends, thoughtfully, in
The joy of truth,

  Yet they were sad, now that
The evening had come. For to
Be pure is a skill, a life that has a heart, in
The presence of such a face, and outlasts the middle.
But much is to be avoided. Too much
Of love, though, where there is idolatry,
Is dangerous, strikes home most. But those men were loath
To part from the face of the Lord
And from their homeland. Inborn
Like fire in iron was this, and beside them
Walked, like a plague, the loved one's shadow.
Therefore he sent them
The Spirit, and mightily trembled
The house and God's thunder-storms rolled
Distantly rumbling, creating men, as when dragons' teeth,
                                    of glorious fate,

Andenken

Der Nordost wehet,
Der liebste unter den Winden
Mir, weil er feurigen Geist
Und gute Fahrt verheißet den Schiffern.
Geh aber nun und grüße
Die schöne Garonne,
Und die Gärten von Bourdeaux
Dort, wo am scharfen Ufer
Hingehet der Steg und in den Strom
Tief fällt der Bach, darüber aber
Hinschauet ein edel Paar
Von Eichen und Silberpappeln;

Noch denket das mir wohl und wie
Die breiten Gipfel neiget
Der Ulmwald, über die Mühl',
Im Hofe aber wächset ein Feigenbaum.
An Feiertagen gehn
Die braunen Frauen daselbst
Auf seidnen Boden,
Zur Märzenzeit,
Wenn gleich ist Nacht und Tag,
Und über langsamen Stegen,
Von goldenen Träumen schwer,
Einwiegende Lüfte ziehen.

Es reiche aber,
Des dunkeln Lichtes voll,
Mir einer den duftenden Becher,
Damit ich ruhen möge; denn süß
Wär' unter Schatten der Schlummer.
Nicht ist es gut,
Seellos von sterblichen
Gedanken zu seyn. Doch gut
Ist ein Gespräch und zu sagen

Remembrance

The north-easterly blows,
Of winds the dearest to me
Because a fiery spirit
And happy voyage it promises mariners.
But go now, go and greet
The beautiful Garonne
And the gardens of Bordeaux,
To where on the rugged bank
The path runs and into the river
Deep falls the brook, but above them
A noble pair of oaks
And white poplars look out;

Still well I remember this, and how
The elm wood with its great leafy tops
Inclines, towards the mill,
But in the courtyard a fig-tree grows.
On holidays there too
The brown women walk
On silken ground,
In the month of March,
When night and day are equal
And over slow footpaths,
Heavy with golden dreams,
Lulling breezes drift.

But someone pass me
The fragrant cup
Full of the dark light,
So that I may rest now; for sweet
It would be to drowse amid shadows.
It is not good
To be soulless
With mortal thoughts. But good
Is converse, and to speak

Des Herzens Meinung, zu hören viel
Von Tagen der Lieb',
Und Thaten, welche geschehen.

Wo aber sind die Freunde? Bellarmin
Mit dem Gefährten? Mancher
Trägt Scheue, an die Quelle zu gehn;
Es beginnet nemlich der Reichtum
Im Meere. Sie,
Wie Mahler, bringen zusammen
Das Schöne der Erd' und verschmähn
Den geflügelten Krieg nicht, und
Zu wohnen einsam, jahrlang, unter
Dem entlaubten Mast, wo nicht die Nacht durchglänzen
Die Feiertage der Stadt,
Und Saitenspiel und eingeborener Tanz nicht.

Nun aber sind zu Indiern
Die Männer gegangen,
Dort an der luftigen Spiz'
An Traubenbergen, wo herab
Die Dordogne kommt,
Und zusammen mit der prächt'gen
Garonne meerbreit
Ausgehet der Strom. Es nehmet aber
Und giebt Gedächtniß die See,
Und die Lieb' auch heftet fleißig die Augen,
Was bleibet aber, stiften die Dichter.

Der Ister

Jezt komme, Feuer!
Begierig sind wir
Zu schauen den Tag,
Und wenn die Prüfung
Ist durch die Knie gegangen,

The heart's opinion, to hear many tales
About the days of love
And deeds that have occurred.

   But where are the friends? Where Bellarmine
And his companion? Many a man
Is shy of going to the source;
For wealth begins in
The sea. And they,
Like painters, bring together
The beautiful things of the earth
And do not disdain winged war, and
To live in solitude, for years, beneath the
Defoliate mast, where through the night do not gleam
The city's holidays
Nor music of strings, nor indigenous dancing.

   But now to Indians
Those men have gone,
There on the airy peak
On grape-covered hills, where down
The Dordogne comes
And together with the glorious
Garonne as wide as the sea
The current sweeps out. But it is the sea
That takes and gives remembrance,
And love no less keeps eyes attentively fixed,
But what is lasting the poets provide.

The Ister*

   Now come, fire!
We are impatient
To look upon Day,
And when the trial
Has passed through the knees

          *The classical name for the Danube.

Mag einer spüren das Waldgeschrei.
Wir singen aber vom Indus her
Fernangekommen und
Vom Alpheus, lange haben
Das Schikliche wir gesucht,
Nicht ohne Schwingen mag
Zum Nächsten einer greifen
Geradezu
Und kommen auf die andere Seite.
Hier aber wollen wir bauen.
Denn Ströme machen urbar
Das Land. Wenn nemlich Kräuter wachsen
Und an denselben gehn
Im Sommer zu trinken die Thiere,
So gehn auch Menschen daran.

Man nennet aber diesen den Ister.
Schön wohnt er. Es brennet der Säulen Laub,
Und reget sich. Wild stehn
Sie aufgerichtet, untereinander; darob
Ein zweites Maas, springt vor
Von Felsen das Dach. So wundert
Mich nicht, daß er
Den Herkules zu Gaste geladen,
Fernglänzend, am Olympos drunten,
Da der, sich Schatten zu suchen
Vom heißen Isthmos kam,
Denn voll des Muthes waren
Daselbst sie, es bedarf aber, der Geister wegen,
Der Kühlung auch. Darum zog jener lieber
An die Wasserquellen hieher und gelben Ufer,
Hoch duftend oben, und schwarz
Vom Fichtenwald, wo in den Tiefen
Ein Jäger gern lustwandelt
Mittags, und Wachstum hörbar ist
An harzigen Bäumen des Isters,

One may perceive the cries in the wood.
But, as for us, we sing from the Indus,
Arrived from afar, and
From the Alpheus, long we
Have sought what is fitting,
Not without wings may one
Reach out for that which is nearest
Directly
And get to the other side.
But here we wish to build.
For rivers make arable
The land. For when herbs are growing
And to the same in summer
The animals go to drink,
There too will human kind go.

   This one, however, is called the Ister.
Beautifully he dwells. The pillars' foliage burns,
And stirs. Wildly they stand
Supporting one another; above,
A second measure, juts out
The roof of rocks. No wonder, therefore,
I say, this river
Invited Hercules,
Distantly gleaming, down by Olympus,
When he, to look for shadows,
Came up from the sultry isthmus,
For full of courage they were
In that place, but, because of the spirits,
There's need of coolness too. That is why that hero
Preferred to come here to the well-springs and yellow banks,
Highly fragrant on top, and black
With fir woods, in whose depths
A huntsman loves to amble
At noon, and growth is audible
In resinous trees of the Ister,

Der scheinet aber fast
Rükwärts zu gehen und
Ich mein, er müsse kommen
Von Osten.
Vieles wäre
Zu sagen davon. Und warum hängt er
An den Bergen gerad? Der andre
Der Rhein ist seitwärts
Hinweggegangen. Umsonst nicht gehn
Im Troknen die Ströme. Aber wie? Ein Zeichen braucht es
Nichts anderes, schlecht und recht, damit es Sonn
Und Mond trag' im Gemüth', untrennbar,
Und fortgeh, Tag und Nacht auch, und
Die Himmlischen warm sich fühlen aneinander.
Darum sind jene auch
Die Freude des Höchsten. Denn wie käm er
Herunter? Und wie Hertha grün,
Sind sie die Kinder des Himmels. Aber allzugedultig
Scheint der mir, nicht
Freier, und fast zu spotten. Nemlich wenn

Angehen soll der Tag
In der Jugend, wo er zu wachsen
Anfängt, es treibet ein anderer da
Hoch schon die Pracht, und Füllen gleich
In den Zaum knirscht er, und weithin hören
Das Treiben die Lüfte,
Ist der zufrieden;
Es brauchet aber Stiche der Fels
Und Furchen die Erd',
Unwirthbar wär es, ohne Weile;
Was aber jener thuet der Strom,
Weis niemand.

Yet almost this river seems
To travel backwards and
I think it must come from
The East.
Much could
Be said about this. And why does
It cling to the mountains, straight? The other,
The Rhine, has gone away
Sideways. Not for nothing rivers flow
Through dry land. But how? A sign is needed,
Nothing else, plain and honest, so that
Sun and moon it may bear in mind, inseparable,
And go away, day and night no less, and
The Heavenly feel warm one beside the other.
That also is why these are
The joy of the Highest. For how
Would he get down? And like Hertha* green
They are the children of Heaven. But all too patient
He seems to me, not
More free, and nearly derisive. For when

Day is due to begin
In youth, where it starts
To grow, another already there
Drives high the splendour, and like foals
He grinds the bit, and far off the breezes
Can hear the commotion,
If he is contented;
But the rock needs incisions
And the earth needs furrows,
Would be desolate else, unabiding;
Yet what that one does, the river,
Nobody knows.

*According to Tacitus, the *terra mater* of the ancient Germans.

Mnemosyne
DRITTE FASSUNG

Reif sind, in Feuer getaucht, gekochet
Die Frücht und auf der Erde geprüfet und ein Gesez ist
Daß alles hineingeht, Schlangen gleich,
Prophetisch, träumend auf
Den Hügeln des Himmels. Und vieles
Wie auf den Schultern eine
Last von Scheitern ist
Zu behalten. Aber bös sind
Die Pfade. Nemlich unrecht,
Wie Rosse, gehn die gefangenen
Element' und alten
Geseze der Erd. Und immer
Ins Ungebundene gehet eine Sehnsucht. Vieles aber ist
Zu behalten. Und Noth die Treue.
Vorwärts aber und rükwärts wollen wir
Nicht sehn. Uns wiegen lassen, wie
Auf schwankem Kahne der See.

Wie aber liebes? Sonnenschein
Am Boden sehen wir und trokenen Staub
Und heimatlich die Schatten der Wälder und es blühet
An Dächern der Rauch, bei alter Krone
Der Thürme, friedsam; gut sind nemlich
Hat gegenredend die Seele
Ein Himmlisches verwundet, die Tageszeichen.
Denn Schnee, wie Majenblumen
Das Edelmüthige, wo
Es seie, bedeutend, glänzet auf
Der grünen Wiese
Der Alpen, hälftig, da, vom Kreuze redend, das
Gesezt ist unterwegs einmal
Gestorbenen, auf hoher Straß

*Mnemosyne**
THIRD VERSION

Ripe are, dipped in fire, cooked
The fruits and tried on the earth, and it is law,
Prophetic, that all must enter in
Like serpents, dreaming on
The mounds of heaven. And much
As on the shoulders a
Load of logs must be
Retained. But evil are
The paths, for crookedly
Like horses go the imprisoned
Elements and ancient laws
Of the earth. And always
There is a yearning that seeks the unbound. But much
Must be retained. And loyalty is needed.
Forward, however, and back we will
Not look. Be lulled and rocked as
On a swaying skiff of the sea.

But how, my dear one? On the ground
Sunshine we see and the dry dust
And, a native sight, the shadows of forests, and on roof-tops
There blossoms smoke, near ancient crests
Of the turrets, peaceable; for good indeed
When, contradicting, the soul
Has wounded one of the Heavenly, are the signs of day.
For snow, like lilies of the valley
By indicating where
The noble-minded is, shines brightly
On the green meadow
Of the Alps, half melted, where
Discoursing of the cross which once was placed
There on the wayside for the dead,

*'Memory': the Mother of the Muses.

Ein Wandersmann geht zornig,
Fern ahnend mit
Dem andern, aber was ist diß?

   Am Feigenbaum ist mein
Achilles mir gestorben,
Und Ajax liegt
An den Grotten der See,
An Bächen, benachbart dem Skamandros.
An Schläfen Sausen einst, nach
Der unbewegten Salamis steter
Gewohnheit, in der Fremd', ist groß
Ajax gestorben
Patroklos aber in des Königes Harnisch. Und es starben
Noch andere viel. Am Kithäron aber lag
Elevtherä, der Mnemosyne Stadt. Der auch als
Ablegte den Mantel Gott, das abendliche nachher löste
Die Loken. Himmlische nemlich sind
Unwillig, wenn einer nicht die Seele schonend sich
Zusammengenommen, aber er muß doch; dem
Gleich fehlet die Trauer.

High up, in anger, distantly divining
A traveller walks
With the other, but what is this?

   Beside the fig-tree
My Achilles has died and is lost to me,
And Ajax lies
Beside the grottoes of the sea,
Beside brooks that neighbour Scamandros.
Of a rushing noise in his temples once,
According to the changeless custom of
Unmoved Salamis, in foreign parts
Great Ajax died,
Not so Patroclus, dead in the King's own armour.
And many others died. But by Cithaeron there stood
Eleutherae, Mnemosyne's town. From her also
When God laid down his festive cloak, soon after did
The powers of Evening sever a lock of hair. For the Heavenly, when
Someone has failed to collect his soul, to spare it,
Are angry, for still he must; like him
Here mourning is at fault.

FRAGMENTS OF OTHER HYMNS

(1800–1805)

Deutscher Gesang

Wenn der Morgen trunken begeisternd heraufgeht
Und der Vogel sein Lied beginnt,
Und Stralen der Strom wirft, und rascher hinab
Die rauhe Bahn geht über den Fels,
Weil ihn die Sonne gewärmet.

Und der
Verlangend in anders Land
Die Jünglinge

Und das Thor erwacht und der Marktplaz,
Und von heiligen Flammen des Heerds
Der röthliche Duft steigt, dann schweigt er allein,
Dann hält er still im Busen das Herz,
Und sinnt in einsamer Halle.

Doch wenn

dann sizt im tiefen Schatten,
Wenn über dem Haupt die Ulme säuselt,
Am kühlathmenden Bache der deutsche Dichter
Und singt, wenn er des heiligen nüchternen Wassers
Genug getrunken, fernhin lauschend in die Stille,
Den Seelengesang.
Und noch, noch ist er des Geistes zu voll,
Und die reine Seele

Bis zürnend er
Und es glühet ihm die Wange vor Schaam,
Unheilig jeder Laut des Gesangs.

Doch lächeln über des Mannes Einfalt
Die Gestirne, wenn vom Orient her
Weissagend über den Bergen unseres Volks
Sie verweilen
Und wie des Vaters Hand ihm über den Loken geruht,
In Tagen der Kindheit,

German Song

When drunkenly inspiring the morning rises
And the bird begins his tune,
And the river flashes beams and more quickly takes
Its rough course over the rock,
Because the sun has warmed it.

And the
Longing to go to another land
The youths

And the gate awakens and the market-place,
And from holy flames of the hearth
The reddish odour rises, then he alone is silent,
Then quiet in his bosom he keeps his heart
And ponders in the solitary hall.

But when

then in the deep shade, when
Above his head the elm tree rustles,
By the stream that breathes out coolness the German poet sits
And sings, when of the hallowed sober water
Enough he has drunk, listening far out into silence,
The song of the soul.
And still, still his mind is too full of thought,
And his pure soul

Until in anger he
And his cheeks are flushed with shame,
Unholy every note of his song.

Yet the planets smile at the man's
Simplicity when, come from the East,
They linger prophesying above
Our people's mountains
And as his father's hand had rested upon his locks
In childhood days,

So krönet, daß er schaudernd es fühlt
Ein Seegen das Haupt des Sängers,
Wenn dich, der du
Um deiner Schöne willen, bis heute,
Nahmlos geblieben o göttlichster!
O guter Geist des Vaterlands
Sein Wort im Liede dich nennet.

Heimath

Und niemand weiß

Indessen laß mich wandeln
Und wilde Beeren pflüken
Zu löschen die Liebe zu dir
An deinen Pfaden, o Erd'

Hier wo – – –
            und Rosendornen
Und süße Linden duften neben
Den Buchen, des Mittags, wenn im falben Kornfeld
Das Wachstum rauscht, an geradem Halm,
Und den Naken die Ähre seitwärts beugt
Dem Herbste gleich, jezt aber unter hohem
Gewölbe der Eichen, da ich sinn
Und aufwärts frage, der Glokenschlag
Mir wohlbekannt
Fernher tönt, goldenklingend, um die Stunde, wenn
Der Vogel wieder wacht. So gehet es wohl.

A blessing, so that he feels a shiver,
Now crowns the singer's head,
When you that for
Your beauty's sake, till today, have been
Kept nameless, O most divine,
Good spirit of our homeland,
When you his word names in song.

Home

And no one knows

But meanwhile let me walk
And pick wild berries
To quench my love for you
Upon your paths, O Earth

Here where
            and thorns of roses
And sweet lime-trees give out their fragrance
Beside the beeches, at noon, when in the yellowish cornfield
There is a whisper of growth, by the straight stalk,
And the ear inclines its neck to one side
Like autumn, but now beneath
The oaks' high vault, where I ponder
And question heavenward, the stroke of the bell,
Familiar to me,
Rings out from afar, with a golden ring, at the hour when
The bird's awake once more. Then all is well.

Wenn nemlich der Rebe Saft . . .

Wenn nemlich der Rebe Saft,
Das milde Gewächs suchet Schatten
Und die Traube wächset unter dem kühlen
Gewölbe der Blätter,
Den Männern eine Stärke,
Wohl aber duftend den Jungfraun,
Und Bienen,
Wenn sie, vom Wohlgeruche
Des Frühlings trunken, der Geist
Der Sonne rühret, irren ihr nach
Die Getriebenen, wenn aber
Ein Stral brennt, kehren sie
Mit Gesumm, vielahnend
                darob
            die Eiche rauschet,

Auf falbem Laube . . .

Auf falbem Laube ruhet
Die Traube, des Weines Hoffnung, also ruhet auf der Wange
Der Schatten von dem goldenen Schmuk, der hängt
Am Ohre der Jungfrau.

Und ledig soll ich bleiben
Leicht fanget aber sich
In der Kette, die
Es abgerissen, das Kälblein.

Fleißig

For when the grape-vine's sap . . .

For when the grape-vine's sap,
That gentle plant, looks for shade
And the grape grows beneath the cool
Involutions of the leaves,
To men a source of strength,
But to young women pleasantly fragrant,
And bees
When, drunken with the fragrance
Of Spring, they are stirred
By the spirit of the sun,
Driven on, they fumble for it,
But when a ray burns,
Buzzing, they turn back,
Divining much
            above it
        the oak-tree rustles,

On fallow foliage . . .

On fallow foliage rests
The grape, the hope of wine, and so on the cheek rests
The shadow of the gold ornament that hangs
On the young woman's ear.

And I must not get married
Yet easily in the chain
It has torn off, the little
Calf entangles itself.

Busy

Es liebet aber der Sämann
Zu sehen eine,
Des Tages schlafend über
Dem Strikstrumpf.

Nicht will wohllauten
Der deutsche Mund
Aber lieblich
Am stechenden Bart rauschen
Die Küsse.

Was ist der Menschen Leben . . .

Was ist der Menschen Leben   ein Bild der Gottheit.
Wie unter dem Himmel wandeln die Irrdischen alle, sehen
Sie diesen. Lesend aber gleichsam, wie
In einer Schrift, die Unendlichkeit nachahmen und den Reichtum
Menschen. Ist der einfältige Himmel
Denn reich? Wie Blüthen sind ja
Silberne Wolken. Es regnet aber von daher
Der Thau und das Feuchte. Wenn aber
Das Blau ist ausgelöschet, das Einfältige, scheint
Das Matte, das dem Marmelstein gleichet, wie Erz,
Anzeige des Reichtums.

Was ist Gott? . . .

Was ist Gott? unbekannt, dennoch
Voll Eigenschaften ist das Angesicht
Des Himmels von ihm. Die Blize nemlich
Der Zorn sind eines Gottes. Jemehr ist eins
Unsichtbar,   schiket es sich in Fremdes. Aber der Donner
Der Ruhm ist Gottes. Die Liebe zur Unsterblichkeit
Das Eigentum auch, wie das unsere,
Ist eines Gottes.

But the sower
Loves to see a woman
Fallen asleep in the daytime
Over a half-knitted stocking.

The German mouth
Will yield no euphony
But brushing the prickly beard
Charmingly patter
The kisses.

What is the life of men . . .

What is the life of men   an image of the godhead.
As all the earthly move under heaven they see
This heaven. But reading, so to speak,
As though in a script, men imitate
Infinity and riches. Is simple heaven
Rich, then? Surely like blossoms are
Silvery clouds. Yet from there it is that dew and
Moisture rain down. But when
The blueness is extinguished, the simpleness,
Then shines the pale hue that resembles marble, like ore,
An indication of riches.

What is God? . . .

What is God? Unknown, and yet
Full of qualities is the face
Of heaven with him. For lightning flashes
And wrath are a god's. The more a thing
Is invisible   into foreignness it goes forth. But thunder
Fame are God's. And love of immortality
Possessions, too, such as ours,
Are a god's.

An die Madonna

Viel hab' ich dein
Und deines Sohnes wegen
Gelitten, o Madonna,
Seit ich gehöret von ihm
In süßer Jugend;
Denn nicht der Seher allein,
Es stehen unter einem Schiksaal
Die Dienenden auch. Denn weil ich

Und manchen Gesang, den ich
Dem höchsten zu singen, dem Vater
Gesonnen war, den hat
Mir weggezehret die Schwermuth.

Doch Himmlische, doch will ich
Dich feiern und nicht soll einer
Der Rede Schönheit mir
Die heimatliche, vorwerfen,
Dieweil ich allein
Zum Felde gehe, wo wild
Die Lilie wächst, furchtlos,
Zum unzugänglichen,
Uralten Gewölbe
Des Waldes,
        das Abendland,

                und gewaltet über
Den Menschen hat, statt anderer Gottheit sie
Die allvergessende Liebe.

    Denn damals sollt es beginnen
Als

Geboren dir im Schoose
Der göttliche Knabe und um ihn
Der Freundin Sohn, Johannes genannt
Vom stummen Vater, der kühne

To the Virgin Mary

Much I have suffered
On your account
And on your son's, Our Lady,
Since first in my sweet youth
I heard of him;
For not the seer alone,
But even those who serve
A destiny rules. Because I

And many a song which to
The Highest, the Father, I once was
Disposed to sing, was lost
To me, devoured by sadness.

Yet, heavenly one, yet you
I'll celebrate and let no one
Reproach me with
The beauty of native speech,
Now that alone
I go to the field where wild
The lily grows, fearless,
To the inaccessible
Primordial vault
Of the forest,
        the Occident,

                    and over mankind
In place of other deities there reigned
The all-oblivious, Love.

    For then it was to begin
When

Born from within you the boy
Divine and when about him
The son of your friend, named John
By his dumb father, he the bold one

Dem war gegeben
Der Zunge Gewalt,
Zu deuten

Und die Furcht der Völker und
Die Donner und
Die stürzenden Wasser des Herrn.

Denn gut sind Sazungen, aber
Wie Drachenzähne, schneiden sie
Und tödten das Leben, wenn im Zorne sie schärft
Ein Geringer oder ein König.
Gleichmuth ist aber gegeben
Den Liebsten Gottes. So dann starben jene.
Die Beiden,　　　　　so auch sahst
Du göttlichtrauernd in der starken Seele sie sterben.
Und wohnst deswegen

　　　　　　　　　　　und wenn in heiliger Nacht
Der Zukunft einer gedenkt und Sorge für
Die sorglosschlafenden trägt
Die frischaufblühenden Kinder
Kömmst lächelnd du, und fragst, was er, wo du
Die Königin seiest, befürchte.

Denn nimmer vermagst du es
Die keimenden Tage zu neiden,
Denn lieb ist dirs, von je,
Wenn größer die Söhne sind,
Denn ihre Mutter. Und nimmer gefällt es dir
Wenn rükwärtsblikend
Ein Älteres spottet des Jüngern.
Wer denkt der theuern Väter
Nicht gern und erzählet
Von ihren Thaten,

　　　　　　wenn aber Verwegnes geschah,
Und Undankbare haben
Das Ärgerniß　　　　　gegeben

To whom was given
The power of the tongue
To interpret

And the fear of the peoples and
The thunder and
The rushing waters of the Lord.

For good are statutes, but
Like dragons' teeth, they cut
And kill the living, when in anger whetted
By a lowly man or a king.
But equanimity is given
To those most loved by God. So then they died
Those two,   so you also saw
Them die, divinely mourning in your mighty soul.
And for that reason dwell

                    and when in holy Night
Of coming ages someone remembers and
Is troubled for their sake who untroubled sleep
The freshly unfolding children,
Then smiling you come and ask him what,
Where you are Queen, he could fear.

For never you could be moved
To envy the days that are burgeoning,
But always have been pleased
When the sons are greater
Than their mother. And never you approve
When looking backwards
An older one mocks at the younger.
Who does not like to think
Of the dear fathers and tell
About their deeds,

                    but when reckless deeds were done,
And ungrateful men gave cause
For   annoyance

Zu gerne blikt
Dann   zum
Und thatenscheu
Unendliche Reue und es haßt das Alte die Kinder.

Darum beschüze
Du Himmlische sie
Die jungen Pflanzen und wenn
Der Nord kömmt oder giftiger Thau weht oder
Zu lange dauert die Dürre
Und wenn sie üppigblühend
Versinken unter der Sense
Der allzuscharfen, gieb erneuertes Wachstum.
Und daß nur niemals nicht
Vielfältig, in schwachem Gezweige
Die Kraft mir vielversuchend
Zerstreue das frische Geschlecht, stark aber sei
Zu wählen aus Vielem das beste.

Nichts ists, das Böse. Das soll
Wie der Adler den Raub
Mir Eines begreifen.
Die Andern dabei. Damit sie nicht
Die Amme, die
Den Tag gebieret
Verwirren, falsch anklebend
Der Heimath und der Schwere spottend
Der Mutter ewig sizen
Im Schoose. Denn groß ist
Von dem sie erben den Reichtum.
Der

Vor allem, daß man schone
Der Wildniß göttlichgebaut
Im reinen Geseze, woher
Es haben die Kinder
Des Gotts, lustwandelnd unter
Den Felsen und Haiden purpurn blühn
Und dunkle Quellen
Dir, o Madonna und

Too gladly then
Looks   to
And shy of action
Unending remorse and the old will hate the children.

Therefore protect them,
O heavenly one,
Those tender plants, and when
The North Wind comes or poisonous dew wafts
Or too long a drought has lasted
And when in copious flower
They sink beneath the scythe,
The all too sharp, then grant them renewal of growth.
And never, above all,
Attempting much and multifarious
In feeble branches let a power
Disperse the new generation, but strong let it be
Out of many to choose the best.

A mere nothing is Evil. This
As an eagle his prey
Let someone grasp.
The others no less. So that they
Do
Not perplex the nurse
Who gives birth to day,
Wrongly sticking to home and mocking
At hardship, endlessly sit
On their mother's lap. For great
Is he whose wealth they inherit.
He

Above all, let them spare
The wilderness divinely built
In the spirit of pure law,
Whence the God's children have it,
Pleasantly strolling under
The rocks; and heaths are in purple flower
And dark the sources
For you, our Lady, and

Dem Sohne, aber den anderen auch
Damit nicht, als von Knechten,
Mit Gewalt das ihre nehmen
Die Götter.

An den Gränzen aber, wo stehet
Der Knochenberg, so nennet man ihn
Heut, aber in alter Sprache heißet
Er Ossa, Teutoburg ist
Daselbst auch und voll geistigen Wassers
Umher das Land, da
Die Himmlischen all
Sich Tempel

    Ein Handwerksmann.

Uns aber die wir
Daß

Und zu sehr zu fürchten die Furcht nicht!
Denn du nicht, holde

          aber es giebt
Ein finster Geschlecht, das weder einen Halbgott
Gern hört, oder wenn mit Menschen ein Himmlisches oder
In Woogen erscheint, gestaltlos, oder das Angesicht
Des reinen ehrt, des nahen
Allgegenwärtigen Gottes.

Doch wenn unheilige schon
         in Menge
           und frech

For the son, but for the others also,
Lest as from slaves by force
The gods
Should take what is theirs.

But near the frontiers, where lies
The Knochenberg, so now it is called,
But in ancient speech its name
Was Ossa, Teutoburg also
Is there and full of spiritual waters
The country round about, where
The heavenly all
(Built) themselves temples

   An artisan.

But to us who
That

Nor be too greatly afraid of fear!
For, gracious one, not you

           but there is
A gloomy race which does not like to hear
Either a demigod or when with mortals a heavenly being
Appears or in waves, amorphous, nor will honour
The face of him, the pure,
The near and omnipresent God.

But even if the unholy
           in masses
               and insolent

Was kümmern sie dich
O Gesang den Reinen, ich zwar
Ich sterbe, doch du
Gehest andere Bahn, umsonst
Mag dich ein Neidisches hindern.

Wenn dann in kommender Zeit
Du einem Guten begegnest
So grüß ihn, und er denkt,
Wie unsere Tage wohl
Voll Glüks, voll Leidens gewesen.
Von einem gehet zum andern

Noch Eins ist aber
Zu sagen. Denn es wäre
Mir fast zu plözlich
Das Glük gekommen,
Das Einsame, daß ich unverständig
Im Eigentum
Mich an die Schatten gewandt,
Denn weil du gabst
Den Sterblichen
Versuchend Göttergestalt,
Wofür ein Wort? so meint' ich, denn es hasset die Rede, wer
Das Lebenslicht das herzernährende sparet.
Es deuteten vor Alters
Die Himmlischen sich, von selbst, wie sie
Die Kraft der Götter hinweggenommen.

Wir aber zwingen
Dem Unglük ab und hängen die Fahnen
Dem Siegsgott, dem befreienden auf, darum auch
Hast du Räthsel gesendet. Heilig sind sie
Die Glänzenden, wenn aber alltäglich
Die Himmlischen und gemein
Das Wunder scheinen will, wenn nemlich
Wie Raub Titanenfürsten die Gaaben
Der Mutter greifen, hilft ein Höherer ihr.

What do they matter to you
O Song, that are pure; indeed
I die, but you
Follow a different course, in vain
Shall the envious try to impede you.

And if in a coming age
You should meet with a good man,
Then greet him and he will think
How once our days were full
Of joy, of suffering.
From one will go to another

Yet one thing remains
To be said. For almost
Too suddenly
This happiness would have been granted,
This lonely happiness: that, lacking knowledge
Of what is mine
To the shadows I would have turned,
For because you gave
To mortals
The tentative shape of gods,
Why waste a word? So then I thought, for he hates speech
Who husbands the light of life that nourishes the heart.
In ancient times
The heavenly beings themselves interpreted
How they had taken away the strength of the gods.

But we
Wrest from misfortune and hang the flags
Upon the god of victory, the liberator, and that is why
You sent enigmas. Holy are they,
The shining, but when the heavenly
Would seem quotidian and vulgar
The miracle and when, indeed,
Like stolen booty Titanic princes seize
The Mother's gifts, then One who is higher comes to her aid.

Die Titanen

Nicht ist es aber
Die Zeit. Noch sind sie
Unangebunden. Göttliches trift untheilnehmende nicht.
Dann mögen sie rechnen
Mit Delphi. Indessen, gieb in Feierstunden
Und daß ich ruhen möge, der Todten
Zu denken. Viele sind gestorben
Feldherrn in alter Zeit
Und schöne Frauen und Dichter
Und in neuer
Der Männer viel
Ich aber bin allein.

            und in den Ocean schiffend
Die duftenden Inseln fragen
Wohin sie sind.

Denn manches von ihnen ist
In treuen Schriften überblieben
Und manches in Sagen der Zeit.
Viel offenbaret der Gott.
Denn lang schon wirken
Die Wolken hinab
Und es wurzelt vielesbereitend heilige Wildniß.
Heiß ist der Reichtum. Denn es fehlet
An Gesang, der löset den Geist.
Verzehren würd' er
Und wäre gegen sich selbst
Denn nimmer duldet
Die Gefangenschaft das himmlische Feuer.

Es erfreuet aber
Das Gastmahl oder wenn am Feste
Das Auge glänzet und von Perlen
Der Jungfrau Hals.
Auch Kriegesspiel

The Titans

Not yet, however,
The time has come. They still are
Untethered. What's divine does not strike the unconcerned.
Then let them reckon
With Delphi. Meanwhile in festive hours,
And so that I may rest, allow me
To think of the dead. In olden days
Died many generals
And lovely women and poets,
In modern times
A host of men.
But I am on my own.

          and sailing into the ocean
The fragrant islands ask
Where they have gone.

For something of them has been
Preserved in faithful writings
And something in lore of the age.
Much does the God reveal.
For long already the clouds
Have worked upon what's below them,
And holy wilderness, pregnant with much, has grown roots.
Hot is wealth. For we lack
Song that loosens the mind.
It would devour
And would make war on itself
For never the heavenly fire
Will suffer captivity.

Yet men are gladdened by
The banquet, and when in celebration
Our eyes are bright, and with pearls
The virgin's neck.
Martial games no less

und durch die Gänge
Der Gärten schmettert
Das Gedächtniß der Schlacht und besänftiget
An schlanker Brust
Die tönenden Wehre ruhn
Von Heldenvätern den Kindern.
Mich aber umsummet
Die Bien und wo der Akersmann
Die Furchen machet singen gegen
Dem Lichte die Vögel. Manche helfen
Dem Himmel. Diese siehet
Der Dichter. Gut ist es, an andern sich
Zu halten. Denn keiner trägt das Leben allein.

Wenn aber ist entzündet
Der geschäfftige Tag
Und an der Kette, die
Den Bliz ableitet
Von der Stunde des Aufgangs
Himmlischer Thau glänzt,
Muß unter Sterblichen auch
Das Hohe sich fühlen.
Drum bauen sie Häußer
Und die Werkstatt gehet
Und über Strömen das Schiff.
Und es bieten tauschend die Menschen
Die Händ' einander, sinnig ist es
Auf Erden und es sind nicht umsonst
Die Augen an den Boden geheftet.

Ihr fühlet aber
Auch andere Art.
Denn unter dem Maaße
Des Rohen brauchet es auch
Damit das Reine sich kenne.
Wenn aber

Und in die Tiefe greifet
Daß es lebendig werde
Der Allerschütterer, meinen die

                        and through the walks
Of gardens blares
The memory of battle and, soothed
Upon the slender breasts
Of children quiet lie
Loud weapons of their heroic ancestors.
But around me hums
The bee, and where the ploughman draws
His furrows, birds are singing
Against the light. Many give help
To Heaven. And them
The poet sees. It is good to rely
Upon others. For no one can bear this life on his own.

But when the busy day
Has been kindled
And on the chain that
Conducts the lightning
From the hour of sunrise
Glistens heavenly dew,
Among mortals also
What is high must feel at home.
That is why they build houses
And the workshop's astir
And over currents the ship.
And, bartering, men hold out
Their hands to one another; pensive it is
On earth, and not for nothing
Are eyes fixed on the ground.

Yet you also sense
A different kind.
For measure demands that
Crudity, coarseness exist, so that
What is pure shall know itself.
But when

And down into the depth
To make it come to life,
Reaches he who shakes all things,

Es komme der Himmlische
Zu Todten herab und gewaltig dämmerts
Im ungebundenen Abgrund
Im allesmerkenden auf.
Nicht möcht ich aber sagen
Es werden die Himmlischen schwach
Wenn schon es aufgährt.
Wenn aber
          und es gehet

An die Scheitel dem Vater, daß

          und der Vogel des Himmels ihm
Es anzeigt. Wunderbar
Im Zorne kommet er drauf.

Einst hab ich die Muse gefragt . . .

Einst hab ich die Muse gefragt, und sie
Antwortete mir
Am Ende wirst du es finden.
Kein Sterblicher kann es fassen.
Vom Höchsten will ich schweigen.
Verbotene Frucht, wie der Lorbeer, aber ist
Am meisten das Vaterland. Die aber kost'
Ein jeder zulezt,

Viel täuschet Anfang
Und Ende.
Das lezte aber ist
Das Himmelszeichen, das reißt
       und   Menschen
Hinweg. Wohl hat Herkules das
Gefürchtet. Aber da wir träge

They believe the Heavenly comes
Down to the dead, and mightily
In the unfettered abyss,
The all-perceiving, light breaks.
But I do not wish to say
That the Heavenly are growing weak
Though now it erupts.
But when

            and it rises

Up to the partings of the Father's hair, so that

            and the bird of Heaven
Makes it known to him. Then
Marvellous in anger he comes.

At one time I questioned the Muse . . .

At one time I questioned the Muse, and she
Replied to me,
In the end you will find it.
No mortal can grasp it.
About the Highest I will not speak.
But, like the laurel, forbidden fruit
Your country is, above all. To be tasted last
By any man,

Beginning and end
Greatly deceive us.
The last thing, however, is
The heavenly sign; it sweeps
        and   men
Away. Of this even Hercules
Was doubtless afraid. But since we are

Geboren sind, bedarf es des Falken, dem
Befolgt' ein Reuter, wenn
Er jaget, den Flug.

Im   wenn
Und der Fürst

            und Feuer und Rauchdampf blüht
Auf dürrem Rasen
Doch ungemischet darunter
Aus guter Brust, das Labsaal
Der Schlacht, die Stimme quillet des Fürsten.

Gefäße machet ein Künstler.
Und es kauffet

                    wenn es aber
Zum Urteil kommt
Und keusch hat es die Lippe
Von einem Halbgott berührt

Und schenket das Liebste
Den Unfruchtbaren
Denn nimmer, von nun an
Taugt zum Gebrauche das Heilge.

Wenn aber die Himmlischen . . .

Wenn aber die Himmlischen haben
Gebaut, still ist es
Auf Erden, und wohlgestalt stehn
Die betroffenen Berge. Gezeichnet

Born lazy, the hawk is needed,
Whose flight, when he hunts,
A horseman follows.

In the   when
And the prince

          and fire and smoke are in flower
On a dry lawn
Yet unmingled on to it wells,
From a good breast, the battle's
Refreshment, the voice of the prince.

An artist makes vessels.
And they are bought

                but when
It comes to the judgement
And chastely it has been touched
By the lip of a demigod

And never now will he
Give away what's dearest to him
To those unfruitful, from now on
The holy is fit for use.

But when the heavenly . . .

But when the heavenly
Have built, it is quiet
On earth, and well-fashioned stand
The mountains they struck. Their brows

Sind ihre Stirnen. Denn es traf
Sie, da den Donnerer hielt
Unzärtlich die gerade Tochter
Des Gottes bebender Stral
Und wohl duftet gelöscht
Von oben der Aufruhr.
Wo inne stehet, beruhiget, da
Und dort,   das Feuer.
Denn Freude schüttet
Der Donnerer aus und hätte fast
Des Himmels vergessen
Damals im Zorne, hätt ihn nicht
Das Weise gewarnet.
Jezt aber blüht es
Am armen Ort.
Und wunderbar groß will
Es stehen.
Gebirg hänget   See,
Warme   Tiefe   es Kühlen aber die Lüfte
Inseln und Halbinseln,
Grotten zu beten,

Ein glänzender Schild
Und schnell, wie Rosen,

                          oder es schafft
Auch andere Art,
Es sprosset aber

                    viel üppig neidiges
Unkraut, das blendet, schneller schießet
Es auf, das ungelenke, denn es scherzet
Der Schöpferische, sie aber
Verstehen es nicht. Zu zornig greifft
Es und wächst. Und dem Brande gleich,
Der Häußer verzehret, schlägt
Empor, achtlos, und schonet
Den Raum nicht, und die Pfade bedeket,
Weitgährend, ein dampfend Gewölk
                    die unbeholfene Wildniß.

Are marked. For they were hit,
When the straight daughter untenderly
Held back the Thunderer,
By the god's tremulous ray
And rebellion quenched from above
Exhales a good fragrance.
Where within, assuaged, here
And there,   is the fire.
For joy the Thunderer
Pours out and almost would have
Forgotten heaven at that time,
Enraged, if the wise had not
Warned him.
But now it blossoms
In a place of dearth.
And wonderfully great
Desires to stand.
Alpine ranges hang   sea,
Warm   deep   but the breezes cool
Islands and peninsulas,
Grottoes to pray,

A gleaming shield
And quick, like roses,

                    or else
A different manner creates,
But there sprouts

                    very lushly an envious
Weed that dazzles, faster it shoots
Up, the awkward, for the creative
Is joking, but they
Do not understand. Too wrathfully
It grips and grows. And like a conflagration
That devours houses, it flares
Up, heedless, and does not spare
Space and a steaming cloud,
Widely in ferment, covers
                    the helpless wilderness.

So will es göttlich scheinen. Aber
Furchtbar ungastlich windet
Sich durch den Garten die Irre,
Die augenlose, da den Ausgang
Mit reinen Händen kaum
Erfindet ein Mensch. Der gehet, gesandt,
Und suchet, dem Thier gleich, das
Nothwendige. Zwar mit Armen,
Der Ahnung voll, mag einer treffen
Das Ziel. Wo nemlich
Die Himmlischen eines Zaunes oder Merkmals,
Das ihren Weg
Anzeige, oder eines Bades
Bedürfen, reget es wie Feuer
In der Brust der Männer sich.

Noch aber hat andre
Bei sich der Vater.
Denn über den Alpen
Weil an den Adler
Sich halten müssen, damit sie nicht
Mit eigenem Sinne zornig deuten
Die Dichter, wohnen über dem Fluge
Des Vogels, um den Thron
Des Gottes der Freude
Und deken den Abgrund
Ihm zu, die gelbem Feuer gleich, in reißender Zeit
Sind über Stirnen der Männer,
Die Prophetischen, denen möchten
Es neiden, weil die Furcht
Sie lieben, Schatten der Hölle,

Sie aber trieb,
Ein rein Schiksaal
Eröffnend   von
Der Erde heiligen Tischen
Der Reiniger Herkules,
Der bleibet immer lauter, jezt noch,
Mit dem Herrscher, und othembringend steigen
Die Dioskuren ab und auf,

So it would seem divine. But
Dreadfully inhospitable through
The garden confusion winds,
The eyeless, when with clean hands
Scarcely a man can find
The way out. He goes, on a mission,
And, like an animal, searches
For what is needed. True, with his arms,
Full of foreknowledge, one may attain
The goal. For where
The heavenly need a fence or a sign
To mark their
Way, or a bath,
There is a stirring like fire
In the hearts of those men.

Yet others the Father
Keeps at his side.
For above the alps,
Because by the eagle
They must be guided, lest with their own minds
In fury they interpret,
The poets, they dwell above
The bird's flight, around the throne
Of the god of joy
And cover the abyss
For him, they who like yellow fire, when time is in spate,
Are above the brows of those men,
The prophetic, would begrudge
It them, because they love
Fear, shades of hell,

But they were driven away,
Opening up a pure
Fate, from
The holy tables of earth,
By Hercules the cleanser
Who, candid always, remains, even now,
With the ruler, and, breath-bearing, still
The Dioscuri descend and rise

An unzugänglichen Treppen, wenn von himmlischer Burg
Die Berge fernhinziehen
Bei Nacht, und hin
Die Zeiten
Pythagoras

Im Gedächtniß aber lebet Philoktetes,

Die helfen dem Vater.
Denn ruhen mögen sie. Wenn aber
Sie reizet unnüz Treiben
Der Erd' und es nehmen
Den Himmlischen
                    die Sinne, brennend kommen
Sie dann,

Die othemlosen –

Denn es hasset
Der sinnende Gott
Unzeitiges Wachstum.

Der Adler

Mein Vater ist gewandert, auf dem Gotthard,
Da wo die Flüsse, hinab,
Wohl nach Hetruria seitwärts,
Und des geraden Weges
Auch über den Schnee,
Zu dem Olympos und Hämos
Wo den Schatten der Athos wirft,
Nach Höhlen in Lemnos.
Anfänglich aber sind
Aus Wäldern des Indus
Starkduftenden

On inaccessible steps, when from the heavenly fortress
The mountains draw far away
By night, and away
The times
Of Pythagoras

In remembrance, though, lives Philoctetes,

Those help the Father.
For they like to rest. But when
They are roused by mischievous
Happenings on earth and the heavenly
Are robbed
                            their senses, burning then
They come,

The breathless –

For the pondering god
Hates
Untimely growth.

The Eagle

My father roamed, up on the Gotthard,
Where the rivers are, downward,
Perhaps to Etruria, sideways,
And by the straight way too
Over the snow,
To Olympus and Haemus
Where Athos casts its shadow,
To caves in Lemnos.
In the beginning, though,
My parents came
Out of the forests of the Indus,

Die Eltern gekommen.
Der Urahn aber
Ist geflogen über der See
Scharfsinnend, und es wunderte sich
Des Königes goldnes Haupt
Ob dem Geheimniß der Wasser,
Als roth die Wolken dampften
Über dem Schiff und die Thiere stumm
Einander schauend
Der Speise gedachten, aber
Es stehen die Berge doch still,
Wo wollen wir bleiben?

Der Fels ist zu Waide gut,
Das Trokne zu Trank.
Das Nasse aber zu Speise.
Will einer wohnen,
So sei es an Treppen,
Und wo ein Häuslein hinabhängt
Am Wasser halte dich auf.
Und was du hast, ist
Athem zu hohlen.
Hat einer ihn nemlich hinauf
Am Tage gebracht,
Er findet im Schlaf ihn wieder.
Denn wo die Augen zugedekt,
Und gebunden die Füße sind,
Da wirst du es finden.
Denn wo erkennest,

The strongly fragrant.
But the first forefather
Flew across the sea,
Pondering sharply, and the golden head
Of the king was full of wonder
At the mystery of the waters,
When red the clouds were steaming
Above the ship, and the animals,
Dumbly gazing at one another,
Gave thought to food, but
Nonetheless the mountains stand still,
Where shall we settle?

The rock is good for pasture,
What is dry, for drink.
But what is wet, for food.
If someone wishes to dwell,
Let it be on steps
And where a small house hangs down
Near water, there spend your days.
And what is yours
Is to draw breath.
For if someone has brought it
Up to the top by day,
In sleep he finds it again.
For where the eyes are covered
And the feet are bound,
There you will find it.
For where will you recognize,

Ihr sichergebaueten Alpen . . .

Ihr sichergebaueten Alpen!
Die

Und ihr sanftblikenden Berge,
Wo über buschigem Abhang
Der Schwarzwald saußt,
Und Wohlgerüche die Loke
Der Tannen herabgießt,
Und der Nekar

       und die Donau!
Im Sommer liebend Fieber
Umherwehet der Garten
Und Linden des Dorfs, und wo
Die Pappelweide blühet
Und der Seidenbaum
Auf heiliger Waide,

Und

Ihr guten Städte!
Nicht ungestalt, mit dem Feinde
Gemischet unmächtig

Was
Auf einmal gehet es weg
Und siehet den Tod nicht.
Wann aber

Und Stutgard, wo ich
Ein Augenbliklicher begraben
Liegen dürfte, dort,
Wo sich die Straße
Bieget, und
      um die Weinstaig,

You firmly built alps . . .

You firmly built alps!
That

And you mildly glancing mountains,
Where over the bushy slope
The Black Forest rushes
And the fir tree's curl
Pours down pleasing odours
And the Neckar

   and the Danube!
In summer the garden wafts
About a loving fever,
And the village's lindens, and where
The black poplar blossoms
And the white mulberry
On a holy pasture,

And

You good cities!
Not misshapen, mingled with
The enemy, powerless

Which
All at once it goes away
And does not see death.
But when

And Stuttgart, where
A momentary one I might be allowed
To lie buried, at the place
Where the road
Bends, and
  around the Weinstaig,

Und der Stadt Klang wieder
Sich findet drunten auf ebenem Grün
Stilltönend unter den Apfelbäumen

Des Tübingens   wo
Und Blize fallen
Am hellen Tage
Und Römisches tönend ausbeuget der Spizberg
Und Wohlgeruch

Und Tills Thal, das

Das Nächste Beste
DRITTE FASSUNG

      offen die Fenster des Himmels
Und freigelassen der Nachtgeist
Der himmelstürmende, der hat unser Land
Beschwäzet, mit Sprachen viel, unbändigen, und
Den Schutt gewälzet
Bis diese Stunde.
Doch kommt das, was ich will,
Wenn
Drum wie die Staaren
Mit Freudengeschrei, wenn auf Gasgogne, Orten, wo viel Gärten sind,
Wenn im Olivenland, und
In liebenswürdiger Fremde,
Springbrunnen an grasbewachsnen Wegen
Die Bäum unwissend in der Wüste
Die Sonne sticht,
Und das Herz der Erde thuet
Sich auf, wo um
Den Hügel von Eichen
Aus brennendem Lande
Die Ströme und wo
Des Sonntags unter Tänzen

And the city's hubbub meets
Itself once more down below on the level sward
Quietly sounding among the apple trees

Of Tübingen   where
And in day's full glare
Lightning flashes fall
And the Spitzberg, resounding, yields Roman lore
And pleasing odour

And Thill's valley, which

Whatever is Nearest
THIRD VERSION

      opened the windows of Heaven
And let loose the spirit of Night
Who takes Heaven by storm – he has talked over
Our country, with many languages, unrestrained, and
Has rolled his ball of rubble
Up to this hour.
Yet what I want shall come
When
Therefore like the starlings
With jubilant cries, when in Gascony, places with many gardens,
When in the olive country, and
In lovable foreign parts,
Fountains by pathways overgrown with grass
The trees ignorant in the desert
Are stung by the sun,
And the heart of Earth
Opens up, where round
The hill of oaks
From a burning land
The rivers and where
On Sundays amid dances

Gastfreundlich die Schwellen sind,
An blüthenbekränzten Straßen, stillegehend.
Sie spüren nemlich die Heimath,
Wenn grad   aus falbem Stein,
Die Wasser silbern rieseln
Und heilig Grün sich zeigt
Auf feuchter Wiese der Charente,

Die klugen Sinne pflegend.   wenn aber
Die Luft sich bahnt,
Und ihnen machet waker
Scharfwehend die Augen der Nordost, fliegen sie auf,
Und Ek um Eke
Das Liebere gewahrend
Denn immer halten die sich genau an das Nächste,
Sehn sie die heiligen Wälder und die Flamme, blühendduftend
Des Wachstums und die Wolken des Gesanges fern und athmen
     Othem
Der Gesänge. Menschlich ist
Das Erkentniß. Aber die Himmlischen
Auch haben solches mit sich, und des Morgens beobachten
Die Stunden und des Abends die Vögel. Himmlischen auch
Gehöret also solches. Wolan nun. Sonst in Zeiten
Des Geheimnisses hätt ich, als von Natur, gesagt,
Sie kommen, in Deutschland. Jezt aber, weil, wie die See
Die Erd ist und die Länder, Männern gleich, die nicht
Vorüber gehen können, einander, untereinander
Sich schelten fast, so sag ich. Abendlich wohlgeschmiedet
Vom Oberlande biegt sich das Gebirg, wo auf hoher Wiese die Wälder
     sind wohl an
Der bairischen Ebne. Nemlich Gebirg
Geht weit und streket, hinter Amberg sich und
Fränkischen Hügeln. Berühmt ist dieses. Umsonst nicht hat
Seitwärts gebogen Einer von Bergen der Jugend
Das Gebirg, und gerichtet das Gebirg
Heimatlich. Wildniß nemlich sind ihm die Alpen und
Das Gebirg, das theilet die Tale und die Länge lang
Geht über die Erd. Dort aber

Hospitable are the thresholds
On streets all hung with garlands, quietly moving.
For it is home that they sense
When straight   from dun-coloured stone
The waters trickle silver
And holy green appears
On a sodden meadow of the Charente,

Cultivating the prudent senses.   but when
The air becomes passable
And the north-easterly, sharply blowing,
Makes bold their eyes, they fly off
And corner by corner
Perceiving that which is dearer to them,
For always they are guided by that which is nearest,
They see the holy woods and the flame, fragrantly blossoming,
Of growth and the clouds of song far away, and breathe the breath

Of songs. Human it is
To perceive, to seek knowledge. But the Heavenly too
Have something like it about them, and in the mornings observe
The hours, and at nightfall the birds. To the Heavenly, therefore, too
This appertains. Very well, then. Before, at times when
The secret was kept, as though by nature, I should have said,
They are coming, in Germany. But now, because the earth
Is like the sea and the countries are like men
Who cannot pass one another, but almost
Are scolding one another, I speak. Nocturnally, well forged
By highlands the mountain range bends, where on the alpine pasture
     the woods are
Near the Bavarian plain. For mountain ranges
Extend far off and stretch beyond Amberg and
Franconian hills. Famous these are. Not for nothing
Did someone bend sideways from mountains of youth
The range and turned it to face
Towards home. For wilderness are the alps to him and
The range that divides the valleys and sprawled full length
Runs across the earth. But there

Gehn mags nun. Fast, unrein, hatt sehn lassen und das Eingeweid
Der Erde.   Bei Ilion aber
War auch das Licht der Adler. Aber in der Mitte
Der Himmel der Gesänge. Neben aber
Am Ufer zornige Greise, der Entscheidung nemlich, die alle
Drei unser sind.

Kolomb

Wünscht' ich der Helden einer zu seyn
Und dürfte frei, mit der Stimme des Schäfers, oder eines Hessen,
Dessen eingeborner Sprach, es bekennen
So wär' es ein Seeheld. Thätigkeit, zu gewinnen nemlich
Ist das freundlichste, das
Unter allen

Heimische Wohnung und Ordnung, durchaus bündig,
Dürre Schönheit zu lernen und Gestalten
In den Sand gebrannt
Aus Nacht und Feuer, voll von Bildern, reingeschliffenes
Fernrohr, hohe Bildung, nemlich für das Leben
Den Himmel zu fragen.

Wenn du sie aber nennest
Anson und Gama, Äneas
Und Jason, Chirons
Schüler in Megaras Felsenhöhlen, und
Im zitternden Reegen der Grotte bildete sich ein Menschenbild
Aus Eindrüken des Walds, und die Tempelherren, die gefahren
Nach Jerusalem Bouillon, Rinaldo,
Bougainville [Entdekungsreisen
als Versuche, den hesperischen
orbis gegen den
orbis der Alten zu bestimmen]

Now let it run. Almost, impurely, it showed and the entrails
Of Earth.   Near Ilion, however,
The light of the eagles was too. But in the midst
The heaven of songs. But near-by
Angry old men on the shore, of decision, that is,
Which all three are ours.

Colombo

If I desired to be one of the heroes
And freely, with the shepherd's voice or a Hessian's,
His native speech, could profess it
A seaman hero I'd be. For action, to gain is
The most amiable thing
Of all

Indigenous dwelling and order, thoroughly compact,
To learn sparse beauty and figures
Burnt into sand
Out of night and fire, full of images, telescope
Polished until it's true, high expertise, that is, for life
To question the sky.

But if you name them
Anson and Gama, Aeneas
And Jason, Chiron's
Pupil in Megara's caves in the rocks, and
In tremulous rain of the grotto a man's image is formed
From the forest's impressions, and the Templars who travelled
To Jerusalem Bouillon, Rinaldo,
Bougainville   [voyages of discovery
as attempts to distinguish
the hesperian orbis from
the orbis of the ancients]

Gewaltig ist die Zahl
Gewaltiger aber sind sie selbst
Und machen stumm

        die Männer.

Dennoch

Und hin nach Genua will ich
Zu erfragen Kolombos Haus
Wo er, als wenn
Eins der Götter eines wäre und wunderbar
Der Menschen Geschlecht,
In süßer Jugend gewohnet. Licht
Aber man kehret
Wesentlich um, wie ein
Bildermann, der stehet
Vorm Kornhaus, von Sicilien her vieleicht
Und die Bilder weiset der Länder
Der Großen auch
Und singet der Welt Pracht,

        so du
Mich aber fragest

So weit das Herz
Mir reichet, wird es gehen
Nach Brauch und Kunst.
Zu Schiffe aber steigen
ils crient rapport, ils fermes maison
'tu es un saisrien'

Mighty is their number
But more mighty are they themselves
And strike dumb

        the men.

And yet

And over to Genoa I want to go
To ask my way to Colombo's house
Where he, as though
One were one of the gods and marvellous
Were human kind,
Dwelled in sweet youth. Light
But one turns
About essentially, like a
Picture man who stands
In front of the cornhouse, from Sicily perhaps
And shows pictures of the countries
And of the great
And sings the world's glory,

        but if
You ask me

As far as my heart
Reaches, it will go
As custom and art command.
But they embark
ils crient rapport, ils ferment maison
'tu es un saisrien'

Ein Murren war es, ungedultig, denn
Von wengen geringen Dingen
Verstimmt wie vom Schnee war
Die Gloke, womit
Man läutet
Zum Abendessen
Die Erde zornig und eilte, während daß sie schrien
Manna und Himmelsbrod
Mit Prophezeiungen und
Großem Geschrei, des Gebets mit Gunst.
Sauer wird mir dieses wenig
Geduld und Gütigkeit mein Richter und Schuzgott
Denn Menschen sind wir
Und sie glaubten, sie seien Mönche.
Und einer, als Redner
Auftrat uns als Pfarherr
Im blauen Wamms
entière personne content de son
âme difficultés connaissance
rapport tire

Doch da hinaus, damit
Vom Plaze
Wir kommen, also rief
Gewaltig richtend
Die Gesellen die Stimme des Meergotts,
Die reine, daran
Heroen erkennen, ob sie recht
Gerathen oder nicht –

Stürzet herein, ihr Bäche
Von Leib und Gottes Gnad und Glük im seinen,
Kräfte zu begreiffen, o ihr Bilder
Der Jugend, als in Genua, damals
Der Erdkreis, griechisch, kindlich gestaltet,
Mit Gewalt unter meinen Augen,
Einschläfernd, kurzgefaßtem Mohngeist gleich mir
Erschien

A murmur it was, impatient, for
By a few trifling matters
Put out of tune as by snow was
The bell with which
One rings
For supper
The earth grew angry, and hurried, while they cried
Manna and bread from Heaven
With prophecies and
Great outcry, of prayer with grace.
This irks me, little
Patience and goodness my judge and tutelary god
For we are human
And they thought they were monks.
And one as orator
As vicar appeared to us
In a blue doublet
entière personne content de son
âme difficultés connaissance
rapport tire

But out that way, so
That we'll get
Moving, thus
Mightily judging
The sea-god's voice called
The companions, pure voice
By which heroes recognize
Whether they've turned out right
Or not –

Rush in, you streams
Of love and God's mercy and bliss in what's his,
To understand powers, o you images
Of youth when in Genoa, then
The terrestrial orb, Greek, childlike in shape
By force under my eyes
Lulling to sleep, like the spirit of poppies compressed
Appeared to me

Das bist du ganz in deiner Schönheit apocalyptica

moments tirées hautes sommeils der Schiffer
Kolombus aber beiseit Hypostasierung des vorigen orbis
Naiveté der Wissenschaft
Und seufzeten miteinander, um die Stunde,
Nach der Hizze des Tags.
lui a les pleures

Sie sahn nun

Es waren nemlich viele,
Der schönen Inseln.
                    damit
Mit Lissabon

Und Genua theilten;

Denn einsam kann
Von Himmlischen den Reichtum tragen
Nicht eins; wohl nemlich mag
Den Harnisch dehnen
                    ein Halbgott, dem Höchsten aber
Ist fast zu wenig
Das Wirken   wo das Tagslicht scheinet,
Und der Mond,

                    Darum auch

                        so

Nemlich öfters, wenn
Den Himmlischen zu einsam
Es wird, daß sie
Allein zusammenhalten

                    oder die Erde; denn allzurein ist
Entweder

                    Dann aber

That is wholly you in your beauty apocalyptica.

moments tirées hautes sommeils the mariner
Colombo apart, though, hypostasis of the previous orbis
naïveté of science
And sighed among themselves, at the hour
After the day's heat.
lui a les pleures

Now they saw

For they were many,
The lovely isles.
              so that
With Lisbon

And Genoa shared;

For lonely not one
Can endure the wealth
Of the heavenly; for indeed
              a demigod
Can stretch the armour, but
To the Highest
Such working is almost too little
Where daylight shines
And the moon

          And therefore

             so

For often, when
The heavenly grow
Too lonely, so that
Alone they hold together

          or Earth; for all too pure is
Either

          But then

Wenn über dem Weinberg ...

Wenn über dem Weinberg es flammt
Und schwarz wie Kohlen
Aussiehet um die Zeit
Des Herbstes der Weinberg, weil
Die Röhren des Lebens feuriger athmen
In den Schatten des Weinstoks. Aber
Schön ists, die Seele
Zu entfalten und das kurze Leben

Vom Abgrund nemlich ...

Vom Abgrund nemlich haben
Wir angefangen und gegangen
Dem Leuen gleich, in Zweifel und Ärgerniß,
Denn sinnlicher sind Menschen
In dem Brand
Der Wüste
Lichttrunken und der Thiergeist ruhet
Mit ihnen. Bald aber wird, wie ein Hund, umgehn
In der Hizze meine Stimme auf den Gassen der Gärten
In denen wohnen Menschen
In Frankreich
Der Schöpfer
Frankfurt aber, nach der Gestalt, die
Abdruk ist der Natur zu reden
Des Menschen nemlich, ist der Nabel
Dieser Erde, diese Zeit auch
Ist Zeit, und deutschen Schmelzes.
Ein wilder Hügel aber stehet über dem Abhang
Meiner Gärten. Kirschenbäume. Scharfer Othem aber wehet
Um die Löcher des Felses. Allda bin ich
Alles miteinander. Wunderbar
Aber über Quellen beuget schlank
Ein Nußbaum und   sich. Beere, wie Korall

When there's a flaming . . .

When there's a flaming above the vineyard
And black as coal
The vineyard looks, around the
Autumn season, because
More fierily breathe the pipes of life
In the grapevine's shadows. But
Lovely it is to unfold
The soul and our brief life

For from the abyss . . .

For from the abyss we
Began and have walked like
The lion, in doubt and annoyance,
For more sensual are men
In the blaze
Of deserts,
Drunk with light, and the spirit of animals
Joins in their rest. But soon like a dog my voice
Will walk in the heat through the alleys of gardens
In which men and women live
In France
The creator
Frankfurt, though to speak according to the shape
Of nature's imprint, human nature, I mean,
Is the navel of this earth, our time too
Is time, and of German mould.
But a wild hill looms above the slope of
My gardens. Cherry-trees. A sharp breath, however,
Blows around the holes of the rock. And there I am
All things at once. But wonderfully
Over well-springs there slenderly bends
A nut tree and   Berries like coral

Hängen an dem Strauche über Röhren von Holz,
Aus denen
Ursprünglich aus Korn, nun aber zu gestehen, bevestigter Gesang von
    Blumen als
Neue Bildung aus der Stadt, wo
Bis zu Schmerzen aber der Nase steigt
Citronengeruch auf und das Öl, aus der Provence, und es haben diese
Dankbarkeit mir die Gasgognischen Lande
Gegeben. Gezähmet aber, noch zu sehen, und genährt hat mich
Die Rappierlust und des Festtags gebraten Fleisch
Der Tisch und braune Trauben, braune
                        und mich leset o
Ihr Blüthen von Deutschland, o mein Herz wird
Untrügbarer Krystall an dem
Das Licht sich prüfet wenn   Deutschland

Narcyssen . . .

Narcyssen Ranunklen und
Siringen aus Persien
Blumen Nelken, gezogen perlenfarb
Und schwarz und Hyacinthen,
Wie wenn es riechet, statt Musik
Des Eingangs, dort, wo böse Gedanken,
Liebende mein Sohn vergessen sollen einzugehen
Verhältnisse und diß Leben
Christophori   der Drache vergleicht der Natur
Gang und Geist und Gestalt.

Hang on the shrub above wooden gutters
From which
Originally of corn, but now to be confessed, fortified song of flowers

As new education from town, where
To the point of pain in the nose
A smell of lemons rises and of oil, from Provence, and it is
The Gascon regions that have given me
This thankfulness. But what tamed me, still to be seen, and fed me
Is love of rapiers and the holiday's roast meat
The table and brown grapes, brown ones
                              and read me, gather me O
You flowers of Germany, O my heart is turning
To crystal that cannot lie, in which
The light is tested when   Germany

Narcissi . . .

Narcissi, ranunculi and
Syringas from Persia
Carnations, bred
Flowers pearl-coloured
And black and hyacinths
As when there's a smell, instead of music
Of entry, there, where an evil thought,
                  my son
Lovers should forget to enter into
Relationships and this life
                              Christopher's
Dragon   compares with nature's
Gait and spirit and shape

Zu Sokrates Zeiten

Vormals richtete Gott.

                       Könige.

                Weise.

                    wer richtet denn izt?

Richtet das einige
   Volk? die heilge Gemeinde?
   Nein! o nein! wer richtet denn izt?
                ein Natterngeschlecht!   feig und falsch
                  das edlere Wort nicht mehr
             Über die Lippe
O im Nahmen

                               ruf ich

        Alter Dämon! dich herab

Oder   sende
   Einen Helden

Oder
   die Weisheit.

Griechenland
DRITTE FASSUNG

O ihr Stimmen des Geschiks, ihr Wege des Wanderers
Denn an der Schule Blau,
Fernher, am Tosen des Himmels
Tönt wie der Amsel Gesang
Der Wolken heitere Stimmung gut

In Socrates' Time

At one time God judged.

                    Kings.

              Wise men.

                   who, then, judges now?

Does the unanimous
   people? the holy community?
   No, oh no! who, then, judges now?
                    a generation of vipers!   cowardly and lying
                         the nobler word no more
                    Passes the lip
O in the name
                                                    I call
            you down to us, ancient Daemon

Or   send
     A hero

Or
     Wisdom.

Greece
THIRD VERSION

O you voices of fate, you ways of the wanderer!
For amid the blue of the school,
From afar, amid the uproar of heaven
Rings out like the blackbird's song
The clouds' happy mood, well

Gestimmt vom Daseyn Gottes, dem Gewitter.
Und Rufe, wie hinausschauen, zur
Unsterblichkeit und Helden;
Viel sind Erinnerungen. Wo darauf
Tönend, wie des Kalbs Haut
Die Erde, von Verwüstungen her, Versuchungen der Heiligen
Denn anfangs bildet das Werk sich
Großen Gesezen nachgehet, die Wissenschaft
Und Zärtlichkeit und den Himmel breit lauter Hülle nachher
Erscheinend singen Gesangeswolken.
Denn fest ist der Erde
Nabel. Gefangen nemlich in Ufern von Gras sind
Die Flammen und die allgemeinen
Elemente. Lauter Besinnung aber oben lebt der Aether. Aber silbern
An reinen Tagen
Ist das Licht. Als Zeichen der Liebe
Veilchenblau die Erde.
Zu Geringem auch kann kommen
Großer Anfang.
Alltag aber wunderbar zu lieb den Menschen
Gott an hat ein Gewand.
Und Erkentnissen verberget sich sein Angesicht
Und deket die Lüfte mit Kunst.
Und Luft und Zeit dekt
Den Schröklichen, daß zu sehr nicht eins
Ihn liebet mit Gebeten oder
Die Seele. Denn lange schon steht offen
Wie Blätter, zu lernen, oder Linien und Winkel
Die Natur
Und gelber die Sonnen und die Monde,
Zu Zeiten aber
Wenn ausgehn will die alte Bildung
Der Erde, bei Geschichten nemlich
Gewordnen, muthig fechtenden, wie auf Höhen führet
Die Erde Gott. Ungemessene Schritte
Begränzt er aber, aber wie Blüthen golden thun
Der Seele Kräfte dann der Seele Verwandtschaften sich zusammen,
Daß lieber auf Erden
Die Schönheit wohnt und irgend ein Geist
Gemeinschaftlicher sich zu Menschen gesellet.

Tempered by the existence of God, the thunder-storm.
And calls, like looking out, for
Immortality and heroes;
Memories are many. Where ringing out
On it, as on the calf's hide,
The earth, proceeding from devastations, temptations of the saints,
For at the beginning the work is shaped,
Pursues great laws, and knowledge
And tenderness and the width of heaven, all wrapping, later becoming
Visible, sing clouds of song.
For firmly fixed is the navel
Of Earth. For captive in banks of grass are
The flames and the common
Elements. But above, all reflection, lives Aether. But silver
On pure days
Is light. As a sign of love
Violet-blue the earth.
A great beginning can come
Even to humble things.
Everyday but marvellous, for the sake of men,
God has put on a garment.
And his face is withheld from the knowing
And covers the winds with art.
And air and time cover
The terrible one, so that not too much a man
With prayers shall love him.
Or else the soul. For long already like leaves,
To learn, or like lines and angles,
Nature lies open
And more yellow the suns and the moons,
But at times
When the ancient knowledge of earth is in danger
Of going out, amid histories, that is, grown, come to pass
And boldly fencing, as on high places God
Leads on the Earth. Unmeasured paces, though,
He limits, but like blossoms golden then
The faculties, affinities of the soul consort
So that more willingly
Beauty dwells on earth and one or the other spirit
More communally joins in human affairs.

Süß ists, dann unter hohen Schatten von Bäumen
Und Hügeln zu wohnen, sonnig, wo der Weg ist
Gepflastert zur Kirche. Reisenden aber, wem,
Aus Lebensliebe, messend immerhin,
Die Füße gehorchen, blühn
Schöner die Wege, wo das Land

Sweet it is then to dwell under the high shade
Of trees and hills, sunny, where the road
Is paved to church. To travellers, though,
To him whose feet, from love of life,
Measuring all along, obey him,
More beautifully blossom the roads, where the land

LAST POEMS
(1807–1843)

Wenn aus der Ferne . . .

Wenn aus der Ferne, da wir geschieden sind,
  Ich dir noch kennbar bin, die Vergangenheit
    O du Theilhaber meiner Leiden!
      Einiges Gute bezeichnen dir kann,

So sage, wie erwartet die Freundin dich?
  In jenen Gärten, da nach entsezlicher
    Und dunkler Zeit wir uns gefunden?
      Hier an den Strömen der heilgen Urwelt.

Das muß ich sagen, einiges Gutes war
  In deinen Bliken, als in den Fernen du
    Dich einmal fröhlich umgesehen
      Immer verschlossener Mensch, mit finstrem

Aussehn. Wie flossen Stunden dahin, wie still
  War meine Seele über der Wahrheit daß
    Ich so getrennt gewesen wäre?
      Ja! ich gestand es, ich war die deine.

Wahrhafftig! wie du alles Bekannte mir
  In mein Gedächtniß bringen und schreiben willst,
    Mit Briefen, so ergeht es mir auch
      Daß ich Vergangenes alles sage.

Wars Frühling? war es Sommer? die Nachtigall
  Mit süßem Liede lebte mit Vögeln, die
    Nicht ferne waren im Gebüsche
      Und mit Gerüchen umgaben Bäum' uns.

Die klaren Gänge, niedres Gestrauch und Sand
  Auf dem wir traten, machten erfreulicher
    Und lieblicher die Hyacinthe
      Oder die Tulpe, Viole, Nelke.

If from the distance . . .

If from the distance where we went separate ways
   I'm recognizable to you still, the past,
      O you the sharer of my sufferings,
         Still can convey to you something pleasant,

Then tell me how your girl friend awaits you now?
   In those same gardens where after horrible
      And darkened years once more we're meeting,
         Here by the holy primaevum's rivers.

This much I'm bound to say, something good there was
   About your glances when in the distances
      For once you cheerfully looked round, you
         Man always shut like a clam, of gloomy

Appearance. How the hours slipped away, how calm
   My soul was at the thought of the truth that I
      Had been so long and wholly parted?
         Yes, I confessed, I was yours entirely.

Indeed! As you are trying to bring and write
   These well-known things all back to my memory,
      With letters, so it is with me, and
         All that is past I now freely speak of.

Was it in spring? In summer? The nightingale
   Lived sweetly singing with other birds that were
      Not far away within the thicket,
         And there was fragrance of trees around us.

The clear-cut pathways, shrubs rather low and sand
   On which we walked were made more agreeable,
      More charming by the hyacinth or
         Tulip, the violet or carnation.

Um Wänd und Mauern grünte der Epheu, grünt'
    Ein seelig Dunkel hoher Alleeen. Offt
        Des Abends, Morgens waren dort wir
            Redeten manches und sahn uns froh an.

In meinen Armen lebte der Jüngling auf,
    Der, noch verlassen, aus den Gefilden kam,
        Die er mir wies, mit einer Schwermuth,
            Aber die Nahmen der seltnen Orte

Und alles Schöne hatt' er behalten, das
    An seeligen Gestaden, auch mir sehr werth
        Im heimatlichen Lande blühet
            Oder verborgen, aus hoher Aussicht,

Allwo das Meer auch einer beschauen kann,
    Doch keiner seyn will. Nehme vorlieb, und denk
        An die, die noch vergnügt ist, darum,
            Weil der entzükende Tag uns anschien,

Der mit Geständniß oder der Hände Druk
    Anhub, der uns vereinet. Ach! wehe mir!
        Es waren schöne Tage. Aber
            Traurige Dämmerung folgte nachher.

Du seiest so allein in der schönen Welt
    Behauptest du mir immer, Geliebter! das
        Weist aber du nicht,

Auf die Geburt eines Kindes

Wie wird des Himmels Vater schauen
Mit Freude das erwachs'ne Kind,
Gehend auf blumenreichen Auen,
Mit andern, welche lieb ihm sind.

On walls and housefront ivy grew green, green too
  A blissful darkness made by tall avenues.
    There we spent many mornings, evenings,
      Said this and that and exchanged glad glances.

In my embrace it was that the youth revived
  Who, still forsaken, came from the very fields
    He showed to me, with such deep sadness,
      But all the names of those curious places

And all the lovely things, he remembers still
  Which, very dear to me also, are in bloom
    On blessèd shores, our native country,
      Or else concealed, from a high perspective,

Wherever men can look at the ocean too,
  But no one wants to be. Now excuse me, think
    Of her who still is glad because that
      Day so enchanting shone down upon us

Which started with confessions or holding hands
  And which united us. But ah, woe is me.
    Those days were beautiful. However,
      Sad was the twilight that followed after.

That you're so much alone in this lovely world,
  You always claim, my darling, but as for that,
      You cannot know . . .

On the Birth of a Child

How will the heavenly Father see,
With what delight, the child more grown
Walking through wildflowers of the lea
With others dear to it, not alone.

Indessen freue dich des Lebens,
Aus einer guten Seele kommt
Die Schönheit herrlichen Bestrebens,
Göttlicher Grund dir mehr noch frommt.

Das Angenehme dieser Welt

Das Angenehme dieser Welt hab' ich genossen,
Die Jugendstunden sind, wie lang! wie lang! verflossen,
April und Mai und Julius sind ferne,
Ich bin nichts mehr, ich lebe nicht mehr gerne!

An Zimmern

Die Linien des Lebens sind verschieden
Wie Wege sind, und wie der Berge Gränzen.
Was hier wir sind, kan dort ein Gott ergänzen
Mit Harmonien und ewigem Lohn und Frieden.

Überzeugung

Als wie der Tag die Menschen hell umscheinet,
Und mit dem Lichte, das den Höh'n entspringet,
Die dämmernden Erscheinungen vereinet,
Ist Wissen, welches tief der Geistigkeit gelinget.

Das Fröhliche Leben

Wenn ich auf die Wiese komme,
Wenn ich auf dem Felde jezt,
Bin ich noch der Zahme, Fromme
Wie von Dornen unverlezt.

Meanwhile be glad that you are living,
From a good soul there issues forth
The beauty of a noble striving,
Divine ends grant still greater worth.

The world's agreeable things . . .

The world's agreeable things were mine to enjoy,
The hours of youth, how long have they been gone!
Remote is April, May, remote July,
I'm nothing now, and listless I live on.

To Zimmer

The lines of life are various; they diverge and cease
Like footpaths and the mountains' utmost ends.
What here we are, elsewhere a God amends
With harmonies, eternal recompense and peace.

Conviction

Like the bright day that shines on human kind
And with a light of heavenly origin
All things obscure and various gathers in,
Is knowledge, deeply granted to the mind.

The Merry Life

When I come to walk the meadow,
Later, reach the field below,
Still I am the tame, the pious,
As by thorns uninjured go.

Mein Gewand in Winden wehet,
Wie der Geist mir lustig fragt,
Worinn Inneres bestehet,
Bis Auflösung diesem tagt.

O vor diesem sanften Bilde,
Wo die grünen Bäume stehn,
Wie vor einer Schenke Schilde
Kann ich kaum vorübergehn.
Denn die Ruh an stillen Tagen
Dünkt entschieden treflich mir,
Dieses mußt du gar nicht fragen,
Wenn ich soll antworten dir.

Aber zu dem schönen Bache
Such' ich einen Lustweg wohl,
Der, als wie in dem Gemache,
Schleicht durch's Ufer wild und hohl,
Wo der Steg darüber gehet,
Geht's den schönen Wald hinauf,
Wo der Wind den Steg umwehet,
Sieht das Auge fröhlich auf.

Droben auf des Hügels Gipfel
Siz' ich manchen Nachmittag,
Bei des Thurmes Glokenschlag,
Und Betrachtung giebt dem Herzen
Frieden, wie das Bild auch ist,
Und Beruhigung den Schmerzen,
Welche reimt Verstand und List.

Holde Landschaft! wo die Straße
Mitten durch sehr eben geht,
Wo der Mond aufsteigt, der blasse,
Wenn der Abendwind entsteht,
Wo die Natur sehr einfältig,
Wo die Berg' erhaben stehn,
Geh' ich heim zulezt, haushältig,
Dort nach goldnem Wein zu sehn.

In the wind my garment flutters
While I gaily think upon
What our inner life consists of
Till its dissolution's dawn.

Oh before this gentle image
Where the green trees line the sky
As before a tavern's emblem
Hardly I can just pass by.
For the peace on days all quiet
Is true excellence, in my view;
This you should not even ask me
If I am to answer you.

But towards the lovely brook now
For a pleasant path I peer
Which, as in a fine apartment,
Creeps through banks all wild and sheer,
Where the footbridge runs across it,
To the lovely woodland ways
Where the breeze blows round the footbridge
Upward happily I gaze.

Sitting on that hilltop yonder
After noon I spend my time,
And I hear the clock tower chime,
Contemplation gives the heart a
Peace, whatever bodes the while,
And a soothing of the sorrows
That our reason rhymes with guile.

Dearest landscape! where the roadway
Runs right through, all level, straight,
Where the moon, the pale, is rising
When the evening wind's in spate,
Where nature's mind is very simple,
Lofty mountains loom and shine,
I go home at last, domestic,
There to see to golden wine.

Der Spaziergang

Ihr Wälder schön an der Seite,
Am grünen Abhang gemahlt,
Wo ich umher mich leite,
Durch süße Ruhe bezahlt
Für jeden Stachel im Herzen,
Wenn dunkel mir ist der Sinn,
Den Kunst und Sinnen hat Schmerzen
Gekostet von Anbeginn.
Ihr lieblichen Bilder im Thale,
Zum Beispiel Gärten und Baum,
Und dann der Steg der schmale,
Der Bach zu sehen kaum,
Wie schön aus heiterer Ferne
Glänzt Einem das herrliche Bild
Der Landschaft, die ich gerne
Besuch' in Witterung mild.
Die Gottheit freundlich geleitet
Uns erstlich mit Blau,
Hernach mit Wolken bereitet,
Gebildet wölbig und grau,
Mit sengenden Blizen und Rollen
Des Donners, mit Reiz des Gefilds,
Mit Schönheit, die gequollen
Vom Quell ursprünglichen Bilds.

Der Frühling

Es kommt der neue Tag aus fernen Höhn herunter,
Der Morgen der erwacht ist aus den Dämmerungen,
Er lacht die Menschheit an, geschmükt und munter,
Von Freuden ist die Menschheit sanft durchdrungen.

The Walk

You wayside woods, well painted
On the green and sloping glade
Where I conduct my footsteps
With lovely quiet repaid
For every thorn in my bosom,
When dark are my mind and heart
Which paid from the beginning
In grief for thought and art.
You graceful views in the valley,
For instance garden and tree
And then the footbridge, the narrow,
The stream one can hardly see,
How beautiful, clear from the distance
These glorious pictures shine
Of the landscape I like to visit
When the weather is mild and fine.
The deity kindly escorts us,
At first with unblemished blue,
Later with clouds provided,
Well rounded and grey in hue,
With scorching flashes and rolling
Of thunder, and charm of the fields,
With beauty the bubbling source of
The primal image yields.

Spring

New day descends from many a distant height,
The morning woken out of twilight shades.
It laughs to human folk adorned and bright,
Gently with joys their hearts and minds pervades.

Ein neues Leben will der Zukunft sich enthüllen,
Mit Blüthen scheint, dem Zeichen froher Tage,
Das große Thal, die Erde sich zu füllen,
Entfernt dagegen ist zur Frühlingszeit die Klage.

Mit Unterthänigkeit
d: 3ten März 1648   Scardanelli

Der Sommer

Wenn dann vorbei des Frühlings Blüthe schwindet,
So ist der Sommer da, der um das Jahr sich windet.
Und wie der Bach das Thal hinuntergleitet,
So ist der Berge Pracht darum verbreitet.
Daß sich das Feld mit Pracht am meisten zeiget,
Ist, wie der Tag, der sich zum Abend neiget;
Wie so das Jahr verweilt, so sind des Sommers Stunden
Und Bilder der Natur dem Menschen oft verschwunden.

d. 24 Mai
   1778   Scardanelli

Der Sommer

Noch ist die Zeit des Jahrs zu sehn, und die Gefilde
Des Sommers stehn in ihrem Glanz, in ihrer Milde;
Des Feldes Grün ist prächtig ausgebreitet,
Allwo der Bach hinab mit Wellen gleitet.

So zieht der Tag hinaus durch Berg und Thale,
Mit seiner Unaufhaltsamkeit und seinem Strale,
Und Wolken ziehn in Ruh', in hohen Räumen,
Es scheint das Jahr mit Herrlichkeit zu säumen.

Mit Unterthänigkeit
d. 9ten Merz   Scardanelli

A new life to the future shows its will,
With blossom, with the signs of happy days
The valley's width, the whole earth seems to fill,
While far away in springtime sorrow stays.

                   Your humble servant
March 3rd 1648   Scardanelli

Summer

When then the blooms of springtime disappear,
Summer is here, that winds around the year.
And as the brook winds down the valley-side
So mountain splendour round it stretches wide.
The utmost splendour field and meadow bring,
Is like the day, that bends to evening;
While the year lingers on, for men a summer's day
And nature's images often will fade away.

May 24th
    1778   Scardanelli

Summer

Still you can see the season, and the field
Of summer shows its mildness and its pride.
The meadow's green is splendidly outspread
Where down the brook and all its wavelets glide.

So now the day moves on through hill and valley,
Not to be stopped and in its beam arrayed,
And clouds move calmly on through lofty space
As though the year in majesty delayed.

                Your humble and obedient servant
March 9th   Scardanelli

Der Herbst

Das Glänzen der Natur ist höheres Erscheinen,
Wo sich der Tag mit vielen Freuden endet,
Es ist das Jahr, das sich mit Pracht vollendet,
Wo Früchte sich mit frohem Glanz vereinen.

Das Erdenrund ist so geschmükt, und selten lärmet
Der Schall durchs offne Feld, die Sonne wärmet
Den Tag des Herbstes mild, die Felder stehen
Als eine Aussicht weit, die Lüffte wehen

Die Zweig' und Äste durch mit frohem Rauschen
Wenn schon mit Leere sich die Felder dann vertauschen,
Der ganze Sinn des hellen Bildes lebet
Als wie ein Bild, das goldne Pracht umschwebet.

d. 15ten Nov.
1759

Der Winter

Wenn ungesehn und nun vorüber sind die Bilder
Der Jahreszeit, so kommt des Winters Dauer,
Das Feld ist leer, die Ansicht scheinet milder,
Und Stürme wehn umher und Reegenschauer.

Als wie ein Ruhetag, so ist des Jahres Ende,
Wie einer Frage Ton, daß dieser sich vollende,
Alsdann erscheint des Frühlings neues Werden,
So glänzet die Natur mit ihrer Pracht auf Erden.

Mit Unterthänigkeit
d. 24 April   Scardanelli
1849

Autumn

Nature's bright gleam is higher revelation,
Where amid many joys the day comes to its end,
It is the year in glorious consummation,
Where fruit with cheerful brightness, gleaming, blend.

Earth's globe is thus adorned, with rare alarms
Of noise through open fields, the sunshine warms
The day of autumn mildly, fields lie so
That widely they are viewed, the breezes blow

Through twigs and branches, rustling cheerfully,
Though then to emptiness the fields give way.
The total meaning of this picture lives, as might
A picture framed in glory, golden light.

Nov 15th
1759

Winter

When past, unseen the season's images are,
Winter's duration comes to us again;
The field is bare, the view seems milder far,
And gales blow round about and showers of rain.

A day of rest, such is the year's conclusion,
A question's tone that seeks a complement.
Then to our eyes the Spring's new growth is lent –
So Nature shines on earth in her profusion.

Your humble and obedient servant
April 24th   Scardanelli
1849

Der Frühling

Wenn aus der Tiefe kommt der Frühling in das Leben,
Es wundert sich der Mensch, und neue Worte streben
Aus Geistigkeit, die Freude kehret wieder
Und festlich machen sich Gesang und Lieder.

Das Leben findet sich aus Harmonie der Zeiten,
Daß immerdar den Sinn Natur und Geist geleiten,
Und die Vollkommenheit ist Eines in dem Geiste,
So findet vieles sich, und aus Natur das Meiste.

                                        Mit Unterthänigkeit
d. 24 Mai   Scardanelli
   1758

Spring

When springtime from the depth returns to life,
Men are amazed, and from their minds aspire
New words, and happiness once more is rife,
And festive music rings from house and choir.

Life finds itself in seasonal harmonies,
That ever Nature, Spirit might attend our thought,
And *one* within our minds perfection is;
So, most of all from Nature, much to itself is brought.

Your humble and obedient servant

May 24th   Scardanelli
  1758

INDEX OF GERMAN FIRST LINES

Als wie der Tag die Menschen hell umscheinet, 328
Alter Vater! Du blikst immer, wie ehmals, noch, 68
Auf falbem Laube ruhet 268

Da ich ein Knabe war, 26
Das Angenehme dieser Welt hab' ich genossen, 328
Das Glänzen der Natur ist höheres Erscheinen, 336
Das Leben suchst du, suchst, und es quillt und glänzt 4
Denn, wie wenn hoch von der herrlichgestimmten, der Orgel 176
Der himmlischen, still wiederklingenden, 208
Der Nordost wehet, 250
Des Ganges Ufer hörten des Freudengotts 16
Des Ganges Ufer hörten des Freudengotts 78
Die Linien des Lebens sind verschieden 328
Deine Freundin, Natur! leidet und schläft und du 12
Drinn in den Alpen ists noch helle Nacht und die Wolke, 158
Du seiest Gottes Stimme, so glaub' ich sonst 82
Du schweigst und duldest, denn sie verstehn dich nicht, 64
Du schweigst und duldest, und sie versteh'n dich nicht, 6
Du waltest hoch am Tag' und es blühet dein 74

Echo des Himmels! heiliges Herz! warum, 72
Einen vergänglichen Tag lebt' ich und wuchs mit den Meinen, 70
Einig zu seyn, ist göttlich und gut; woher ist die Sucht denn 18
Einsam stand ich und sah in die Afrikanischen dürren 136
Einst hab ich die Muse gefragt, und sie 286
Es kommt der neue Tag aus fernen Höhn herunter, 332

Froh kehrt der Schiffer heim an den stillen Strom, 12
Froh kehrt der Schiffer heim an den stillen Strom, 54
Fürchtet den Dichter nicht, wenn er edel zürnet, sein Buchstab 18

Geh unter, schöne Sonne, sie achteten 42
Glükseelig Suevien, meine Mutter, 182
Größers wolltest auch du, aber die Liebe zwingt 58

Hast du Verstand und ein Herz, so zeige nur eines von beiden, 2

Heilig Wesen! gestört hab' ich die goldene 8
Heilige Gefäße sind die Dichter, 4
Heilige Unschuld, du der Menschen und der 76
Himmlische Liebe! zärtliche! wenn ich dein 94
Hinunter sinket der Wald, 172
Hoch auf strebte mein Geist, aber die Liebe zog 10

Ihr kalten Heuchler, sprecht von den Göttern nicht! 16
Ihr milden Lüfte! Boten Italiens! 66
Ihr sichergebaueten Alpen! 298
Ihr Städte des Euphrats! 170
Ihr Wälder schön an der Seite, 332
Ihr wandelt droben im Licht 24
Im dunkeln Epheu saß ich, an der Pforte 196
In deinen Thälern wachte mein Herz mir auf 52
In jüngern Tagen war ich des Morgens froh, 8
In seiner Fülle ruhet der Herbsttag nun, 36
Ist nicht heilig mein Herz, schöneren Lebens voll, 10

Jezt komm und hülle, freundlicher Feuergeist, 96
Jezt komme, Feuer! 252

Kaum sproßten aus den Wassern, o Erde, dir 22
Kehren die Kraniche wieder zu dir, und suchen zu deinen 110
Komm und besänftige mir, die du einst Elemente versöhntest 2

Lange lieb' ich dich schon, möchte dich, mir zur Lust, 50
Lieben Brüder! es reift unsere Kunst vielleicht, 14

Mein Vater ist gewandert, auf dem Gotthard, 294
Mit gelben Birnen hänget 170

Nah ist 230
Narcyssen Ranunklen und 314
Nicht ist es aber 282
Nicht sie, die Seeligen, die erschienen sind, 188
Noch freundlichzögernd scheidet vom Auge dir 40
Noch ist die Zeit des Jahrs zu sehn, und die Gefilde 334
Nur Einen Sommer gönnt, ihr Gewaltigen! 6

O Hofnung! holde! gütiggeschäffige! 96
O ihr Stimmen des Geschiks, ihr Wege des Wanderers 316
offen die Fenster des Himmels 300

Reif sind. in Feuer getaucht. gekochet 258

Rings um ruhet die Stadt; still wird die erleuchtete Gasse, 150

Schönes Leben! du lebst, wie die zarten Blüthen im Winter, 2
Schönes Leben! du liegst krank, und das Herz ist mir 12
Send' ihr Blumen und Frücht' aus nieversiegender Fülle, 8
Sieh! dein Liebstes, Natur, leidet und schläft und du 60
Sind denn dir nicht bekannt viele Lebendigen? 98
Sind denn dir nicht verwandt alle Lebendigen? 100
Spottet ja nicht des Kinds, wenn es mit Peitsch' und Sporn 14
Spottet nimmer des Kinds, wenn noch das albernne 44

Tägliche geh' ich heraus, und such' ein Anderes immer, 126
Trennen wollten wir uns? wähnten es gut und klug? 62

Und niemand weiß 266

Viel hab' ich dein 272
Viele versuchten umsonst das Freudigste freudig zu sagen 18
Voll Güt' ist; keiner aber fasset 242
Vom Abgrund nemlich haben 312
Vom Thaue glänzt der Rasen; beweglicher 32
Vor seiner Hütte ruhig im Schatten sizt 30
Vormals richtete Gott. 316

Warum bist du so kurz? liebst du, wie vormals, denn 10
Warum huldigest du, heiliger Sokrates, 18
Was ist der Menschen Lebel   ein Bild der Gottheit. 270
Was ist es, das 218
Was ist es, das 224
Was ist Gott? unbekannt, dennoch 270
Was schläfst du, Bergsohn, liegest in Unmuth, schief, 104
Was schläfst und träumst du, Jüngling, gehüllt in dich, 102
Wenn aber die Himmlischen haben 288
Wenn aus der Ferne, da wir geschieden sind, 324
Wenn aus der Tiefe kommt der Frühling in das Leben, 338
Wenn dann vorbei des Frühlings Blüthe schwindet, 334
Wenn der Morgan trunken begeisternd heraufgeht 264
Wenn ich auf die Wiese komme, 328
Wenn ihr Freunde vergeßt, wenn ihr den Künstler höhnt, 14
Wenn ihr Freunde vergeßt, wenn ihr die Euern all, 56
Wenn nemlich der Rebe Saft, 268
Wenn über dem Weinberg es flammt 312
Wenn ungesehen und nun voruber sind die Bilder 336
Wie eng begränzt ist unsere Tageszeit. 48
Wie wenn am Feiertage. das Feld zu sehn 172

Wie wird des Himmels Vater schauen 326
Wieder ein Glük ist erlebt. Die gefährliche Dürre geneset, 142
Wißt! Apoll ist der Zeitungsschreiber geworden 2
Wo bist du? Jugendliches! das immer mich 86
Wo bist du? Nachdenkliches! das immer muß 90
Wo bist du? trunken dämmert die Seele mir 16
Wohl manches Land der lebenden Erde möcht' 34
Wünscht' ich der Helden einer zu seyn 304

Zu lang schon waltest über dem Haupte mir 28

INDEX OF ENGLISH FIRST LINES

Aged father, you gaze now as you did before 69
Amid dark ivy I was sitting, at 197
And no one knows 267
Are the cranes returning to you, and the mercantile vessels 111
As on a holiday, to see the field 173
At one time God judged. 317
At one time I questioned the Muse, and she 287
At peace the ploughman sits in the shade outside 31
At rest in fulness, calm lies in the autumn day, 37

Beautiful being, you live as do delicate blossoms in winter, 3
Being at one is godlike and good, but human, too human, the mania 19
Bliss of the heavenly Muse who on elements once imposed order, 3
But when the heavenly 289

Cold hypocrites, of gods do not dare to speak! 17
Content the boatman turns to the river's calm 13
Content the boatman turns to the river's calm 55

Daily I search, now here, now there my wandering takes me 127
Dearest one, you lie sick, so that with weeping my 13
Do not laugh at the child when with his whip and spurs 15
Down slopes the forest 173

Echo of Heaven, heart that is hallowed, why, 73

For as when high from the gloriously voiced, the organ 177
For from the abyss we 313
For when the grape-vine's sap, 269

Go down, then, lovely sun, for but little they 43

Has love not hallowed, filled with new life my heart, 11
High my spirit aspired, truly, however, love 11
High up in day you govern, your law prevails, 75
Holy being, I know, often I've troubled your 9
Holy Socrates, why always with deference 19

How narrowly confined is our day-time here. 47
How will the heavenly Father see, 327

If from the distance where we went separate ways 325
If I desired to be one of the heroes 305
If you drop an old friend if, O you grateful ones, 57
If you drop an old friend, laugh at the artist and 15
In my boyhood days 27
In younger days each morning I rose with joy, 9
Innocence, you the holy, dearest and nearest 77
Is not all that's alive close and akin to you, 99

Latest news: Apollo's become the god of journalists, press men, 3
Like the bright day that shines on human kind 329
Lonely I stood and looked out into African desert, unbroken 137
Long I have loved you, and now for my own delight 51

Many have tried, but in vain, with joy to express the most joyful; 19
More you also desired, but every one of us 59
Most happy Swabia, my mother, 183
Most kind is; but no one by himself 243
Much I have suffered 273
My father roamed, up on the Gotthard, 295

Narcissi, ranunculi and 315
Nature, look, your most loved drowses and ails, and you 61
Nature, she who's your friend drowses and ails, and you 13
Nature's bright gleam is higher revelation, 337
Near is 231
Never fear the poet when nobly he rages; his letter 19
Never laugh at the child, seeing the silly one 45
New day descends from many a distant height, 333
Not them, the blessed, who once appeared, 189
Not yet however, 283
Now come, fire! 253

O heavenly love, the tender, if you I should 95
O hope, benignly active one, dear to men, 97
O you voices of fate, you ways of the wanderer! 317
Of the living are not many well-known to you? 101
On fallow foliage rests 269
Once again a joy has been lived. The dangerous dryness recovers 143
One summer only grant me, you powerful Fates 7
opened the windows of Heaven 301

Poets are holy vessels 5

Quite soon, dear brothers, perhaps our art, 15

Ripe are, dipped in fire, cooked 259
Round us the town is at rest; the street, in pale lamplight, falls quiet 151

Send her flowers and fruit from inexhaustible fulness, 9
So, we wanted to part? Thought it both good and wise? 63
Still kindly lingering the year from your eye departs, 41
Still you can see the season, and the field 335

The banks of Ganges heard how the god of joy 17
The banks of Ganges heard how the god of joy 79
The lines of life are various; they diverge and cease 329
The north-easterly blows, 251
The voice of God I called you and thought you once, 83
The world's agreeable things were mine to enjoy, 329
There in the Alps a gleaming night still delays and, composing 159
Too long above my head you have governed there, 29
True, on this living earth there are many lands 35

What is God? Unknown, and yet 271
What is it that 219
What is it that 225
What is the life of men   an image of the godhead. 231
When drunkenly inspiring the morning rises 265
When I come to walk the meadow, 329
When past, unseen the season's images are, 337
When scarcely from the waters, O Earth, for you 23
When springtime from the depth returns to life, 339
When then the blooms of springtime disappear, 335
When there's a flaming above the vineyard 313
Where are you? Dazzled, drunken my soul grows faint 17
Where are you, thought-infusing, which at this time 91
Where are you, youthful herald who always once 87
Why do you sleep and dream, in yourself wrapped up, 103
Why do you sleep, lie crooked, ill-humoured here, 105
'Why so brief now, so curt? Do you no longer, then, 11
With dew the lawn is glistening; more nimbly now, 33
With heavenly, quietly echoing, 209
With my own kind I lived and could grow for a day that was fleeting 71
With yellow pears hangs down 171

You cities of Euphrates. 171

You come now, friendly spirit of fire, and wrap 97
You firmly built alps! 299
You gentle breezes, heralds of Italy, 67
You look for life, you look and from deeps of Earth 5
You suffer and keep silent and, strange to them, 7
You suffer and keep silent, unknown to them, 65
You walk above in the light, 25
You wayside woods, well painted 333
Your banks and dells awakened my heart to life, 53
You've a head *and* a heart? Reveal only one of them, I say; 3

INDEX OF GERMAN TITLES

Abbitte 8
Abschied, Der 62
Abendphantasie 30
Adler, Der 294
Ahnenbild, Das 68
Am Quell der Donau 176
An die Deutschen 14
An die Deutschen 44
An die Hofnung 96
An die Jungen Dichter 14
An die Madonna 272
An die Parzen 6
An Diotima 2
An Ihren Genius 8
An Unsere Grossen Dichter 16
An Zimmern 328
Andenken 250
Angenehme dieser Welt . . .
    Das 328
Archipelagus, Der 110
Auf die Geburt eines Kindes 326
Auf falbem Laube . . . 268

Beschreibende Poësie, Die 2
Blinde Sänger, Der 86
Blödigkeit 100
Brot und Wein 150
Buonaparte 4

Chiron 90

Da Ich ein Knabe War . . . 26
Deutscher Gesang 264
Dichterberuf 78
Dichtermuth 98
Diotima 2
Diotima 6

Diotima 65

Ehmals und Jezt 8
Einst hab ich die Muse
    gefragt . . . 286
Einzige, Der 218
Einzige, Der 224
Empedokles 4
Entschlafenen, Die 70
Ermunterung 72

Friendensfeier 208
Fröhliche Leben, Das 328
Frühling, Der 332
Frühling, Der 338

Ganymed 104
Gefesselte Strom, Der 102
Geh unter, schöne Sonne . . . 42
Germanien 188
Griechenland 316
Gute Glaube, Der 12
Guter Rath 2

Hälfte des Lebens 170
Heidelberg 50
Heimath 266
Heimath, Die 12
Heimath, Die 54
Heimkunft 158
Herbst, Der 336
Hyperions Schiksaalslied 24

Ihr sichergebaueten Alpen . . . 298
Ihre Genesung 12
Ihre Genesung 60
Ister, Der 252

Kolomb 304
Kürze, Die 10

Lebensalter 170
Lebenslauf 10
Lebenslauf 58
Liebe, Die 56

Main, Der 34
Mein Eigentum 36
Menons Klagen um Diotima 126
Mensch, Der 22
Menschenbeifall 10
Mnemosyne 258
Morgens, Des 32

Nächste Beste, Das 300
Narcyssen . . . 314
Natur und Kunst 74
Nekar, Der 52

Patmos 230
Patmos 242
Prinzessin Auguste von
    Homburg , Der 40

Rhein, Der 196
Rousseau 48
Rükkehr in die Heimath 66

Saturn und Jupiter 74
Scheinheiligen Dichter, Die 16
Sokrates und Alcibiades 18
Sommer, Der 334
Sommer, Der 334

Sonnenuntergang 16
Sophokles 18
Spaziergang, Der 332
Stimme des Volks 82
Stutgard 142

Thränen 94
Titanen, Die 282

Überzeugung 328
Unter den Alpen gesungen 76
Unverzeihliche, Das 14

Vom Abgrund nemlich . . . 312
Vulkan 96

Wanderer, Der 136
Wanderung, Die 182
Was ist der Menschen
    Leben . . . 270
Was ist Gott? . . . 270
Wenn aber die
    Himmlischen . . . 288
Wenn aus der Ferne . . . 324
Wenn nemlich der Rebe
    Saft . . . 268
Wenn über dem Weinberg . . . 312
Wie wenn am Feiertage . . . 172
Winkel von Hahrdt, Der 172
Winter, Der 336
Wurzel Alles Übels 18

Zeitgeist, Der 28
Zu Sokrates Zeiten 316
Zürnende Dichter, Der 18

INDEX OF ENGLISH TITLES

Ages of Life, The 171
Ancestral Portrait, The 69
Angry Poet, The 19
Archipelago, The 111
As on a holiday . . . 175
At one time I questioned the
  Muse . . . 287
At the Source of the Danube 177
Autumn 337

Blind Singer, The 87
Bonaparte 5
Bread and Wine 151
Brevity 11
But when the heavenly . . . 289

Celebration of Peace 209
Chiron 91
Colombo 305
Conviction 329
Course of Life, The 11
Course of Life, The 59

Departed, The 71
Descriptive Poetry 3
Diotima 3
Diotima 7
Diotima 65

Eagle, The 295
Empedocles 5
Evening Fantasy 31
Exhortation 73

Farewell, The 63
Fettered River, The 103
For from the abyss . . . 313

For when the grape-vine's
  sap . . . 269

Ganymede 105
German Song 265
Germania 189
Go down, then, lovely sun . . . 43
Good Advice 3
Good Faith 13
Greece 317

Half of Life 171
Heidelberg ALCAIC VERSION 51
Her Recovery 13
Her Recovery 61
Home 13
Home 55
Home 267
Homecoming 159
Human Applause 11
Hyperion's Song of Fate 25

If from the distance . . . 325
In my boyhood days 27
In Socrates' Time 317
In the Morning 33
Ister, The 253

Journey, The 183

Love 57

Man 23
Menon's Lament for Diotima 127
Merry Life, The 329
Mnemosyne 259
My Possessions 37

Narcissi . . . 315
Nature and Art 75
Neckar, The 53
Nook at Hardt, The 173

On fallow foliage . . . 269
On the Birth of a Child 327
Only One, FIRST VERSION 219
Only One, SECOND VERSION 225

Patmos 231
Patmos 243
Plea for Forgiveness 9
Poet's Courage, The 99
Poet's Vocation, The 79

Remembrance 251
Return to the Homeland 67
Rhine, The 197
River Main, The 35
Root of All Evil, The 19
Rousseau 47

Sanctimonius Poets, The 17
Saturn and Jupiter 75
Socrates and Alcibiades 19
Sophocles 19
Spirit of the Age, The 29
Spring 333
Spring 339
Stuttgart 143
Summer (24.5.1778) 335
Summer (9.3.1840) 335
Sung beneath the Alps 77

Sunset 17

Tears 95
Then and Now 9
Timidness 101
Titans, The 283
To Diotima 3
To Her Genius 9
To Hope 97
To Our Great Poets 17
To Princess Augusta of
    Homburg 41
To the Fates 7
To the Germans 15
To the Germans 45
To the Virgin Mary 273
To the Young Poets 15
To Zimmer 329
Traveller, The 137

Unpardonable, The 15

Voice of the People 83
Vulcan 97

Walk, The 333
What is God? . . . 271
What is the life of men . . . 271
Whatever is Nearest 301
When there's a flaming . . . 313
Winter 337
World's agreeable things, The 331

You firmly built alps . . . 299